THE WIGAN SHEDS
VOLUME ONE
SPRINGS BRANCH
MOTIVE POWER DEPOT

One of my earliest memories of Springs Branch was when my grandfather, a railway shunter, took me one day to look over the wall in Cecil Street. This was the view I was treated to - looking across the face of the shed whilst soaking up the atmosphere of the place. I was soon to learn that it was also the vantage point for those boys who hadn't been able to get around the shed. This 1961 photograph coincided with a time of much change. One of the last two ex-Great Central J10's, No **65157,** dominates the foreground and lies rusting away, awaiting removal to Gorton for scrapping. Beyond is the new No 2 shed which is nearing completion with the scaffolding erected to finish the front roof section. Behind this is the brick wall forming No 1 shed with the old Moss Pits in the far distance beyond the main line. However this was no ordinary week as the Wigan townsfolk were gearing themselves up for Saturday's Rugby League Challenge Cup Final at Wembley Stadium. No less than four visiting Jubilees - Nos **45632 *Tonga*** (24L - in view), 45620 *North Borneo* (16A), 45671 *Prince Rupert* (6G) and 45653 *Barham* (24E) are in attendance ready to haul supporters trains the following day. Despite winning the Challenge Cup many times, this wasn't to be Wigan's year as they lost 6 - 12 to arch rivals St. Helens.   **13TH MAY 1961** ● **JOHN BURGESS**

CHRIS COATES

THE WIGAN SHEDS
VOLUME ONE
SPRINGS BRANCH
MOTIVE POWER DEPOT

First published 2010

ISBN 0 9543128 4 8

All rights reserved. No part of this book may be reproduced or transmitted in any form by any means, electronic or mechanical, including photocopying, recording or by any information storage + retrieval system, without prior permission from the Publisher in writing.

© Steam Image 2010

Published by Steam Image, PO Box 90, Cheadle Hulme, Cheshire SK8 6WZ & printed by Deanprint Ltd, Stockport, Cheshire SK3 0PR.

FOREWORD

This book has been over 15 years in the making. Originally it was to be a personal record of a shed which I visited regularly and in those early days had little detailed information other than a few visit logs and some rather poor photographs. I set about finding out anything and everything about the shed, the men and how it all operated. As I immersed myself in the task, I enjoyed the hospitality of many enginemen on my visits who were always enthusiastic, despite my continual quest for detailed memories of their past. Gradually the information started to build up and I began to understand how the depot operated. Unfortunately this whetted my appetite to find out even more. Several times the question would be asked ... *and what are you going to do with all this information?* It had never been my intention to produce a book but, as a few railwaymen made comment, *If anyone was going to do a book on the shed then it would have to be Chris Coates.* So, unwittingly, I had created my own monster and was now somewhat obliged to take it to the next stage and eventually to print. Enter Paul Shackcloth, my friend from the Manchester Locomotive Society, who ably assisted me in creating something that was eventually suitable for publication. It proved to be a mammoth task deciding what would be included and what would have to be left out, such was the wealth of material that had been accumulated. I have tried to strike a happy medium between including enough detail to satisfy most readers whilst not getting too bogged down with endless documentation. Railway terminology occasionally appears in the text, mainly within the tabular matter, which I trust is decipherable. For those unfamiliar, . is am and / pm. I have structured the book into sections which are in a loosely chronological order and cover the areas of operation and employment. Whilst steam naturally predominates, the final years section also caters for the diesel era and new Maintenance Depot.

The main reason for producing this book was to illustrate, both in photographs and text, just how a large engine shed operated in the steam era. I wanted to capture both the shed life and atmosphere of how the depot functioned on a daily basis, how and why the engines were allocated and utilised and what the men actually did.

DEDICATION

I dedicate this book to the railwaymen of Springs Branch who were so forthcoming in sharing their memories with me. Some have suffered more than one visit in my quest for accurate details, yet it has been a pleasure to be in their company. I have immense respect for the generations of enginemen of Springs Branch whose toil, sweat and companionship was remarkable. We shall not see the likes of them again.

ACKNOWLEDGEMENTS

A great many Springs Branch men and women have been invaluable by way of both offering assistance and sharing their experiences. Those who have been primarily involved include Fred Banks, Eric Clayton, Arthur Edwards, Derek Gibson, Alan Grundy, Arthur Pollard and Tommy Sutch. Others who have helped in one way or another include Jack Ashley, Bill Baxendale, Ronnie Bentley, Fred Darbyshire, Ron Davies, Kate Devaney, Harry Edwards, Alan Fieldhouse, Randy Fitzpatrick, Jack Green, Peter Hampson, Tommy Hunt, Charlie Leatherbarrow, Jack Jolley, Alf Jones, J Lawnsborough, Jimmy Lincoln, Bill Paxford, Jack Perkins, Ernie Phillips, Frank Prestt, Ronnie Reed, Bill Sanderland, Tony Taylor and J M White (Neville). A book such as this is always reliant on its photographic content and candidate pictures have been submitted from a great number of sources. In this respect I must extend special thanks to John Burgess, Peter Fitton, Tom Heavyside, Allan Heyes and Bob Kimmins (Les Riley) for access to their impressive collections. Other contributors include Bill Ashcroft, Pat Avery, Len Ball, Brian Barlow, Arnold Battson, E Bellass, Rod Blencowe, H K Boulter, John Bretherton, Allan Brown, J Buckley, Malcolm Capstick, Richard Casserley, D Cousins, A B Cross, John Daniels, J Davenport, F Dean, Gerry Drought, Alan Edwards, Ray Farrell, N Fields, Richard Freeman, A C Gilbert, Tony Gillett, A N H Glover, P Gratton, BKB Green, D Hampson, L Hanson, G Harrop, N Harrop, C Hawkins, Arthur Haynes, I G Holt, H Hunt, P Hutchinson, D Ingham, G P Keane, Steve Leyland, D Long, John Loughman, B Lowe, Robin Lush, E McDermott, B Magilton, Bob Maxwell, G Newall, P Nightingale, J Peden, W Potter, Danny Preston, Bev Price, S Price, B Roberts, A Sommerfield, Colin Stacey, Jeremy Suter, Mike Taylor, Mrs M Taylor, P Ward, T G Wassell, M Welch, H F Wheeler, G Whitehead, J P Wilson, P Wilson, David Young, members of both the LNWR and Manchester Locomotive Societies, David Postle at the Kidderminster Railway Museum and the staff at Wigan Archive Services. Other valuable assistance came from Richard Strange (Steam Railway Research Society) and Ted Talbot. To all I offer my sincere thanks. Inevitably there is the odd anonymous shot included which can only be credited to the collector. If any have inadvertently slipped the net, please accept my apologies.

Finally, I must thank my wife Jean for her constant support and encouragement, especially as I seemed to spend each spare moment glued to the computer. Also thanks to the Railwaymen from the *Upper Morris Street Working Mens Club* without whose assistance and support this book would not have become a reality.

NOVEMBER 2010 ● CHRIS COATES

CONTENTS

INTRODUCTION	5
BUILDINGS AND INFRASTRUCTURE	7
LOCOMOTIVES IN LNWR DAYS	23
LOCOMOTIVES IN LMS DAYS	27
LOCOMOTIVES IN BR DAYS	31
LOCOMOTIVES AWAY FROM HOME	55
VISITING LOCOMOTIVES	58
STAFF AND ADMINISTRATION	65
PASSENGER WORKINGS	97
FREIGHT WORKINGS	121
TRIP, SHUNT AND BANKING WORKINGS	137
ACCIDENTS, INCIDENTS AND FOLKLORE	159
THE FINAL YEARS	163
LOCOMOTIVE ALLOCATIONS	173

An unidentified 'Super D' climbs the bank past Rylands Siding.

c1959 ● AUTHOR'S COLLECTION

The lure of the engine shed. When Flight Lieutenant Aidan Fuller introduced *The British Locomotive Shed Directory* in 1948, he opened up whole new horizons for the budding trainspotter. Whilst he forcibly stressed that these directions did not grant permission to enter such premises, permission to do so without a permit was frequently refused on a busier weekday but very often granted on a much quieter Sunday. Although Springs Branch didn't quite have the pulling power of, say, Crewe (North) - it was always regarded as an attractive proposition, mainly because of the visiting engines which could be found, often including a rare 'namer'. Making use of the directory, such a visit was made by Paul Shackcloth on May 10th 1964 and the engines duly logged below. On this occasion, permission was sought and granted with the proviso that he was to report his departure to the shed office.

> **SPRINGS BRANCH 10A. (Wigan)**
> The shed is on the east side of the main line about one mile south of Wigan North Western Station. The yard is partially visible from the line.
> Turn right outside Wigan North Western Station into Wallgate, and turn right into King Street. Continue into Darlington Street, and turn right into Warrington Lane. Continue along Warrington Road for about one mile, and turn right into Morris Street. The shed entrance is at the end of this cul-de-sac. Walking time 30 minutes.

The relevant extract from the directory.

A large proportion of Springs Branch enginemen lived within walking distance of the shed - which of course made life easier for the 'knocker up'. Others had bicycles but those living further afield made use of the local bus services (and trams before that). Both the Wigan Corporation and Lancashire United Transport operated along the Warrington Road from the Town Centre and perhaps the most popular - certainly the most intensive service - was the No 12 to Abram. In February 1965, the Wigan Corporation fleet consisted of 160 buses all of which carried a distinctive crimson and white livery. Here, No **67 (EJP 508)**, a 1959 built Leyland Titan PD3/2 with Northern Counties bodywork returns to the bus station on service No 12. The vehicle has just passed under Scholes Bridge which carries the Wigan Central to Glazebrook line.

c1965 ● ABCROSS

INTRODUCTION

The first coal mine in Wigan opened in 1450 and coal production gradually increased using the only available method of transport, the horse drawn cart. Later, canals were built and this allowed a much better distribution of coal; however, it wasn't until the railways arrived that the Wigan Coalfield was fully exploited, when, at its peak, there were over 1000 pit shafts within 5 miles of Wigan Town Centre. The huge coal seams that existed under this area of Lancashire were to prove pivotal to the creation and expansion of the railways in the Wigan area and the subsequent infrastructure that appeared to support these operations.

When the Liverpool & Manchester Railway opened in 1830, further lines were proposed to extend the system, one of which was to Wigan. The Wigan Branch Railway Company was approved in 1830 to construct a 7 mile line from Parkside to Wigan, but it was also to include a 3 mile branch from a point known locally as Ince Mill (Springs Branch) to New Springs (Aspull), known thereafter as the Springs Branch which eventually opened in 1838. The main railway system then continued to expand with further extensions to Preston (The North Union Railway) and later to Birmingham, London and Scotland, and, in 1846, it was all amalgamated to form the London & North Western Railway.

Coal operations around Wigan were becoming increasingly lucrative and the area around Springs Branch, the point where the New Springs line branched off the main line, was to change dramatically from the original two track railway of the 1830's, such was the demand for coal as the Industrial Revolution gained momentum. The Springs Branch itself became an artery into colliery systems and wagon repair yards and gradually the whole Wigan area became a complex network of standard and colliery lines, such that many pits had access to more than one Railway Company for the dispatch of its coal. In 1840, the UK produced about 34 million tons of coal but this was to rise to 242 million in 1905 and 680 million by 1918 before falling away. The Lancashire coalfield produced about 10% of all UK coal and it is understandable that this massive growth in production would have placed huge demands on the railways. Approximately 25% of this coal was exported, although this would have been most prevalent in areas such as South Wales.

Stanier locos crowd the corridor across the front of No 1 shed.   21ST JANUARY 1967 ● ALLAN HEYES

As the railways grew, so did the support facilities, and the original small wagon repair works, goods yards and engine sheds were gradually expanded or replaced by new and larger buildings. Over the years there have been at least 15 different engine shed buildings at Wigan and of these, the Great Central (Wigan Junction Railway) was the smallest concern with just one shed building at Lower Ince. The Liverpool & Bury Railway (later Lancashire & Yorkshire) also had one small shed with a further three small sheds erected by the L&Y until it built the eight road shed at Pagefield and later replaced this with the fourteen road shed at Prescott St that survived until 1964. The remaining eight shed buildings were all associated with the LNWR/BR or its constituents, with two early engine shed buildings close to Wigan NW station and seven at Springs Branch.

Of all these engine shed buildings, four survived into the British Railways era in 1948. The smallest was the Great Central depot at Lower Ince, servicing just over a dozen locos and closed in 1952. The ex-L&Y (Central Division) shed could boast 50 to 60 locomotives and survived until 1964. The importance of the Wigan area to the LNWR is reflected in the eventual size of Springs Branch shed with, at one time, an allocation of over 130 engines. Even as late as 1961, it could still boast of over 80 engines on its books and it continued to maintain steam engines until the end of 1967. Even then Springs Branch was starting a new chapter with the official opening of its modern Diesel Maintenance depot in 1968, a facility that operated well into the 1990's, outliving virtually all its rivals.

This is the story of Springs Branch Motive Power Depot. Not just a photographic record of the Locomotives, the Buildings and the Men, but an in-depth study into how it functioned with all aspects of the depot's operations described in detail.

Whether the current depot will survive the ongoing changes in railway operations remains unclear, but at the time of writing it is still housing locomotives for D.B Schenker (the new Company) and still doing some repair work. I wonder if there are any other depots that could claim over 170 years of servicing railway locomotives on the same site - there will not be many.

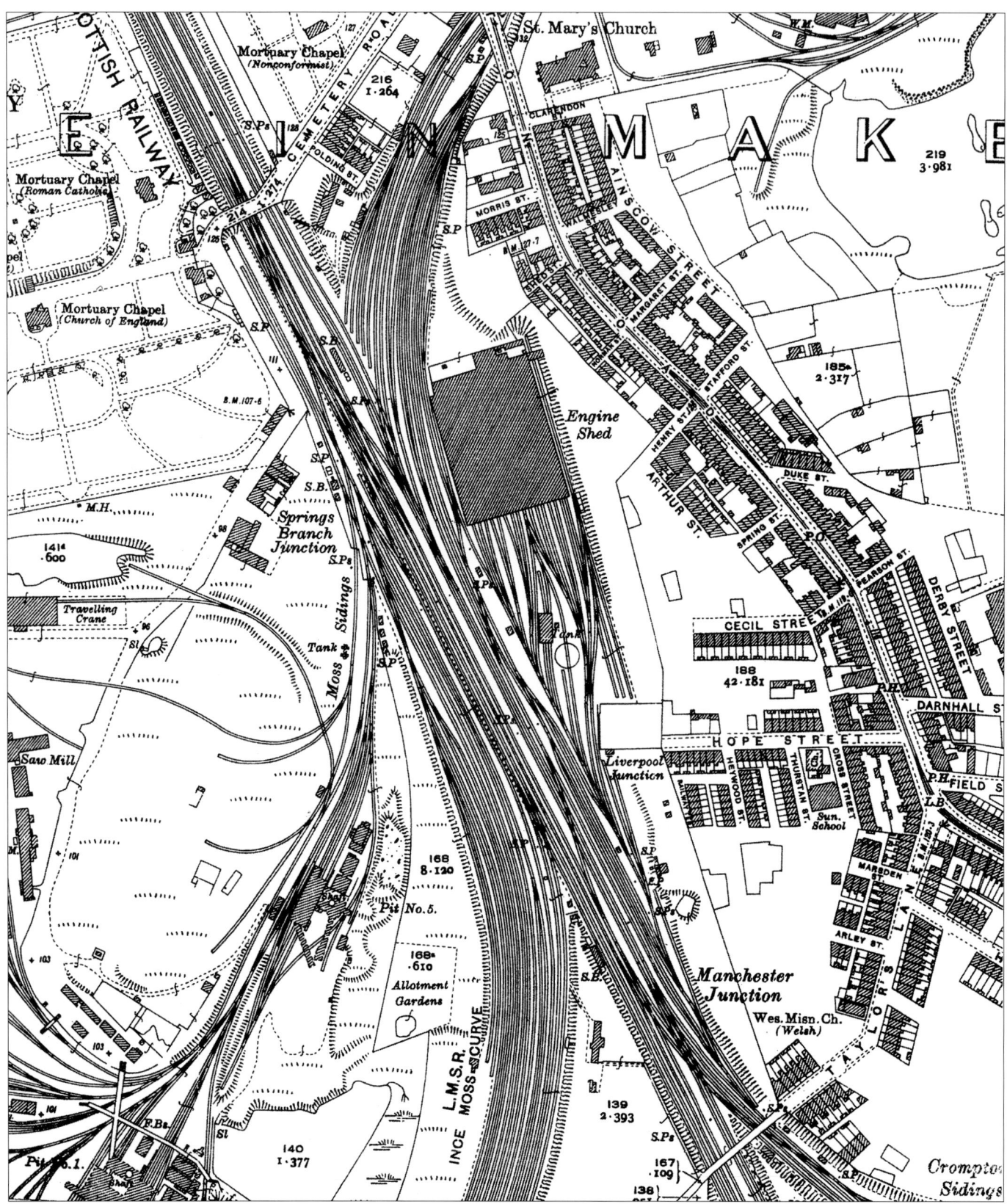

The general view of the area around the shed in 1929 with the turntable and coal stage in the centre of the yard. A few years later, the 1935 LMS modernisation scheme would significantly improve the layout for loco coaling and disposal. The block of land at the bottom of Hope St was bought and this enabled the new layout to be created. There is also a Shed Street on the map which was the original entrance to Springs Branch before Morris Street was used.

BUILDINGS AND INFRASTRUCTURE

The first engine shed at Springs Branch, built in the late 1840's, was in fact the third such building on this line in the area, the two previous locomotive sheds being built near to North Western station. The building was very close to where the larger sheds were later constructed, but a bit further round the actual Springs Branch itself. A coaling stage was provided to the south of the two road shed and a small turntable was sited in the fork of the Springs Branch and main line. The capacity of this brick building was a mere 6 locos and within years of its construction was deemed totally inadequate. Although a new engine shed was proposed, a partial solution was a temporary wooden building which was erected to the south of the existing structure, but the whole arrangement was inadequate as at this time there were 16 locomotives working from the shed with work for 6 more.

In 1867, it was eventually agreed to build new premises to house 24 locomotives on land close to the present site yet 18 months later the only progress was the land being cleared ready for construction. Mr. Ramsbottom, CME of the LNWR recommended that the building should now house 40 locomotives at an estimate of £17,000 which included a new coaling stage, 42ft turntable and office facilities, The coal stage was later modified to include a 64,000 gallon water tank above. The plans were approved in December 1868 and the new 8 road, twin hipped shed was completed in 1869. It had been built to the standard Ramsbottom design with a twin parallel hipped roof supported by cast iron columns and brick walls with a timber roof and doors and was the eighth such shed to be constructed by the LNWR in the 1857 to 1871 period. The earlier shed remained in use for a little while. It was reported that the floor of the new 1869 No 1 shed was made of wood from old wheel centres. In LNWR days, Springs Branch was given the shed code 25 which was carried, on small enamel plates, inside the cabs of its locos. At this time the four road shed at Blackburn, which had opened in 1882, remained a sub shed of Springs Branch until its closure in 1922 when the L&Y and LNWR amalgamated.

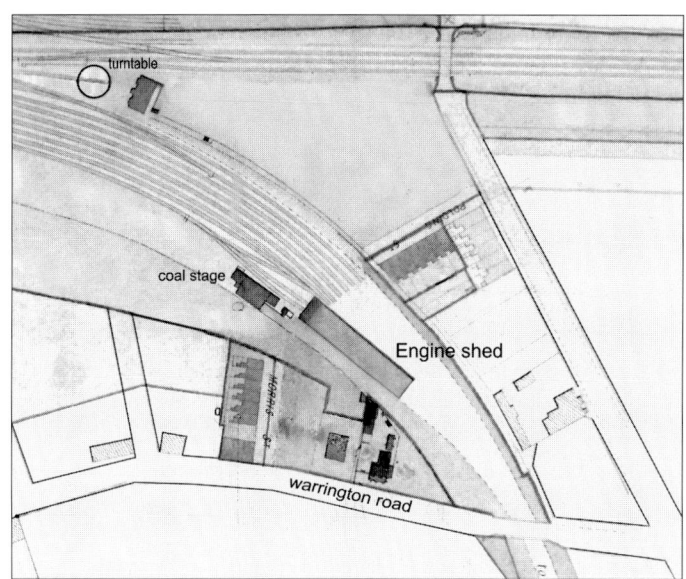

The position of the first Springs Branch shed, coaling stage and turntable around 1850.

A map showing the old and new shed buildings in 1870. The old shed continued to be used after 1869 for a short period as traffic was increasing at a considerable rate. The turntable remained in the fork at this time.
▼

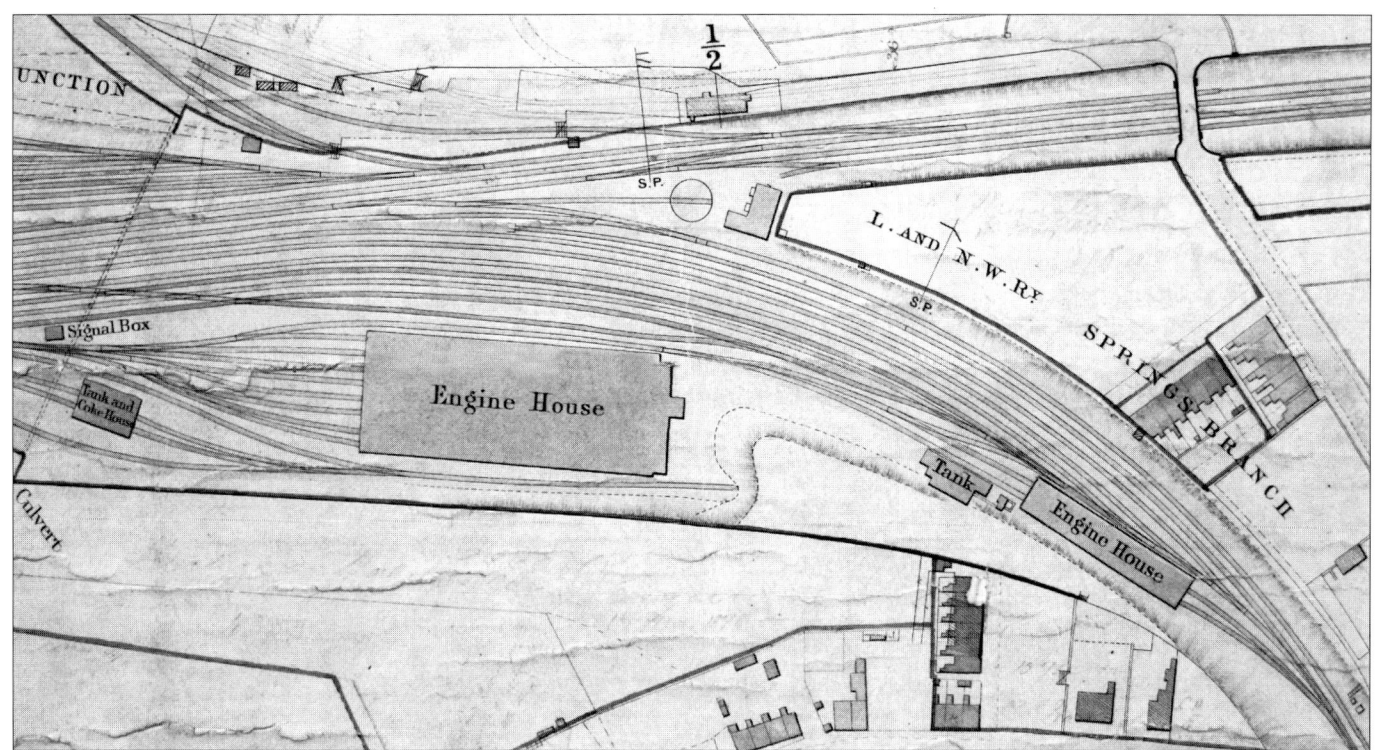

A general view of Nos 1 and 2 sheds in LNWR days showing the original ventilation system.　　c1900 ● A. SOMMERFIELD COLLECTION

Such was the growth of the coal trade that the shed allocation had risen to 86 locomotives by 1881, and the incumbent CME - Mr. Webb, gained approval for a second building (No 2) to be constructed on land adjoining the existing Ramsbottom building. This shed was also of 8 roads but this time with the new Northlight pattern style of wooden roof and beams, supported by cast iron columns and was completed in 1882. The walls and doors were also of wooden construction, taking into consideration potential mining subsidence in the immediate area. The shed was equipped with pits, on all 8 roads, that were 2' 9" below rail level. The internal walls were painted black to a height of 5ft and whitewashed above. The lower portions of the roof columns were also painted white from 1930, probably as a safety aspect. Workshop facilities at the rear of the shed appear to have been included in this project as was a hydraulic wheel drop and shearlegs on Road 10. Once completed, all washouts and repair work was undertaken in No 2 shed.

▲

A similar view of Nos 1 and 2 sheds in LMS days with modified roof vents fitted. Notice the yard lamp, which appears in the LNWR photo *(top)* has been removed and that the point levers have been treated to a coat of paint, presumably to aid visibility at nightfall.

c1930 ● STEAM IMAGE

◄ **Aspinall designed 3F Class 0-6-0 No 12417** stands outside No 1 shed. The same roof vents appear to have quickly suffered from the ravages of incessant smoke. The front columns have already been removed leaving four rectangular holes in the gable ends.

14TH MAY 1938 ● KRM

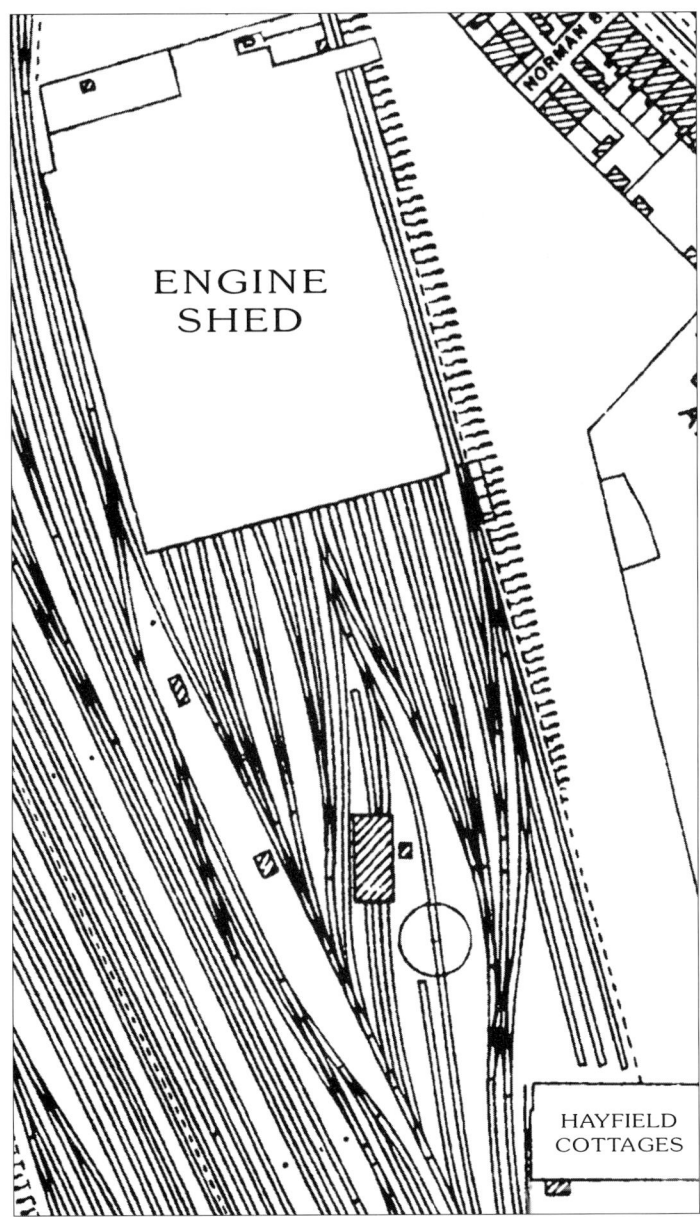

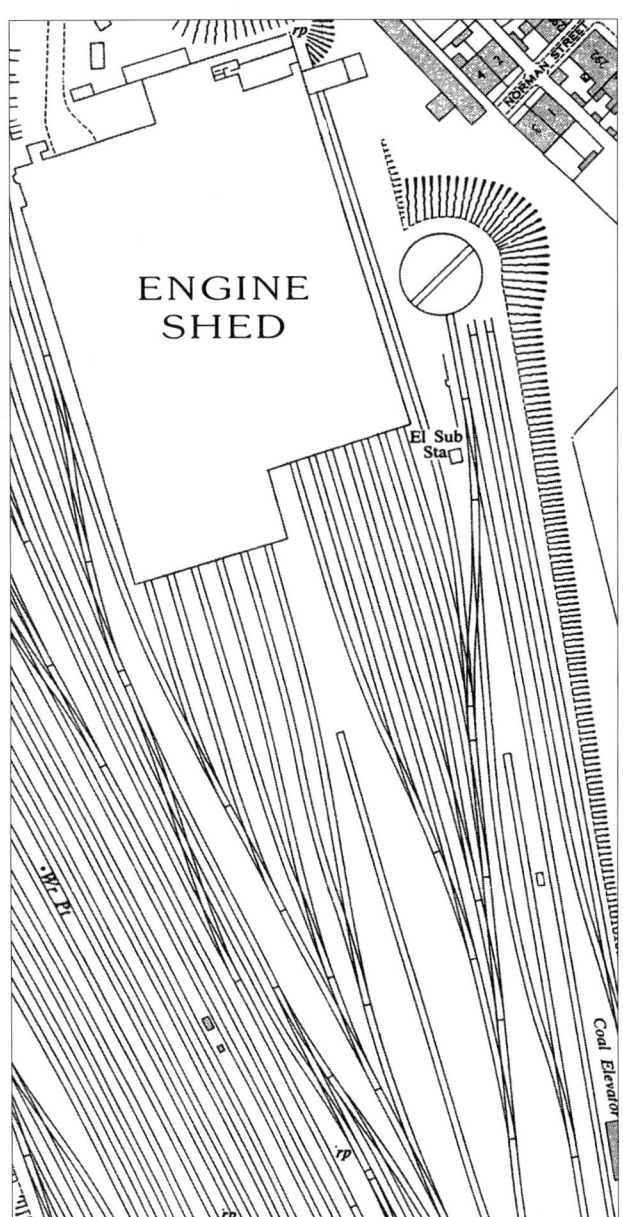

This plan shows the situation up to 1935 just before the old two road coaling stage/water tank/ turntable were cleared away and the land levelled. The area around the south end of the three short sidings (just above Hayfield Cottages) is shown on early maps as a coal stack. At the time of the improvements, both eight roads sheds existed so there were no track changes in the main shed yard, just at the necks. There was obviously considerable additional trackwork required on the east side of the site in the area from the new coaler through to the replacement turntable and provision was also made for two coal storage sidings to be created. The roads were, logically, numbered 1 - 8 and 9 - 16 with 17 the outside road.

The situation from the early 1950's when the eight road No 1 building has been replaced by a six road shed, the tracks of which were now numbered 1 to 6 and 7 to 14 with the outside road becoming Road 15. At this time the track layout in the yard was simplified and the centre terminating road effectively cuts the yard into two necks. By 1961 this had been further modified with the feed to Road 7 (old Road 9) now coming from the left side of the yard as it had done before 1935.

The view in the early days of BR and just prior to work commencing on the rebuild. No 1 shed (left) has suffered badly and the first section is virtually roofless. No 2 (right) shows similar signs of dilapidation. Note that even after 15 years there is still plenty of coal around the area where the original coal stage was situated.

c1950 ● G. NEWALL

Whilst the new No 1 shed was being built in 1951, photographic evidence shows No 2 was also having considerable roof repairs, although to what extent is not known. Certainly the front two sections were either extended or repaired and they are now in corrugated sheeting. It's possible the shed roof was damaged as a result of a fire.

22ND APRIL 1951 ● P. WARD

Some changes to the roof vents of No 1 and No 2 shed appear to have occurred in the early 1900's with the tall stovepipe vents being replaced by louvre types but, apart from gradual dilapidation, very little changed until the late 1940's, by which time No 1 shed was virtually roofless.

Original planning drawings show that No 1 shed at Springs Branch was proposed for reconstruction in 1945 but nothing progressed further than the drawing table. In a letter to the British Transport Commission in March 1950, it was stated: *Between the years 1883 and 1925 the shed was seriously affected by mining subsidence in the area to the extent of 7' 9" at the south-west corner and 2' 4" at the north-east corner and that the structure was beyond further repair and would need to be completely rebuilt.* It was also stated that the site had now settled and that there would be no engineering objection to a new building on the present site. One matter for consideration was that the existing 8 road shed created cramped working conditions with "platforms" only 7' 10" wide, so any new design should have 6 roads with 12' platforms. It was agreed that a new No 1 shed would be built at an estimate of £63,758. On dismantling the old (1869) No 1 shed, the timber was found to be still in good condition so an air raid shelter was converted into a joiners shop and this wood was used by the shed handyman to make window frames for various buildings.

Cauliflower 0-6-0 No 58381 stands outside No 1 shed which appears to be in the process of being dismantled. The loco was at Springs Branch from September 1947 to March 1950 which suggests late 1949/early 1950 for this shot.

c JANUARY 1950 ● G. NEWALL

The new No 1 shed is nearing completion with most of the concrete roof sections in situ. The track alteration will have been completed judging by the clean finish of the yard floor where resident engine No **47877** is stabled.

23RD MAY 1951 ● T. G. WASSELL

In this early 1950's view, No 1 shed is back in action as is No 2 following its roof renovations. Within a rather deserted scene, ex-GC 0-6-0 No **65175** appears stored in the centre of the yard with its chimney 'sacked' whilst another member, No **65189** stands in steam ready for duty. A 'Super D' 0-8-0 in the distance is the only other identifiable loco in view. JULY 1952 ● P. WARD

A side view of No 2 shed with long term resident Stanier 2-6-4T No **42456** on the outside track then known as road 17. Sections of this shed that were replaced or extended in 1951 are clearly seen from this angle.

9TH AUGUST 1953 ● H.C. CASSERLEY

The original eight road No 2 shed. Ex-L&Y Nos **52021** and **52098** and Fairburn Tank No **42266** are the locos identified.

9TH AUGUST 1953 ● H.C. CASSERLEY

11

The new No 1 shed opened in 1951 and was of the standard LMS type then being constructed with concrete columns and roof sections with louvre vents. The walls were then infilled with brick and metal window frames fitted. Included in the cost was an electric wheel drop facility, hoist and illuminated pits plus some new accommodation for stores/offices which was presumably for the fitting staff as the old offices and stores at the rear of the original sheds remained until the 1980's. There were no smoke vents in the rear part of this shed and sliding doors were provided whereby the whole rear section of the shed (the repair area) could be partitioned off from the front section and thus allow for better conditions for the shed repair staff. Virtually all repair work was now done in this building, No 2 being used mainly for stabling locos.

It must be a weekday as the tracks outside No 1 shed are completely empty and the fitters are having a rest in this mid 1960's view. Standard 4-6-0 No **75057** heads a line of engines outside No 2 shed with the oil and tool hut just visible on the left. c1964 ● FRED BANKS

During the winter of 1960-61, the majority of the eight road No 2 shed was demolished apart from the rear sections which housed workshops and stores. A new 4 road shed with a steel frame and a corrugated steel roof and sides was then erected over half the site with the remaining four tracks uncovered. This building was opened in summer 1961 and the remaining outside roads were then provided with electric lighting on steel stanchions.

The vista showing Nos 1 & 2 sheds in August 1962. The foreman's assistant will have decided the locomotives' position and direction depending on their next job. Seemingly just as many are facing in as facing out! Prominent in the background are the sand dryer chimney and, just to its left, the shed water tank. 26TH AUGUST 1962 ● BRIAN BARLOW

NO 1 SHED PLAN

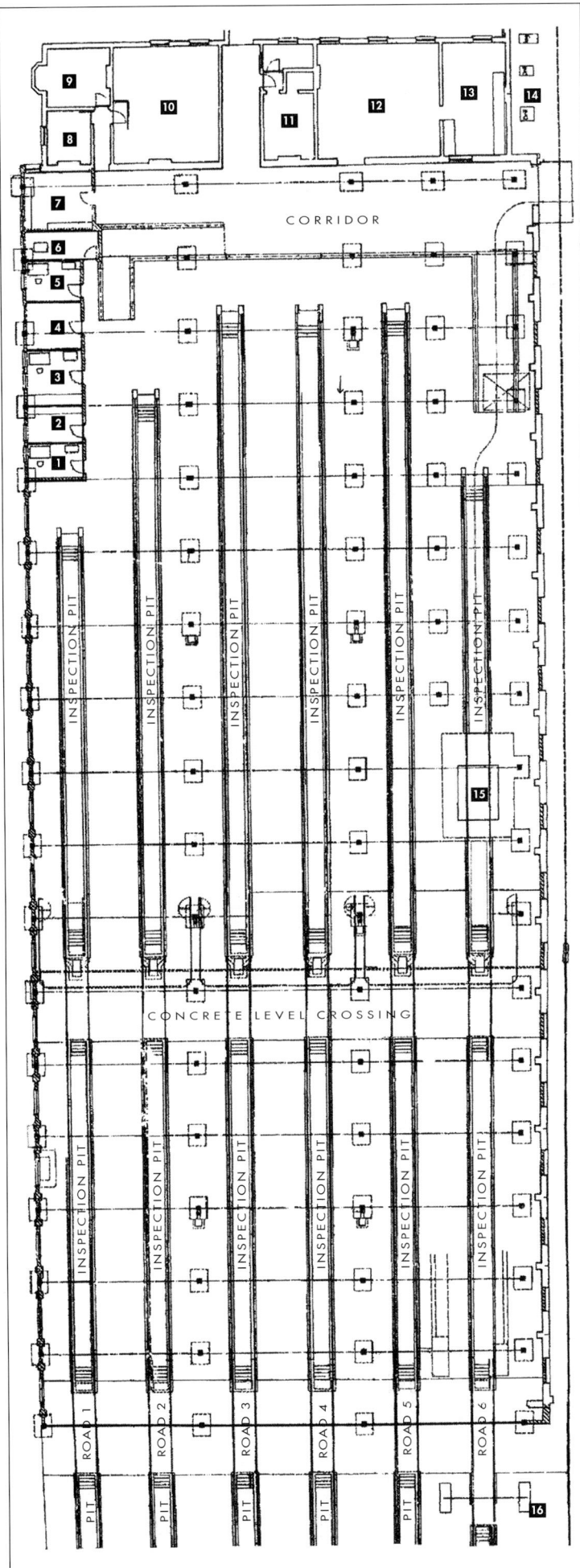

Notable items on the plan of the 1951 building are the Tangent type sliding doors situated one third from the entrance, thus enabling the rear repair section to be isolated from the front part. This rear section also had illuminated inspection pits and no roof vents. Non illuminated pits were also provided in the other section of the shed as well as outside the building on all six roads. Additional concrete supports are evident where the overhead gantry runs from the rear of the wheeldrop to the workshops. The route of this gantry would take it up one of the concrete ramps that ran from the shed floor up to the raised office/workshop corridor. The second ramp was 'L' shaped and ran from the top left corner up to the same corridor. They enabled most heavy items to be moved around on hand trucks. Interestingly, although the plan shows the concrete supports on the right (east) wall being separate from the walls, photographic evidence shows that they were in fact incorporated into the walls in the same way as the west wall.

The original 1869 shed had offices and stores (8 - 13) whereas the new 1951 building had considerably more provision with five new offices which were occupied by the repair staff and, in particular, the hierarchy. Also incorporated in the design was a heating chamber (basically a boiler room) which provided heat to many areas. The shed floor was concrete and generally at sleeper level however it sloped up to track top level at the three crossing points within the shed. Hydrants were available at various points and were used extensively when boiler washouts were being undertaken.

There were six roads and at the end of each a steel rail stop was fitted to both rails to prevent wheels from passing this point. The area along the bottom wall was used for storage lockers. That at the bottom of the shortest track, Road 1, seems to have been a collection point for ladders or staging. In the early 1960's this road was designated for diesel shunter maintenance and the various oils etc. involved with this were stored in this vicinity.

1 FITTERS CUPBOARD
2 FITTERS LOBBY
3 FOREMAN FITTER
4 FITTERS TOOL STORE
5 BOILERSMITHS CUPBOARD
6 HEATING CHAMBER
7 DRIVERS LOBBY
8 ASSISTANT DLS
9 DISTRICT LOCOMOTIVE SUPERINTENDENT
10 GENERAL OFFICE
11 TIME OFFICE
12 STORES
13 STORES
14 WORKSHOP
15 WHEEL DROP
16 OVERHEAD HOIST

◀ **The view inside No 1 shed** with roads 3 to 6 full of locos awaiting or undergoing maintenance. Standard Class 4's seem to dominate with No **76077** discernible on the left and, just in front of this loco, are one set of Tangent sliding doors, the housing for which is seen in the centre of the photo. Typical shed debris is evident with water pipes, etc.

27TH JULY 1966 ● **COLIN STACEY**

▲ **The shortest road, (road No 1)** was originally used for the breakdown crane but was eventually reserved for the diesel shunters. The diesel fitters were housed in the offices beyond this shortened track. Closer examination of the background reveals the left side ramp, the first part of which is visible just to the left of the Jinty.

c1965 ● **FRED BANKS**

◀ **The interior of No 2 shed in the mid 1960's** with coaches occupying road 7. On road 8, Stanier 2-6-4 Tank No **42587** stands over one of the pits in a shed where there isn't much room between those tracks!

c1965 ● **FRED BANKS**

When the new No 1 shed was opened in 1951, the old 1869 offices at the rear were retained, although some new office units were incorporated along the west wall of the new shed, principally for repair staff. The original offices were occupied by the running department with the General Office and Time Office being the most relevant. The main stores were also situated here. Behind No 2 shed was the 1881 building containing the machine shop which incorporated the wheel lathe and other workshop machines. Beyond this was the sand dryer with its distinctive chimney. The staff and operations of these buildings are fully covered in their own chapter.

Looking west along the main corridor with the temporary pay office hut on the left. Immediately right are the stores. To the right of the cabin is the Time Office and at the top right of the picture can be seen the wheel of the overhead pulley system which could haul a wheelset up from road 6 into the machine shop. Motorcycles were obviously starting to replace pushbikes by this time.

1970 ● JOHN BRETHERTON

This photograph down the same corridor gives a better view of the Time Office (right) with the late notices board alongside the desk. On the other side of the opening (still right) are the boards showing the enginemen's rosters for the week. The temporary pay cabin is seen directly left with the steps up to the enginemen's lobby beyond. A War Memorial from the 1914 - 1918 war is believed to have been displayed on a wall in the corridor near the stores.

1970 ● JOHN BRETHERTON

This view shows the roadway from Morris Street leading to the shed entrance (behind the white van). The windows are those of the Time Office (left) and the General Office (right) with the new toilet facility also on the right. An interesting array of cars of the period occupy the foreground.

1970 ● JOHN BRETHERTON

In the Winter of 1960/1, the majority of the eight road No 2 shed was demolished apart from the rear sections which housed workshops and stores. A new 4 road shed with a steel frame and a corrugated steel roof and sides was then erected over half the site with the remaining four tracks uncovered. This building was opened in summer 1961 and the remaining outside roads were then provided with electric lighting on steel stanchions, hovever this building was not to survive for long.

Preparation for the forthcoming Diesel Depot began in 1966 and some tracks in Springs Branch Up Sidings (Engine Shed Sidings) were utilised for the storage of locomotives. Approximately six roads were used for stabling although this area gradually became a collection point for stored engines. More withdrawn locos appeared at Brewery sidings, although these were usually bound for the scrapyard of Central Wagon Works, about ½ mile up the Springs Branch itself. Once all the locomotives had been removed from inside and around No 2 shed, the building was demolished and the area cleared. This work would also require the turntable to be demolished and thereafter locomotives used the Platt Bridge - Ince Moss - Springs Branch triangle to turn.

All change in the Summer of 1966 with the four-road No 2 shed empty and awaiting the demolition crew. The photographer is standing where the old pre-1935 coal stage was situated. Note the diesel fuel road has now been extended and connected to road 6.

JULY 1966 ● FRED BANKS

A superb aerial view of the demolished No 2 shed and its surrounding tracks, only the lighting stanchions and one small wall remain to be tackled. The workshops at the rear have survived again but their days are numbered. It won't take long for the whole area to be cleared and the foundations for the diesel depot to be installed. Just to the right of the water tank are the barracks.

AUGUST 1966 ● FRED BANKS

Engines stabled around the west side of No 1 shed. 8F's Nos **48359** (Left) and **48125** are in the foreground.

11TH MARCH 1967 ● JOHN BURGESS

Soon the steel framework for the new three road diesel maintenance depot was erected and work continued throughout 1967 until the depot officially opened on 3rd April 1968. Additional buildings were also constructed, including new stores, toilets and office block for the clerks. The old workshop section was cleared soon after but the remaining offices at the rear of No 1 shed continued to be used for train crew purposes until the 1980's. Around this time other new buildings for the overhead staff were constructed at the rear of the diesel depot on land originally reserved for additional tracks, allowing the diesel depot to be accessed from both ends, an option that was never progressed.

No 1 shed continued to be used for loco stabling (both steam and diesel) and the shed finally closed to steam on 4th December 1967, although it was summer 1968 before many of the withdrawn steam engines had been removed from site. Springs Branch No 1 shed continued to be used for diesel stabling until problems with the concrete sections in the roof caused the abandonment and subsequent demolition of the building in October 1983. After the rubble was cleared, the tracks continued to serve their original purpose and loco or wagon storage was still evident well into the 21st Century.

The view looking south showing construction of the new Diesel Depot progressing well. Much of the steelwork is in place and the brick walls appear virtually complete. Cladding will create the remaining side sections.

1967 ● FRED BANKS

Steam and diesel operating side by side, each with its own servicing facility. By this time the Class 25's and 40's were arriving in large numbers.

1967 ● LES RILEY

Three Class 25's and a Class 40 stand outside the recently completed diesel depot. To the right of the main building is the stores building whilst the new office accommodation lies just beyond this.

1967 ● LES RILEY

COALING PLANT

The original coal stage, built in 1869, was 30' x 60' in the centre of the shed yard and had the water tank mounted above it. Improvements in 1935 included a new mechanical coaling stage and an electrically operated ash plant. Also a new 100,000 gallon water tower was erected on the hill behind the shed in 1937. On one occasion this tank burst and flooded the shed.

Stanier 8F 2-8-0 No 48509, a visitor from Lancaster (Green Ayre) shed, stands on the through line awaiting its turn at the coaler.
30TH AUGUST 1964 ● ALLAN HEYES

The new coaling plant at Springs Branch was of steel construction with corrugated panels and was one of only two erected on British Railways by Wellman Smith Owen, the other one being at Bescot shed. Although the LMS was mainly installing concrete coaling plants at this time, the use of steel was likely to be due to a geographical fault that ran through this area of the site and may have precluded using concrete and its associated weight. The coaler was of the 'full wagon' lift type with a 25 ton bunker and a shaker. This was a small capacity bunker for this size of depot and again the unstable land may have dictated this. There was one delivery chute which could be turned left or right but only one loco could be coaled at a time. Behind the coaling plant were two loco coal storage sidings, one containing the better quality coal (generally from Chanters Colliery near Atherton) and the other the poorer Garswood Hall Colliery coal. Four additional loco coal storage sidings were situated alongside the shed yard, next to the main line.

◄ **Springs Branch's unusual coaling plant** is shown to full effect here. The bucket scoop could be turned to distribute coal to the left or the right. 2-6-4T No **42426** has just been coaled and will move up to the ash pit disposal area once the WD has cleared away.

c1964 ● FRED BANKS

A rare view of the rear of the coaling apparatus. ► A single wagon would be lifted and its contents emptied into the 25 Ton bunker.

22ND AUGUST 1965 ●
DANNY PRESTON

ASH PITS AND DISPOSAL UNIT

After water and coaling, an engine would be moved up to the ash pit area and would be dealt with over the ash pits, one of which was cleared by the Ash Disposal Hoist. The other ash pits would have to be cleared manually, which meant shoveling the ash onto the ground level then shoveling again into the wagons. A tiring and dirty job, particularly on a windy day!

Fowler 2-6-4T No 42374 has just had the ash removed from its smokebox and ashpan. The structure behind the loco is the mechanical ash pit hoist which, when working properly, would greatly assist the men by clearing the ashes into the waiting wagon. Its reliability was variable in the difficult and dusty conditions that existed.

22ND AUGUST 1965 ● JOHN BURGESS

Standing over the ash pit is a visitor from Speke Junction, 8F No **48060**.

28TH AUGUST 1967 ● DANNY PRESTON

Ash pit cleaner Alan Edwards.

c1955 ● ALAN EDWARDS COLLECTION

The flood of ash which cascades from the firebox into the pit can be detected between the rear driving wheels of Stanier 2-6-4T No **42587**.

22ND AUGUST 1965 ● ROBIN LUSH

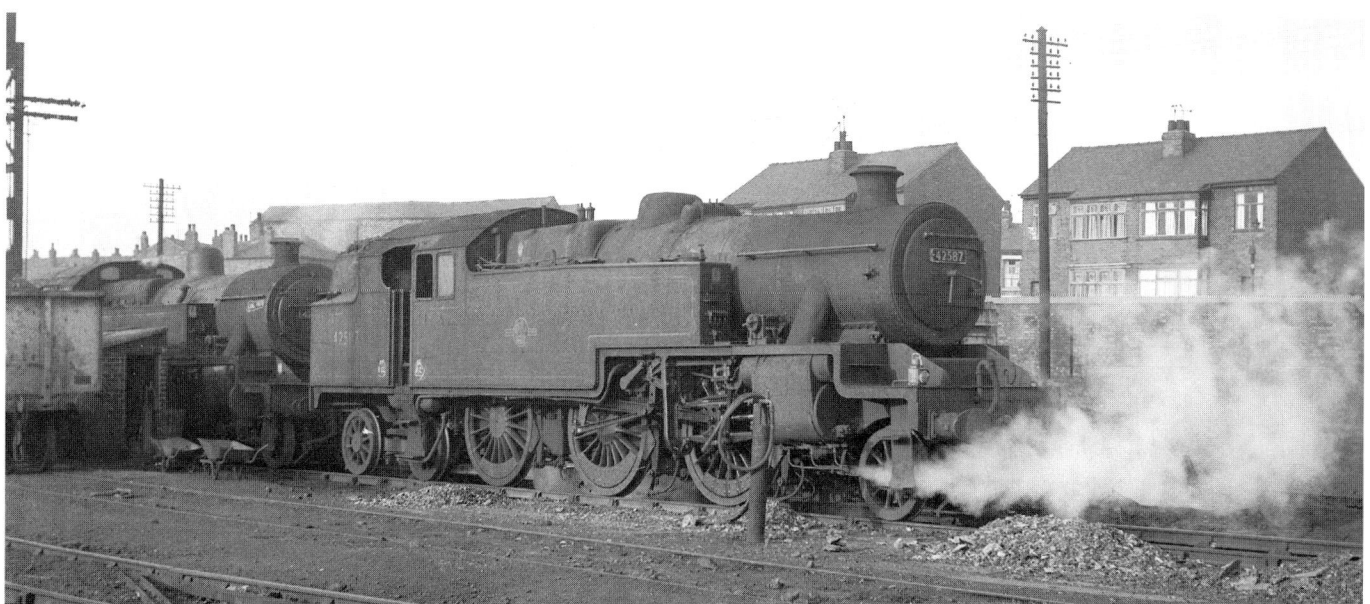

TURNTABLE

The first turntable at Springs Branch, probably dating from 1847, was in the fork formed by the main line and the Springs Branch line itself. This stayed in use even when the new No 1 shed was built and it was not until 1881, when No 2 shed was built that a new 42 ft turntable was then constructed in the centre of the shed yard, almost alongside the original coal/water tank. Finally, in 1935 a new 60ft Gresham & Craven electrically operated turntable was built alongside the rear of No 2 shed, but some engines such as the Princess Royals and the Coronations were still too big to handle. This turntable was removed in 1966 when the Diesel Depot was constructed, and thereafter engines used the Platt Bridge/Ince Moss/Springs Branch triangle to turn.

All sheds had their moments when engines would career across turntables. Springs Branch was no exception and below are a couple of incidents extracted from the foreman's log book dated 1/12/51 and 1/2/52. On another occasion a Super D went right across the turntable and part way up the steep dirt bank leading to the canteen. This was a major challenge for the breakdown team as they couldn't get a crane anywhere near the engine.

▲ **A visiting Caprotti Black 5 No 44753** from Southport stands on the table.   **2ND AUGUST 1964** ● **ALLAN HEYES**

◀ **A rear view of Stanier Class Five No 45278.**
1964 ● **TOM SUTCH**

Extracts from Running Shift Foremans log:

1st December 1951: *Passed Fireman R. Foster in charge of No 5388 (Upperby) overshot on the turntable and became derailed in the sand pit. Engine stopped for repairs to tender brake stretchers.*

1st February 1952: *No 5108 (Crewe South) derailed (bogie wheels) when coming off turntable at 5.10pm. Rerailed - 5.55pm. Care to be used when turning engines and table will require attention first thing Friday morning.*

BREAKDOWN CRANE

During the period between March 1943 and September 1967, there had only been two different steam cranes at Springs Branch and, after the shed closed to steam, a further three examples spent time here before a diesel powered crane arrived in 1977. This crane was the last to work from Springs Branch and left in 1987.

Ex-Caledonian Railway No 1 built 1886 by Cowans Sheldon with a 15 ton lift *(above)* was first on the scene. It arrived in March 1943 from Llandudno Junction shed and was renumbered MP42 by the LMS and RS1029/15 by BR. It lasted until July 1959 when it was withdrawn. c.1950 ● G.P. KEANE

A Ransome Rapier crane built 1942 of 30 ton capacity and BR number RS1067/30 followed. It arrived in 1962 from Wellingborough shed and left in September 1967, being scrapped two years later.

A Cowans Sheldon 30 ton crane built 1961 arrived in November 1968 from Carnforth having previously been at Hellifield. This carried the number RS1087/30 and departed in April 1973 for Bletchley. This crane was later purchased by the Keighley & Worth Valley Railway where it sees regular use.

Another Cowans Sheldon crane RS1001/50, built 1931 was next to arrive in February 1972. This was a 50 ton capacity type which had previously seen service at Carlisle and then Lostock Hall before leaving in 1979 and was obtained a year later by the Midland Railway Trust, Butterley.

The fifth crane came as a direct replacement for the last one, being an almost identical 50 ton Cowans Sheldon 1931-built unit number RS1005/50. It had previously been at Crewe North, then Crewe South and when it left in 1981 it also later went to the Keighley and Worth Valley Railway.

The final one, a Cowans Sheldon 75 ton diesel crane was numbered ADB966092 and later ADRC96713. This arrived brand new directly from the makers and although the breakdown crew fought hard to retain it, the crane was eventually repossessed and sent to Crewe in 1987, and later to Cardiff. At the time of writing this crane is still operating on the railways.

The Ransome Rapier Crane and supporting vans leave the shed behind Stanier Black Five No **45313**. Notice the Class 1 headlamps.
10TH APRIL 1964 ● JOHN BURGESS

A busy scene at Haworth Yard on the Keighley and Worth Valley Railway. The 30 ton capacity Cowan Sheldon Breakdown Crane *(referred to on page 21)* is in the process of lifting the ex-L&Y 0-6-0ST No **51218** in order to reset the rear wheels/springs etc. This operation has drawn the attention of a large number of observers, many of whom are congregated behind the railings. Those at closer quarters in the yard would represent a major health and safety issue by today's standards.

27TH AUGUST 1979 ● M. WELCH

The steam crane crew saying goodbye to Bill Heyes on his retirement. *(left to right)* Shed Master Fred Livesey, Cliff Lancaster, Eddie McDermott, Bill Heyes, George Davies, Bill Shufflebottom, Arthur Lewis and Derek Gibson.

JANUARY 1976 ● EDDIE McDERMOTT

These extracts from the RSF log books are of interest:

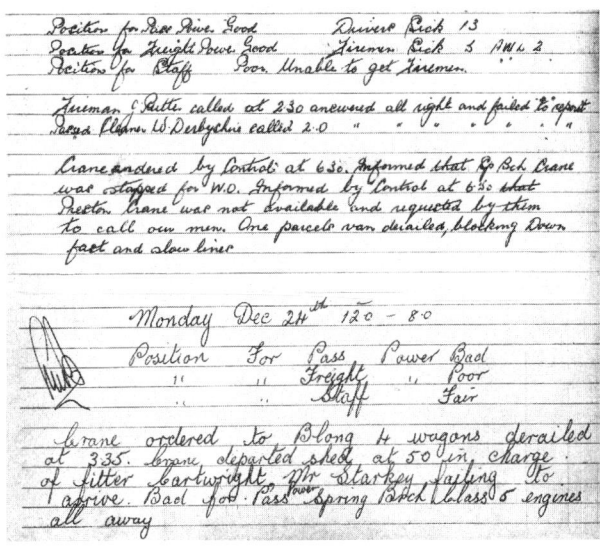

DIESEL FUEL POINT

To allow the growing collection of diesel shunters to be refuelled easily, a diesel fuelling point was added in the centre of the shed yard in the early 1960's. It consisted of two fuel tanks and all manner of associated pumps and pipework. This arrangement remained in use until the newly constructed Diesel Maintenance Depot was opened in 1968 at which time two additional storage tanks were installed alongside the original pair. A new, larger fuelling point was created to the south east of the present one with the original facility being retained for emergency use.

The diesel fuelling point. 2010 ● CHRIS COATES

SPRINGS BRANCH LOCOS IN LNWR DAYS

Although locomotives of the early railway companies would have operated in the Wigan area prior to the LNWR being formed in 1846, this book looks specifically at engines operating from Springs Branch from the turn of the century onwards. The shed was given the code 25 by the LNWR. Referring to the period from 1900, individual shed allocations are difficult to identify, but some details have been discovered for the 1910 to 1919 period. The LNWR policy was to replace engines going into works for overhaul with a similar ex-works locomotive, so individual allocations were continually changing. Certainly most of the notable LNWR passenger and freight classes were, at some stage, allocated to the shed but there would always be an understandable bias towards coal engines.

In 1911 the shed had an allocation of 95 locos including 2 Precedents, 1 Waterloo and 1 Bill Bailey. By October 1913 there were 3 Precedents, 1 Waterloo, 1 Bill Bailey and 1 Experiment amongst a total allocation of 102, but by 1917 this had reduced to 76 and the Precedents now stood at 4. There remained one each of the Waterloo, Experiment and Bill Bailey classes. The most notable changes over these years were the increase in 'Cauliflower' 18" goods engines, the arrival of the 0-8-2 side tanks and the decline of the 0-6-0 square saddle tanks, a very prominent shunting engine in 1911.

ALLOCATION - NOVEMBER 1911

Large Jumbo/Improved Precedent	394 *Eamont*, 2183 *Antelope*
Small Jumbo (Waterloo)	2154 *Loadstone*
5' 6" Tank	151, 255, 662
19" Goods Tender engine	1415, 1613/53, 2003
Bill Bailey Tender engine	606
18" Goods Tender engine	34, 543, 566, 1270, 1475
	1705/19/40, 2315/30/88
DX Goods 0-6-0 Tender engine	3006/22/6/34/8/56/99, 3105/22/32/89
	3269/84, 3309/28, 3330, 3402/36/54
	3501/62
G 0-8-0 Tender engine	1070, 1462, 1539/70/8/82
	1600/64/87/90, 2030
D 0-8-0 Tender engine	2548
F 2-8-0 Tender engine	647
C 0-8-0 Tender engine	1817/44, 2546
B 0-8-0 Tender engine	1240/1
17" Coal Tender engine	27, 45, 83, 99, 104/16/98, 856, 1081
	1345, 2082/8, 2107, 2205/92, 2300
	2338/66, 2409, 3231
Coal Tank	150, 266, 274, 1101
Square Saddle Tank	1096, 1133, 1257, 1317, 2100/8, 2404
LNWR Special Tank 0-6-0	3201, 3204, 3258
TOTAL 95	

ALLOCATION - OCTOBER 1917

Experiment	1490 *Wellington*
Large Jumbo/Improved Precedent	262 *Wheatstone*, 860 *Merrie Carlisle*,
	862 *Balmoral*, 2189 *Avon*
Small Jumbo (Waterloo)	1166 *Wyre*
Superheater Tank	2096
5' 6" Tank	204, 2136, 2145
19" Goods Tender engine	77, 1552
Bill Bailey Tender engine	504
18" Goods Tender engine	22, 195, 319/46, 473/94, 541, 623, 776
	967, 1139, 1264, 1636/46, 1736, 2325/8,
	2464/5/8/72
DX Goods 0-6-0 Tender engine	3067/72/96, 3157/79, 3270, 3301/93
	3457/94
F 2-8-0 Tender engine	647
G 0-8-0 Tender engine	2569, 2654
D 0-8-0 Tender engine	818, 1122, 1816/36/50/95, 2532
B 0-8-0 Tender engine	1044/88, 1231/87, 1436
17" Coal Tender engine	1332, 2072, 2170, 2419, 3075/95
	3100/12, 3397/9
Coal Tank	269
0-8-2 Tank	2277/94
LNWR Special Tank 0-6-0	3052, 3193, 3258, 3540
TOTAL 76	

It is interesting to record that whilst the various classes have remained consistent, there has been a total transformation of the actual stock. ie. no one locomotive features in both lists. Looking at the later LNWR period, the shed was required on every weekday to provide power for the following:

1 - Passenger work (approx. 17)   2 - Freight work (approx. 12)   3 - Trip workings (28)   4 - Shunt workings (14)
5 - Banking engines (9)

This total of 80 locomotives would include about 10 which would be 'foreign engines' on return workings. In addition, a few of the booked workings would allow the engine to move on to other diagrams later in the day. On occasions engines would be loaned or earmarked for excursions, particularly during the summer months. For example on Saturday 16th July 1921, two Springs Branch 19" Goods engines appeared at Colwyn Bay. Just after noon No 1569 headed the 12 coach 08:50 Blackburn to Llandudno whilst No 2586 passed in the opposite direction with the 13:05 Llandudno to Manchester and Oldham, a train with 15 six wheeler coaches.

No 1348 was one of forty five 17" coal engines converted into saddle tanks for shunting duties. They were referred to as the 'Square Saddle Tanks' and in 1911 Springs Branch had seven members on allocation *(see above)*. This particular engine was originally built in September 1891, rebuilt in June 1906 and eventually withdrawn as LMS No 27484 in January 1946. Records indicate that it worked out of Ordsall Lane (by this time a sub shed of Patricroft) and Springs Branch in LNWR days.

c1908 • AUTHOR'S COLLECTION

The principal classes of locomotives working from the shed in the later LNWR period were:

TENDER ENGINES

DX Goods 0-6-0. 943 built 1858-72. Some converted to the Special DX vacuum braked version. 89 passed to LMS
Improved Precedent or Large Jumbo 2-4-0. 166 built 1887-1901. 6' 9" driving wheels. 80 passed to LMS.
Waterloo or Small Jumbo 2-4-0. 90 built 1889-96. 6' 3" driving wheels. 36 passed to LMS.
Jubilee 4-4-0. Most later rebuilt as **Renowns**. 7' 1" driving wheels. 9 passed to LMS.
Bill Bailey 4-6-0. 30 built from 1903.
Precursor 4-4-0. Built from 1904. Some rebuilt & superheated. 6' 9" driving wheels. Approx 58 passed to LMS.
Experiment 4-6-0. Built from 1905. 6' 3" driving wheels. Approx 105 passed to LMS.
George V 4-4-0. Built from 1910.
Prince of Wales 4-6-0. (larger version of George V) built 1911-22. 6' 3" driving wheels. Approx 245 passed to LMS.
17" Coal engine 0-6-0. Built 1873. 4' 3½" wheels. 227 survived into LMS service.
18" Goods engine 0-6-0. Built 1880. 5' 2½" driving wheels, 308 passed to LMS.
19" 4-6-0 Goods (similar to Experiments) 170 built 1906-09 by George Whale, 5' 2½" wheels.
All survived into LMS days and one was reportedly painted red. They had a healthy appetite for coal and water.
'A - G' 0-8-0 and 2-8-0. There were many variants of these large classes.

No 859, a 4 cylinder compound 0-8-0 stands resplendent at the depot in fully lined out livery. They were introduced by Francis Webb in 1901 and later designated 'Class B'.
c1910 ● AUTHOR'S COLLECTION

TANK ENGINES

Special Tank. 0-6-0. Built from 1870 4' 5½" wheels.

Coal Tank. 0-6-2 tank version of the 17" Coal Engine. Built from 1881.

5' 6" 2-4-2 Side Tank. Built 1890-7. 160 built including 40 converted from Precursor 2-4-0's. 5' 6" driving wheels.

Dock Square Saddle Tank 0-4-2. 20 were built from 1896. 4' 5½" driving wheels. Also known as 'Bissel Tanks'

Square Saddle Tank 0-6-0. 45 were created by converting 17" Coal Engines in 1904-5.

Superheater Tank (Prince of Wales tank) 4-6-2 with 5' 6" driving wheels

0-8-2 Shunting Tank (a tank version of the 'G' Class). 30 were built between 1911 and 1917.

Jubilee Class No 1924 *Powerful.* This was originally built as a 4 cylinder compound in 1900 before being modified to a 2 cylinder simple in 1922. Although pictured at Crewe in its rebuilt form, the loco had spent a period allocated to Springs Branch before conversion.
2ND JUNE 1923 ● STEAM IMAGE

No 2190 *Princess Beatrice,* a renewed or Improved Precedent Class more commonly referred to as a 'Large Jumbo' stands in the shed yard. The engine was one of the first to be built in April 1875 and destined to be one the last remaining in service. It became LMS No 5000 in July 1928 and withdrawn four years later.

c1912 ● KRM

Members of the shed staff showing typically stern expressions are featured on this classic portrait of 'B' Class 0-8-0 No **1041**, commonly referred to as a 'piano front'. The loco appears to be in ex-works condition and carrying unlined black livery. Notice the 'Stanley Corn Mill' standing alongside the shed yard.

c1912 ● KRM

SEEN ON SHED ● ONE DAY IN 1919	
5' 6" Tank	202, 408, 2147
17" Coal	1006, 1340, 2375, 2403, 3286/317/459
18" Goods	416, 540, 1701/18/43/98, 2070, 2470
19" Goods	724, 1605
Renown	1901/36
Experiment	1652
Precedent	1189, 1749, 2178
'G' Class	1503
'D' Class	1832/54/7, 2526
'C1' Class	1850
'B' Class	1894
G1	2054
0-8-2 Tank	58, 1185, 1291
4-6-2 Tank	963
SDX	3085/122/225/402
DX	3398, 3457
Others	261, 3092, 3114, 3195, 3267, 3381/9, 3575/98, 3612
TOTAL 56	

Small Jumbo (or Waterloo Class) No 1166 *Wyre*. Records show the loco as being allocated to Springs Branch MPD in October 1917.

c1917 ● REAL PHOTOS

Seen on shed one day in 1919 *(above right)* was this member of the Jubilee Class, No **1901 *Jubilee*.** As the loco was rebuilt as a 2 cylinder simple in April of that year, it cannot be ascertained which version was observed! The photo shows the engine in its original condition.

c1912 ● STEAM IMAGE

0-8-0 No 2655 stands resplendent outside No 2 shed

c1918 ● AUTHOR'S COLLECTION

Springs Branch Locos in LMS Days

The LNWR handed over 3,360 locomotives to the new London Midland & Scottish Railway Company in 1923 but some of these were rather aged and new designs soon appeared. The most common and relevant to Springs Branch were the variants of the 2-6-4 tanks, the Hughes & Stanier Moguls, the Ivatt Class 2's and the Stanier Black 5's and 8's.

A few designs were perpetuated by the LMS such as the Midland 2P's, the 4F's and Jinties and examples of these three classes plus locos of the former L&Y Railway resided at Springs Branch during the LMS period. According to the notes of Mr C. Williams, Springs Branch had 131 engines allocated in early 1928 and this must be as near to the maximum recorded as can be determined.

ALLOCATION - 1928 (Tender Locos: 28.1.28 Tank: 22.2.28)

Prince of Wales	5809 - 5822
George V (and SH Precursor)	3390/1
Precursor (Sat)	5198 - 5200
Experiment	5525/6/8/9
G and D 0-8-0 Tender engines	9131/2/3/5, 9137 - 9158
LNWR 19" Goods Tender engine	8770 - 8778
LNWR 18" Goods Tender engine	8370 - 8375, 8403 - 8415
LNWR 17" Coal Tender engine	8197/8/9, 8200/2 - 8223
B/E/F 4 cyl compounds	9603/6/8/14
5'6" 2-4-2 1P Tank	6723 - 6725
LNWR 0-8-2 Tank	7892/3/4/5
LNWR Special Tank 0-6-0	7269, 7313/6/8/53/6/8
DX Goods 0-6-0 Tender engine	8072, 8084
Fowler 4F 0-6-0	4151 - 4156
Jinty 0-6-0 Tank	16648/9

TOTAL 131

SH - Superheated   Sat - Saturated

ALLOCATION - March 1933

Prince of Wales	5810 - 5822
Precursor (Sat)	5200
G and D 0-8-0 Tender engines	8897, 8908/9/11, 9002/48/96/7/8, 9120/31/6/8 9139/40/2/7 - 50, 9152 - 57, 9178, 9281/2, 9365
LNWR 19" Goods Tender engine	8772 - 8778, 8789, 8848 - 8851
LNWR 18" Goods Tender engine	8409/10/3/7/97/8, 8544
LNWR 17" Coal Tender engines	8193/5, 8204/5/6/8/9/10/1/5
5'6" 2-4-2 1P Tank	6750
LNWR Webb 0-6-2 Tank	6881/3/94
LNWR 0-8-2 Tank	7884/92/3/4/5
LNWR Special Tank 0-6-0	7318/56/8
Hughes Crab	13077/8
Barton Wright 0-6-0	12030/1/2/6/45/53/9/64
L&Y 2-4-2 Tank	10734

TOTAL 96

From 1935 the major changes to the allocation were the huge increase in the numbers of 2-6-4 Tanks between 1941 and 1943. There was a corresponding reduction in Black Five's from twelve down to four, but this had recovered back to nine by 1943. In 1945 over 40% of the total allocation were Super D's. There were also eleven ex-LNWR 0-8-2 Tanks and the Stanier Moguls briefly appeared as did some of the LMS 7F 0-8-0's and finally, a solitary Fowler 4F, No 44470.

DX 0-6-0 No 8084 at Springs Branch MPD.
c1928 ● STEAM IMAGE

LOCOMOTIVE CLASSES ALLOCATED FROM 1935

Ex-LNWR Prince of Wales 4-6-0 tender engine. The allocation was down to eight at the start of 1935 and the last four were all cleared out together in June 1937 to Crewe North and Stafford sheds, ending a long association with this class.

Ex-LNWR 18" Goods tender engine (Cauliflower). The shed had four Cauliflowers in January 1935 but this was down to two in 1942 then the allocation recovered and increased to seven just before Nationalisation before settling back to four engines. The Cauliflowers would, by this stage, be mostly employed in the yards or short trip workings.

Ex-LNWR 17" Coal Tender engine. Five remained by January 1935 but all moved on to Barrow in July 1935. The following year three arrived from Shrewsbury but moved on a month later. The last arrival came from Patricroft in December 1937 and again left for Barrow in September 1946.

Ex-LNWR 19" Goods engines. There were five at the shed at the start of 1935 but just one by 1939. The allocation then improved to three in the mid 1940's with two being passed to BR. Thirteen different engines were allocated from the start of 1935 to Nationalisation.

Ex-LNWR 0-8-2 Tanks. Springs Branch still had five of these heavy shunting locos at the start of 1935 but this had dropped to two by 1939 only to revert to five, briefly, in 1942. The LMS eventually handed over three examples to BR and they spent their time solely employed shunting the Bamfurlong yards.

Ex-LNWR G1, G2 and G2A 0-8-0 Tender engines. The main freight loco throughout the LMS period, there were thirty examples at the shed in January 1935, almost half of the total allocation of sixty nine. This remained fairly static until 1938 when numbers started to fall and reached a record low of sixteen engines in 1942, The sheds workload must then have increased considerably as the depot's general allocation rose to almost ninety by 1945 and thirty seven of these were now G1/G2's. At the start of BR, twenty seven of these locos were still hard at work.

Class F 2-8-0 No 9614 4 cylinder compound with large boiler. Note the old coal stack behind the engine.

c1928 ● STEAM IMAGE

Ex-LNWR 2F 0-6-2 Tanks (Coal Tank). There were none at the start of 1935 then three arrived from Patricroft in May 1938. Over the following years there was always an allocation with nine different engines until 1948, when just one, No 7703, remained to be passed into BR stock.

Ex-MR & LMS 2P 4-4-0 tender engines. No 483 arrived in November 1938 and left a year later. From April 1940, numbers built up to seven within a month and two survived Nationalisation.

LMS 2-6-4 Tanks. The Stanier version began to appear in 1937 and the quantity gradually increased, then decreased leaving only seven on the books by 1948. The first Fowler version appeared in 1947 with three handed over to BR in 1948. None of the Fairburn examples were ever allocated during the LMS period.

LMS 2-6-2 Tanks. First to come for a mere five months was Stanier 3P No 109 from Barrow in September 1937. In 1941, three Fowler 3P's arrived from Bangor in December followed by another from Carnforth in January 1941. There was a bit of activity in 1943 when the three Fowler tanks were swapped with Edge Hill for three Stanier locos, although they left within a few years, leaving none at Nationalisation.

LMS 0-6-0 Jinty. Two locos, Nos 7390/476 arrived from Plodder Lane and Warrington Dallam during 1936, leaving after three and six years respectively. Another, No 7293 came for just one month in 1946 before returning to Preston

LMS Black Fives. The first to arrive were Nos 5126/7/8, brought in from North Wales in October 1935, followed two months later by one from Crewe North. Thereafter the allocation grew steadily and included three brand new locos coming direct to the shed (Nos 5294, 5333 & 5403). After a peak of thirteen at the end of 1939, the numbers decreased and seven remained to be handed over to BR.

Ex-L&Y Barton Wright 0-6-0's. The Barton Wright 2F's were a small versatile tender loco weighing just over 39 tons and dating back to 1887. There were eight of these ex-L&Y engines on the books by 1933, even though Springs Branch was an ex-LNWR shed. This allocation dipped to five then increased to ten by 1937, and eleven by 1942. Loco Nos 12045 and 12064 were the most prominent engines prior to 1948 when eight locos went into BR service.

Ex-L&Y 3F 0-6-0's. The Aspinall 3F's or L&Y 'A' Class as they were best known, date back to 1889. They gradually became a large class of 448 engines but this had dwindled to 245 by nationalisation. Just one appears on the Springs Branch books in January 1935 but within two months more had arrived from Shrewsbury and Abergavenny sheds. The allocation then continued to increase as older ex LNWR locos were withdrawn, with a maximum of thirteen engines allocated in January 1937, thereafter dwindling down to just two by 1948.

Ex-L&Y 2P & 3P 2-4-2 Tanks. There were three locos on allocation at start of 1935 and this rose to five in 1937 and 1938, but during 1939 the class was completely cleared out, only for No 10646 to return in March 1940. When this was exchanged for No 10676 in August 1941, another member, No 10660, also joined the fleet but four months later the 2-4-2's were both transferred away.

SEEN ON SHED ● 5TH APRIL 1931

Prince Of Wales	5750/6, 5810/1/2/3/4/6/7/8/9/22/3
Precedent/Improved Renown	5200
Experiment	5476, 5526/8
G and D 0-8-0's	8909, 9002/3/48/50/85/96/7/8, 9117/20/31/2/3/6/8/9/40/2/5/7/9/53 9154/5/6/7, 9250, 9310/27
LNWR 19" Goods	8707/72/3/4/5/6/7/8/89, 8849/51
LNWR 18" Goods	8404/10/2/3/7/40/79/97/8, 8544
LNWR 17" Coal	8192/5/8, 8204/5/6/8/9/10/1/5/20
5'6" 2-4-2 1P Tank	6725/50
LNWR 0-8-2 Tank	7883/4/92/3/4/5
Special Tank	7356/8
Barton Wright 2F	12015/30/1/2/6/45/53/8/9/64
Aspinall 2-4-2T	10647
Hughes 5P	10414

TOTAL 102

Class 0-6-0 No 8610 stands in the shed yard.

MARCH 1935 ● STEAM IMAGE

17" 0-6-0 Coal Engine No 8309   c1938 ● STEAM IMAGE

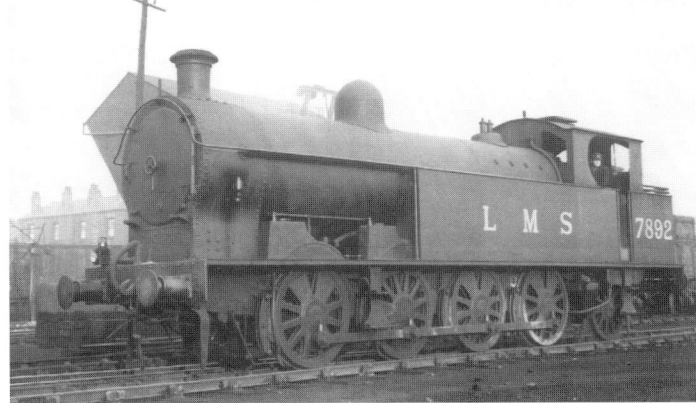
0-8-2 Tank No 7892.   20TH JUNE 1937 ● A.N.H. GLOVER

SPRINGS BRANCH LOCO ALLOCATIONS 1923 - 1948

	DX Goods	Experiment	Precursor (*& George V)	Prince Of Wales	19" Goods	Cauliflower 18"	17" Coal engine	LNWR 7F D/G Type	4 cyl comp (B, E, F)	Special Tank	LNWR 2F 0-6-0ST	0-6-2T (1P)	2-4-2T (1P) 5'6"	L&Y 2-4-2T Wirral	L&Y 2-4-2T	L&Y 0F 0-4-0ST	0-8-2T	L&Y 3F 0-6-0	L&Y 2F 0-6-0	LMS 2-6-4T	LMS 3P 2-6-2T	MR/LMS 2P 4-4-0	Black Five	LMS Jinty	Hughes 2-6-0	Stanier 2-6-0	Fowler 4F	LMS 7F 0-8-0	TOTALS
Feb 1928	2	4	5*	14	9	19	26	26	4	7			3				4							2			6		131
Mar 1933			1	13	12	7	10	30		3		3	1		1		5		8					2					96
Jan 1935				8	5	4	5	30						1	3		5	1	5					2					69
Jan 1936				6	4	4		27			3				3		4	4	7				4	2					68
Jan 1937				4	1	4		27			4			1	3		4	13	8				6	2				4	81
Jan 1938					1	3	1	29			2				5		4	8	10	2	1	1	8	2		2	1		80
1939					2	3	1	28							4		3	8	10	1		2	8	2					72
Jan 1940					1	4	1	27									2	5	10	2			12	1					65
1941					1	4	1	20							1		2	5	10	8		5	4	1					62
1942					3	3	1	23			2						2	6	10	9	3	5	5	1					73
1943					3	3	1	23			3						4	7	11	13	3	4	9						84
1944					3	4	1	26			4						4	4	11	14	2	2	9						84
1945					3	5	1	37			4						4	5	11	8	2	2	7						89
1946					3	7	1	34			2					1	4	4	11	6	2	2	8						85
1947					2	7		28			2						3	3	10	7		3	7						72
1948					2	4		29			1						3	3	9	9		2	7						69

Ex LNWR G2 0-8-0 No 9136 inside No 1 shed.   24TH APRIL 1938 ● L. HANSON

OTHER OCCASIONAL RESIDENTS

Ex-L&Y Hughes 0-8-0 3F's. Four of these were tried at the shed during 1936 and 1937 but none lasted for more than a year.

LMS Hughes 'Crab' 2-6-0's. Two had appeared on the books by 1933 but both left for Abergavenny in May 1935. In October 1935 two more arrived from Dallam but left seven months later for Shrewsbury.

Ex-LNWR 0-8-4 Heavy Shunting Tanks. No 7942 from Dallam and No 7946 from Crewe South spent seven weeks at the shed in 1936, probably being tried at Bamfurlong Yard.

Ex-L&Y Pug 0-4-0 Saddletank. No 11218 arrived in November 1945 from Preston shed. The loco was most likely used at Park Forge, up the Springs Branch, due to the sharp curvature of their track. It appears likely that their own shunting loco was unavailable and the LMS duly obliged by hiring out the 'Pug'. Another duty may have been at Roundhouse Sidings where the LNWR had always employed their smallest loco in the Wigan area. After nine months the engine returned to Preston.

LMS Patriot. Just one named LMS loco, No 5533 *Lord Rathmore* was allocated to the shed in March 1940 but left for Crewe North three months later.

Ex-L&Y/Wirral 2P 2-4-2 Tank. No 6762 was on allocation at the start of 1935 then left for Preston in July 1935 only to return in May 1936 and later depart to Sutton Oak in May 1937. One turn for this loco was the Wigan to Manchester Exchange locals *(see page 99)*.

LNWR 0-6-0 Special Tank. These locos had been regularly allocated to Springs Branch right up to the 1930's, however there were none here at January 1935. Things quickly changed, albeit only briefly, when four arrived in March 1936 from Birkenhead & Llandudno Junction sheds, but within a couple of weeks they were all sent to Speke Junction depot to end the depot's association with this class.

LNWR 2F Saddletank (Square Saddle Tank). Although they had been at Springs Branch up to the late 1920's, there were none of these odd looking engines here at the start of 1935 but three did arrive later from Speke in December 1936. Thereafter a couple were generally on allocation until the last one, No 27469, was transferred to Crewe South in April 1938.

SEEN ON SHED • 28TH MARCH 1936

MR 2P 4-4-0	447, 561
Fowler 2-6-4T	2303, 2400
Stanier 2-6-4T	2455/6/65, 2539/61/3/72
Hughes 2-6-0	2891, 2903
Stanier 2-6-0	2981
Black 5	5019/21, 5127/35/9/99, 5398
Prince of Wales Tank	6953
LNWR Coal Tank	7806
LNWR 0-8-2T	7880/4/92/4
LNWR 18" Goods	8417/22/505/26/98/610/1/756
LNWR 19" Goods	8824/49
LNWR 0-8-0	8911, 9002/38/55/70/80 9105/29/34/6/9/52/3/4/5, 9255/81/2, 9315, 9406
Aspinall 2-4-2T	10639/88
Barton Wright 2F	12016/21/2/3/32/45/53/64
Aspinall 3F	12111/9/34, 12225
Hughes 3F	12585/9
Hughes 7F	12958
Prince of Wales	25725/30, 25812/3/6/8, 27351
LNWR Square Tank	27471/5/7/80/4/92

TOTAL 87

Class 2P 4-4-0 No 695 stands stored in the shed yard with its chimney sacked. The loco arrived in November 1937 and then seemed to be almost shared between Springs Branch and Preston, moving back and forth three times before finally leaving in September 1939. It was mainly used on pilot work, particularly over Shap, but also saw service on local turns such as the Manchester Exchange services. **MARCH 1938 • AUTHOR'S COLLECTION**

◀ **19" Goods 4-6-0 No 8859 prepares to move off shed.** They were a genuine mixed traffic loco widely distributed over the system and were somewhat similar to the 'Experiments' but having smaller wheels. 170 members were built between 1906-1909, all of which survived the Grouping. The last three were scrapped in 1950 (Nos 8801/24/34) but never received their allocated BR numbers. Many were fitted with Belpaire boilers as is the example here. Stanier Class Five No **5403** lurks behind. On 1st September 1947 Nos 8824/34 were reported performing light duties with one designated shed pilot.

c1936 • DAVID YOUNG COLLECTION

Springs Branch Locos in BR Days

Apart from the Super D's, very few ex-LNWR locos survived through to the British Railways era. Four Cauliflowers, three 0-8-2 tanks, two Whale 19 inch Goods and a single 0-6-2 tank were the only others at Springs Branch. They had all gone by 1953, leaving the Super D's to soldier on and represent the ex-LNWR until 1962 when those remaining were withdrawn, apart from a few which were transferred to Bescot shed where they did another two years' work.

The mainstay of the passenger locomotive stud were the 2-6-4 tanks of the Fairburn, Fowler and Stanier variety and the Stanier Black 5's. The ex-Great Central services that were transferred across in 1952 continued from Springs Branch with their J10 locos, followed by the Ivatt 2-6-0's and 2-6-4 tanks, although BR Standard Class 4's and Black 5's did appear at times. When Preston shed caught fire in June 1960, closing fifteen months later, some extra work was transferred to Springs Branch and this resulted in a few Rebuilt Patriots and Royal Scots on the books for the first time, although by July 1964 they too had all gone.

Freight duties were always monopolised by the Super D's with the assistance of a few Black 5's, Ivatt 2-6-0's and the ex-L&Y 0-6-0 tender engines. By 1960 the ex-L&Y 0-6-0's had all gone and, as the Super D's were gradually withdrawn - Fowler 4F 0-6-0's and WD 2-8-0's arrived to take over some of their freight work, supplemented by an increase in the Black 5 allocation. In 1963, BR Standard Class 4 tender engines made a two year appearance before moving on and the same year saw the return of the Stanier Moguls. They could be found on virtually any type of work, supported a year later by the Black 8's. In addition, a few classes made brief appearances such as the Furness 0-6-0 tender engines, the Hughes Crabs and the BR Standard Class 2's and Class 4 2-6-0's, but none stayed very long. Between 1960 and 1966 there were a handful of Jinty 0-6-0T's allocated to Springs Branch which were used for local shunting duties and occasionally the Wigan North Western station pilot. In the final three years of steam, the depot allocation was virtually all Black 5's and Black 8's.

A few ex-LMS 0-6-0 diesel shunters arrived in 1957 and these were supplemented by the similar BR 08 type shunters, with most of these staying after the depot closed to steam in December 1967. A batch of Hunslet 05 diesel shunters arrived in March 1966 but never found favour and in 1967 some BR 03 shunters arrived for several years' work.

By 1967, Class 25 and 40 locomotives had arrived and taken over the depot's work, and the following year saw the official opening of the new Springs Branch Maintenance Depot (as it had now become). By 1984, the Class 20's had ousted both the Sulzers and the 40's and, later still, those Class 20's were superseded by Class 60's shortly before the depot closed in May 1997, mainly due to the closure of the Bickershaw Colliery complex in 1992.

Ex Great Central J10 0-6-0 No **65148** stands in front of the newly built No 1 shed after transfer across from Lower Ince shed.

JULY 1952 • P. WARD

SPRINGS BRANCH IN THE BR PERIOD

There are three main periods of loco allocation and operation concerning the shed, namely:

1 - 1948 to March 1952 (the closure of Lower Ince shed).
2 - March 1952 to April 1964 (taking on the ex-GC work following Lower Ince shed's closure).
3 - From April 1964 (taking on the ex L&Y work following Wigan L&Y shed's closure).

The different classes of loco and numbers allocated are shown in the table below. The shed allocation peaked at 88 when most of Wigan L&Y shed's locos came to Springs Branch upon its closure on 13th April 1964.

LOCO ALLOCATIONS 1948 - 1967

	LMS 3P 2-6-2T	MR 2P	LMS 2-6-4T's	Hughes Mogul	Stanier Mogul	Fowler 4F	Black 5	Rebuilt Patriot	Royal Scot	Ivatt 2-6-0	Jinty	LNWR 0-8-2T	LNW 19" Goods	Black 8	Super D	L&Y 2F 0-6-0	L&Y 3F 0-6-0	MR 2F 0-6-0	Cauliflower	LNW 2F 0-6-2T	GC J10 0-6-0	STD4 4-6-0	STD4 2-6-0	STD2 2-6-0	WD 2-8-0	Diesel Shunters	Totals
July 1948		2	9				9					3	2		27	5	4		4	1							66
July 1949	2	2	8				7					3	1		25	6	5		3								62
July 1950			10				7					3			27	4	6		2								59
July 1951			10				8			1		2			22	4	5		2								54
*July 1952			10				10			1		1			22	4	5		1		13						67
July 1953	1		11				9			3					22	2	7				8						63
July 1954			11				11			3					24	2	6				8						65
July 1955			9				10			4					27	2	6				8						66
July 1956			8				9			5					28		7				9						66
July 1957			11				9			4					29	2					9					7	71
July 1958			11			4	9			5					28						5					6	68
July 1959			7			4	14			4					28						4				4	6	71
July 1960			9			4	18			2	6				22			2			2			2	9	7	83
July 1961			8			8	18			4	5				25						2				8	6	84
July 1962			10			7	19	1	3		5				21									2	14	5	87
July 1963			9	3		10	30	1	1		7														14	5	80
**July 1964			15	3	5	3	17	1	1	7	6										12				13	5	88
July 1965			9		4	2	15			5	5			12											9		61
July 1966			7		3		24			4	3			16											15		72
July 1967							33							25							6				20		84
***Dec 1967							13							18											20		106

*Lower Ince Shed closed 24.3.52   ** Wigan (L&Y) Shed closed 13.4.64   *** The December 1967 total of 106 includes 55 main line diesels allocated

A busy Sunday at Springs Branch with Nos 45305, 42343 and 45114 (a visitor from Aston MPD) in front of No 1 shed. On this date No 45305 had only been officially allocated to Springs Branch the previous week.   **22ND AUGUST 1965** ● **JOHN BURGESS**

THE FAIRBURN, FOWLER & STANIER 2-6-4 TANKS

The first 2-6-4 tanks to arrive at Springs Branch were brand new Stanier locos Nos 2613 and 2614 in January 1937. Thereafter 2-6-4 tanks were continuously allocated for the next 30 years until the last, No 42577, was withdrawn in January 1967. The shed would generally have around 10 'Tanky's' on the books at any one time and most were of the Stanier design but, over the years, both the Fowler and Fairburn types were also represented but surprisingly, the Standard variety didn't feature here. Between 1948 and 1967, 59 different engines were, at various times, on allocation.

At Nationalisation in 1948, Fowler Nos 42303 and 42379 were here, and although they both moved on to other sheds, No 42303 returned for two more periods at the shed in 1960 and 1962. There were no Fowlers at the shed in 1964 but a final batch arrived in May 1965 when Nos 42343, 42369 and 42374 all appeared from Stockport and Gorton but their stay was short and when No 42374 was transferred to Trafford Park in September 1965, that was the end for the Fowler tanks. A total of 9 different Fowlers came and went, with No 42303 being the longest resident with over four years at the shed. By comparison, its nearest rival, No 42327 only had an 18 month stay.

Fowler 2-6-4T No 42343 is stabled on the truncated tracks leading to No 2 shed soon after its transfer from Stockport Edgeley in May 1965. By September it was off to Trafford Park shed.

20TH JUNE 1965 ● DANNY PRESTON

Stanier 2-6-4T No 42572 stands in steam in the shed yard. The loco's presentable condition reveals a fully lined out livery and BR 'ferret and dartboard' on the tank side

22ND MARCH 1959 ● PETER HUTCHINSON

Fairburn 2-6-4T No 42174 was yet another transfer in from Stockport Edgeley in January 1964, staying until it was withdrawn in August 1965. Shortly before its demise it is seen looking towards the ash hoist & coaler.

1965 ● FRED BANKS

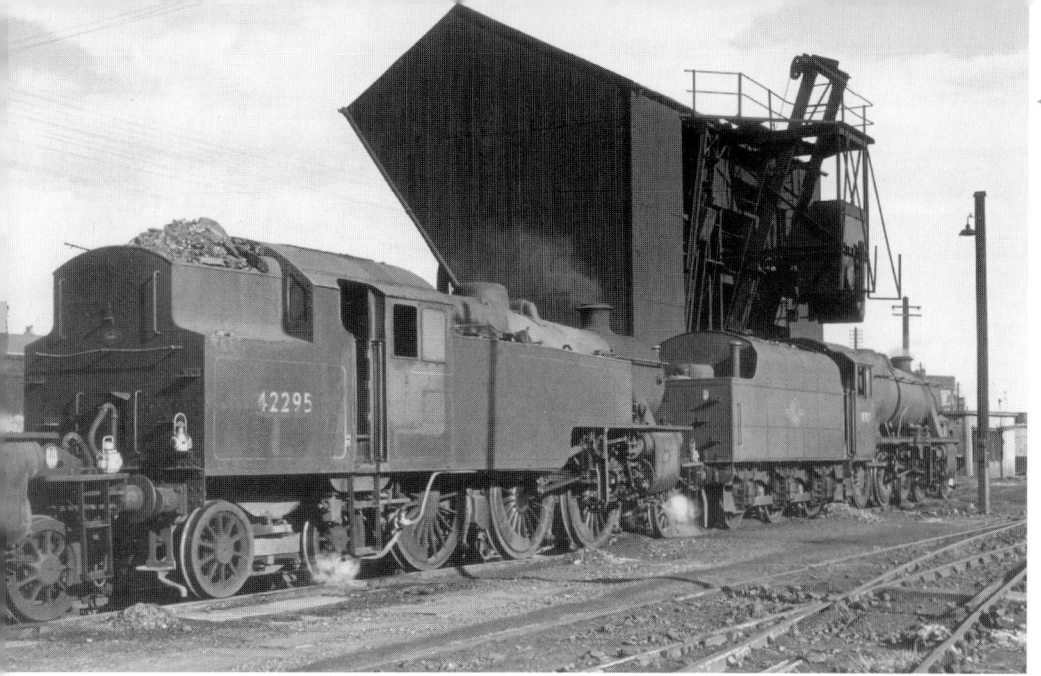

Fairburn 2-6-4 Tank No 42295 has just been coaled and awaits the 'coal & ash' men to move her forward to the ash pits. This loco had an 11 month stay from September 1964 until moving to Lostock Hall in August 1965.

27TH JUNE 1965 ● ALLAN HEYES

Stanier 2-6-4T No 42587 arrived from Kirkby-in-Ashfield in November 1964 and spent two years on allocation before moving on to Birkenhead shed. A visiting Black Five, No 45248 from Crewe South, stands alongside in the shed yard.

2ND APRIL 1965 ● DANNY PRESTON

Similarly, the Fairburn version of the 2-6-4 Tank was scarcely represented at the shed. Three arrived in March 1957, Nos 42119/20 and 42235, the first two leaving after a couple of years with No 42235 staying on to be the longest allocated Fairburn and lasting until November 1966. It was also the loco involved in the Ince Moss Junction incident on 17th February 1958 when it collided with a Black Five. During 1964, Nos 42174 and 42295 arrived and stayed for an 18 month spell, then Wigan L&Y shed closed in April 1964, and several 2-6-4 tanks came across including No 42680, the only one of the latter number series of Fairburn's to be allocated to Springs Branch, but it moved on within one month.

A couple more came, No 42102 in June 1965 and No 42233 a year later but all had gone by the end of 1966. At Springs Branch, the Stanier 2-6-4 Tanks were the mainstay of the local passenger and parcels traffic in the BR period. From 1948 through to 1966 there were forty different Stanier 2-6-4 tanks allocated, and the longest resident, No 42572, was here from February 1942 through to January 1964 when it was withdrawn. Both Nos 42456 and 42465 were allocated for over 16 and 17 years respectively and these are well remembered as 'pet' engines. In January 1967, just 11 months before the shed closed to steam, the last 2-6-4 tank, No 42577 was withdrawn, ending a long association with the type.

One of the locos that arrived with the demise of Wigan L&Y shed, No 42647, is seen stabled on road 5, five months after its arrival. Although Stanier tanks were being withdrawn at this time, No 42647 also moved on to Birkenhead in July 1966.

12TH SEPTEMBER 1964 ● JOHN BURGESS

Seen on Shed - Sunday 12th April 1964 (the day after Wigan L&Y shed closed)

Fairburn 2-6-4T	42174, 42235, 42680	Rebuilt Patriot	45531	Visitors	42148 (10B), 42474 (9H), 42559 (10B),
Stanier 2-6-4T	42426/56/62/5/94, 42554/60/72/89,	Ivatt 2-6-0 2MT	46419/84/6/7		42826 (9B), 44675 (10D), 44727/9 (12A),
	42607/34/64	Jinty	47314/95, 47444/93, 47517, 47603/71		44745 (8M), 44900 (12A), 44958 (8L),
Hughes Crab	42730/4/51, 42894	Std 4 4-6-0	75011/7/9/41/2/4/51/7/9		45375 (8M), 45512 (12B), 45588 (12A),
Stanier Mogul	42948	Std 2 2-6-0	78020/7/37/57/61/2		48512 (8A), 90140 (9J)
LMS 4F	44121, 44246, 44301, 44490	WD 2-8-0	90147/8/57/73/83, 90316/7, 90423/93,	In Transit	42297 (9H), 42644 (9E), 44222 (10G),
Black 5	44823, 45019/24, 45140, 45218/81/96,		90509/85, 90667	from L&Y	44240 (10G), 44544 (9G)
	45425/31/49	Withdrawn	42135, 42569, 44280, 45023		**Total 97**

THE HUGHES CRABS

Being basically an L&Y design, most of the Hughes Crabs that were seen in the North West originated from the ex-L&Y sheds and, whilst not uncommon on the West Coast Main Line, they were only very occasionally allocated to the likes of Springs Branch. In the 1930's, Nos 13077 and 13078 were on the books until May 1935 and Nos 13191 and 13220 again from October 1935 to May 1936, but then there were no allocations until the next Crabs arrived in July 1962 when Nos 42751, 42777 and 42894 all appeared. Most of these stayed around for two years, being joined by Nos 42730, 42734 and 42878 in April 1964 when Wigan L&Y shed closed. Thereafter it was a gradual decline until the last one, No 42878 left for Gorton in October 1964. Although many of the Crabs were being condemned by 1964, none were actually withdrawn from Springs Branch shed itself, although the Central Wagon Works cut up quite a few from other sheds. During their time at Wigan, the Crabs could be found on almost any job and even had occasional sessions on the Wigan - Preston locals.

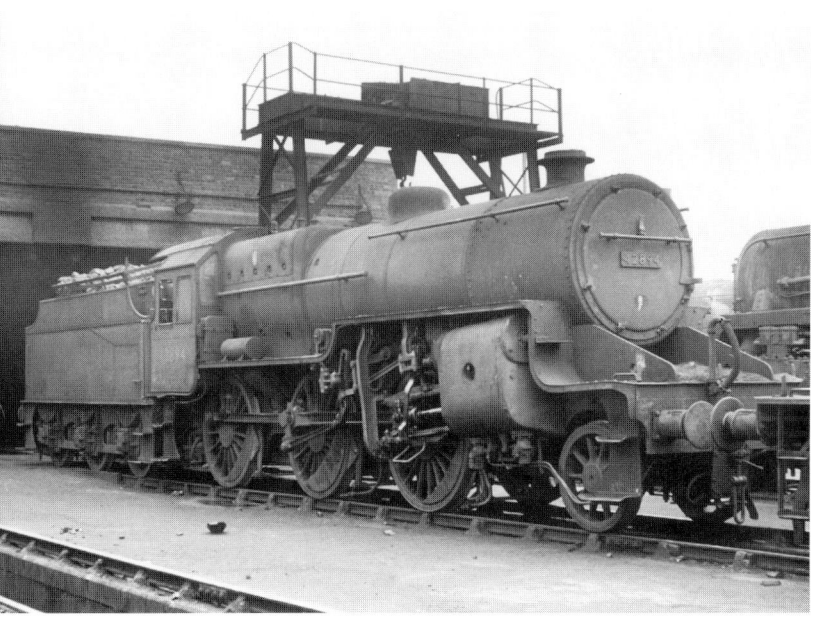

Sporting a painted 8F shedcode, No 42894 stands on road 5 outside No 1 shed with the 5 ton hoist behind. This loco arrived from Stoke in July 1962, staying just over four years before departing for Birkenhead in August 1965.

2ND AUGUST 1964 ● **ALLAN HEYES**

No 42894 is seen once again as it comes off the shed for a local working. It is approaching Cromptons Sidings Signal Box, the access point to the shed.

6TH APRIL 1964 ● **JOHN BURGESS**

35

THE STANIER MOGULS

In the British Railways era, the Stanier Moguls were mostly associated with the likes of Aston, Crewe, Mold Junction and Birkenhead, although a few had been allocated to Springs Branch around 1935-38 but none stayed for longer than five months. There was now a gap of 25 years before they re-appeared on the allocation, when three arrived at the end of 1963 (Nos 42948, 42959 and 42977). There then followed a large influx of the locos in 1964 with Nos 42963 and 42968 arriving in May followed by another five from Aintree shed in July and another from Nuneaton in August. One of the ex-Aintree engines, No 42952 must have been in very poor condition because it was withdrawn within weeks of arriving but the others stayed until Summer 1965 when five were transferred to Gorton shed. This started a decline that was followed by the withdrawal of No 42959 at the end of that year and No 42953 a month later, leaving just Nos 42954 and 42963 at the shed. However, as No 42953 left, No 42968 reappeared and these three continued until they were all gradually withdrawn, the last being No 42954 in February 1967. Only one example escaped the cutter's torch and Springs Branch's No 42968 now resides on the Severn Valley Railway in Shropshire.

The Stanier Moguls, commonly referred to as Stanier Crabs, had a slightly higher tractive effort than a Black Five, were a most useful loco and could be found on virtually any turn. However, in the very final years when larger steam power was readily available, they were often demoted to shunting work, particularly on the Ince Moss pilot turn.

No 42963 has the company of an unidentified Diesel Shunter and WD 2-8-0 in the shed yard.   **15TH AUGUST 1964 ● DANNY PRESTON**

Devoid of shedplate and seemingly stored at the back of the outside shed roads, No **42953** still had 5 months service left at the date of the photograph. The area is obviously a storage point for braziers etc.   **22ND AUGUST 1965 ● JOHN BURGESS**

Sundays were always the favourite day for shed visits and a week before Christmas 1966, No **42968** basks in the winter sun inside No 1 shed in an area used for boiler washouts, hence the pipe on the floor. Although withdrawn two weeks after this photo was taken, the loco evaded the cutter's torch and now resides on the *Severn Valley Railway*.   **18TH DECEMBER 1966 ● PETER FITTON**

THE FOWLER 4F 0-6-0's

Although they were principally a Midland design, this large class of just under 600 locos could be found throughout the BR rail system, yet very few had been allocated to the shed in LMS days. This all changed in 1958, when the demise of the Super D's caused an influx of these engines. Whether they were able to compete with the Super D's is debatable, but they did generally take on the more local freight jobs in the Wigan area, particularly the GC trip workings and even had stints on the banking duties. Known to local enginemen as 'Wuff Wuff's or 'Wuffies', four locos arrived at the shed in 1958 and, over the years, this increased to a maximum of thirteen before slowly petering out. Five engines stayed approximately 4 to 5 years and became well known around the shed. Notable engines were Nos 44490 (1/61 - 8/65), 44303 (3/58 - 9/63), 44280 (3/58 - 12/63), 44121 (5/61 - 1/65) and 44069 (3/58 - 10/63).

The replacement four road No 2 shed has just been completed and the access roads have yet to be cleared. Fowler 4Fs Nos **44069** and **44280** are stabled on roads 10 and 11.

20TH MAY 1961 ● **RICHARD STRANGE**

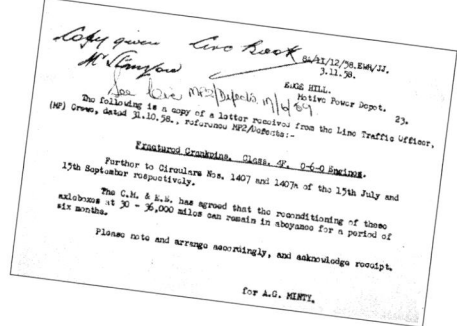

In the later years, Nos 44490 and 44500 are well remembered as the snow plough engines, spending most of their time at the back of the outside shed roads alongside No 2 shed with the plough attachments almost permanently affixed. Whether they ever actually did any snow plough work is unlikely, for the engines never seemed to move and were, in all probability, stored. Serious withdrawals took place from 1963 and many visitors will remember the long line of stored 4F's in the shed yard alongside the main line. Three 4F's did last until 1965 with No 44500 being the final loco on the books at Springs Branch. Although it's doubtful No 44500 did any work in those latter years, it was surprisingly moved to Barrow shed in December 1965 before being officially withdrawn from there in July 1966 and finally cut up at Drapers' scrapyard (Hull) four months later.

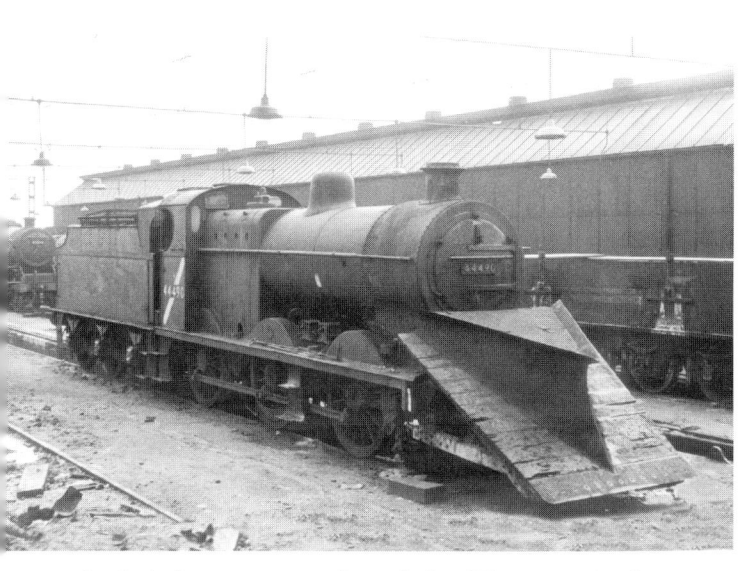

In their latter years, a few of the 4F's were utilised as snow-plough engines, although they are not recorded as ever actually being so employed. No **44490**, complete with diagonal cab side stripe, stands at the bottom of road 14.

1965 ● **ALLAN HEYES**

Uniquely numbered No 44444, known throughout the BR period as 'All the 4's', spent 13 months at Springs Branch after arriving from Aston shed. The engine managed another five months in service here before being withdrawn in August 1963.

23RD MARCH 1963 ● **R. BLENCOWE COLLECTION**

THE STANIER BLACK 5's

Introduced from 1934, the LMS built 842 of the Black 5's and, in the BR era, 84 of them spent some time allocated to Springs Branch, working anything from prestigious passenger trains (The Lakes Express) to local trip workings; they really were 'Jack of all trades'. The shed saw just a few of the Skefko and Timken bearing types, but not the real variants such as the Caprotti or Stephenson valve gear ones, although they did appear as visitors at times, particularly Southport's Caprotti engines.

With just six examples of the class on the shed at the start of the BR era, the allocation gradually built up to 29 Black Fives in 1963 and although this then slowly decreased, the final years saw further transfers and the allocation increased to 33, mainly because there was little else available apart from Black 8's and a few of the standard designs. Of the Black Fives allocated to Springs Branch, there were those that came and went, and those that stayed, the pet one being No 45449 with a continuous span of over 25 years from April 1942 until withdrawn in December 1967 when the shed closed to steam. Also notable are Nos 45314 (12 years) and 45425 (16+ years) which were both withdrawn from the shed. Another, No 45313, had clocked more than 15 years at the shed when it was involved in the Bickershaw accident in February 1965, a collision from which it did not recover and was withdrawn soon after and towed up the incline to the scrapyard of Central Wagon Works. Black 5's from the shed were also used on Royal Train duties and Nos 45425 and 45449 were the regular performers, although No 45408 had also done some of these until it was found to have a cracked frame.

Black Five No 45372 arrived from Longsight on 6th September 1959 and was eventually withdrawn from the shed on 23rd November 1966. The loco is caught moving smartly away one fine Saturday morning.

19TH JUNE 1965 ● JOHN BURGESS

Standing beside Springs Branch's distinctive coal plant is No 44918 which had arrived from Nottingham MPD in February 1965 as a result of increased dieselisation in that area. The stay was short lived and it moved on to Lostock Hall in July 1965, a couple of weeks after this photo was taken.

20TH JUNE 1965 ● DANNY PRESTON

Two of the sheds long term residents, Nos 45431 and 45449 are captured together here on camera. Both locos had previously featured on Royal Train Duties but now, with the end of steam at the shed just five months away, neither engine was to survive beyond this.

3RD JUNE 1967 ● DANNY PRESTON

A view from near the bridge carrying Taylors Lane over the railway. Black Five No **45385** is at the shed throat and going on to the depot. This engine came from Patricroft in October 1963 and was withdrawn from Springs Branch in November 1966. The Up and Down Loop and Manchester lines are below the engine.

29TH FEBRUARY 1964 • JOHN BURGESS

Black Five 4-6-0 No 44683 stands in front of No 1 shed with the newly constructed Diesel Maintenance Depot alongside. This loco only stayed here for six months after arriving from Crewe South in June 1967 and departing for Lostock Hall in December 1967 when the shed closed to steam.

23RD OCTOBER 1967 • DANNY PRESTON

When the shed closed to steam in December 1967, just over a dozen of its Black Fives escaped to survive another eight months elsewhere, but the rest had already worked their last jobs and were earmarked for the cutter's torch. Sadly none of these final locos at Springs Branch were preserved. Another Wigan Black Five was cut up at Central Wagon Works, namely No 45108 which had two spells at the shed, the last one from September 1959 to withdrawal in November 1965. On 30th January 1959, thirty four LMR engines were reported to be ATC (Auto train control) fitted including Springs Branch's No 45026.

Captured on a quiet Monday (for a change), No **45024** is stabled on shed ready for traffic. This loco arrived at the end of 1961 and was withdrawn in May 1967, some six months before the final closure to steam. There was always plenty of work for the Black Fives as they were capable of virtually any job.

28TH JUNE 1965 • DANNY PRESTON

FAST PILOT ON THE TOURIST

Driver Tommy Taylor reports that during the first half of the 20th century, a regular train on the LMS was the night Euston to Aberdeen which was always heavy and frequently needed a pilot engine for the mountain section between Wigan and Carlisle. Springs Branch always provided the crew and engine for this job, the loco varying from a Webb 6ft Jumbo during the first part of the century through Experiment 4-6-0's to Prince of Wales in the early 1930's. *Soon after the 5X's (Jubilees) came into service, I was called out to assist the 'Tourist' to Carlisle. On arriving at Springs Branch shed, I found a brand new 5X ready and prepared to leave for Wigan station where, upon arrival, I was put behind the signalbox to await the train. When the Tourist arrived, 20 minutes late, it too had a 5X on with a Crewe driver who reported his engine was not steaming very well. He passed a remark about Springs Branch men being unable to run fast enough to keep time with an express so I gave him a run to remember. We set off up Boars Head bank at a rate of knots and by Preston the lost time had been recovered. North of here the road is flat and straight so the train flew and, because we were running so fast, I misjudged the speed approaching Lancaster Old Junction, shutting the regulator too late for comfort. We ran round the curve so fast that sparks were flying from the frames due to the wheel tyres touching them, which was rather alarming and shook the Crewe man. We never felt Grayrigg and reduced speed for the curve, then opened up for Shap. We ran through Tebay at over 80 mph and it was obvious that the bush telegraph had been working as all the station staff were on the platform to watch the flyer go through at such unaccustomed speed. The train sailed over Shap and, despite a stand outside Carlisle station, we arrived 10 minutes early. The Crewe man was nowhere to be seen. I would imagine he may reconsider his earlier comment after this run. We hooked off and proceeded to Upperby shed tender first, where we left the engine and climbed into bed at the barracks before 2.30am, happy in the knowledge we had certainly put that man in his place.*

THE PATRIOTS AND ROYAL SCOTS

The type of traffic worked from Springs Branch meant that the shed was never blessed with much in the Class 7 (or higher) range of motive power and so missed out on the more glamorous locomotives. It wasn't until the serious fire at Preston shed in June 1960, resulting in its closure in September 1961, that things changed slightly and five named locos appeared on the shed books, namely Preston's four Royal Scots Nos 46161/5/7/8 and Edge Hill's No 45521. The Royal Scots had worked the Euston turns to and from Preston which also included the Wigan - Chorley ROF workers train in its diagram and these local turns were also taken over by Springs Branch. By the Summer of the following year Nos 46161/5/7 had left for Crewe North shed, but a few months later No 46128 arrived from Crewe North. This stayed for just a few weeks before moving on to Carlisle Kingmoor. The next change brought No 46110 (in July 1963) and No 45531 (October 1963) from Edge Hill to the shed and No 46115 from Longsight in June 1964 to replace No 46168 which had been withdrawn a few weeks earlier. Finally Nos 45531 and 46115 were transferred away to Upperby at the end of July 1964 ending the short but interesting association with these classes. Although Warrington Dallam, a mere eleven miles away, had an allocation of Jubilees, it's surprising that none of this class was ever allocated to Wigan, but Jubilees from many former LMR sheds, particularly Crewe, Dallam, Carnforth and Upperby, were frequent visitors, as were the Preston Jubilees prior to that depot's demise.

In the late 1950's, as part of a Camden engine diagram, a 1B Royal Scot would work the evening workmen only Chorley ROF to Wigan train, stable overnight on the shed, and return the following morning on the Wigan to Chorley ROF train whence it would regain its Blackpool-Euston circuit. Such are the complexities of loco/men diagrams, Preston men worked the Camden loco up to Wigan and Springs Branch men took it back the following morning. On Saturday mornings, when the ROF train didn't operate, the engine did a fill in trip to Manchester Exchange and back.

In the mid 1960's, a few Jubilees, a 'Royal Scot' No 46129 and a Duchess Pacific No 46243 appeared at the shed, but these were all withdrawn examples heading for the nearby scrapyard of Central Wagon Works at Ince.

The shed's longest Class 7P resident, No 46168 *The Girl Guide* sits on the diesel fuel road after withdrawal. It remained here until June 1964 after which it was placed in store at Preston *(see page 55)*. The 'Scot' was eventually towed away for scrapping at Crewe Works.

17TH MAY 1964 • ALLAN HEYES

No 45531 *Sir Frederick Harrison* had been a long standing Edge Hill resident and arrived in October 1963, by which time there was little suitable work remaining on Merseyside. After a nine month period it moved on again to Carlisle Upperby. During both the LMS and BR periods, a great variety of Class 6, 7 and 8 passenger locomotives appeared on shed - either for servicing or repair - and some of these are featured in the 'Visitors' section on Pages 58 - 62.

10TH OCTOBER 1965 • JOHN BURGESS

40

THE IVATT CLASS 2P 2-6-0's

Although only classed as 2P, these versatile little engines were equally at home on local passenger, parcels, or lengthy freight trains and could often be found on the ex-GC lines in the area. Even as late as 1965 there were varied diagrams for these engines including Class 6 freights to Preston and Warrington, a Preston local on Saturdays and a trip working to Southport ... a complete mix! Of the two versions, the BR style didn't make an appearance until May 1960, long after the LMS variety had been associated with the shed.

In total, 19 LMS and 8 BR Ivatt's came and went over the years. Looking at the LMS variety, in BR days the first to appear were Nos 46428 and 46430, arriving from Preston shed in March 1951. Others came and went but they had all disappeared by February 1962. Following a gap of a couple of years, there was a sudden influx of the class on the 12th April 1964 which, surprisingly, had nothing to do with Wigan L&Y's demise that day but was a result of the closure of Lees (Oldham) shed. Another batch came in May 1964 from Derby and Nottingham sheds. In August 1965 a green liveried No 46517 appeared, having originally been a Bristol St Philips Marsh loco but more recently had been allocated to Northwich. Apart from the Patriots and Royal Scots which had now long gone, it was refreshing to have a green loco on shed again. It stayed for over a year at Wigan but was withdrawn at the end of 1966 along with No 46447. This left Nos 46432 and 46515 to carry on until May 1967 before also being withdrawn, just seven months before the end of steam at Springs Branch.

Ivatt No 46434 heads a line of locos in front of No 1 shed. After arriving from Rhyl in October 1953, it spent nearly seven years at Springs Branch before moving on to Carlisle Upperby in May 1960. During its latter period it was often noted on the ex-GC services from Wigan Central station.

17TH JUNE 1959 ● B.K.B. GREEN COLLECTION

A pair of gricers have made careful note of Ivatt 2-6-0 No **46447** standing in the sun outside No 2 shed.

22ND AUGUST 1965 ● JOHN BURGESS

A busy scene at the coaling plant. Replenishing its tender is Ivatt No **46515**, one of a number which carried fully lined green livery, a legacy of Swindon, when allocated to Oswestry.

29TH JUNE 1966 ● TOM HEAVYSIDE

THE 'JINTY' 0-6-0T's

Introduced by the LMS in 1924, the Jintys became a very common sight across much of the BR system with 412 transferring into BR ownership. Springs Branch had three Jintys at the shed before nationalisation, the last leaving in 1946, but it was to be January 1960 before the next allocation arrived when Nos 47392, 47659, 47669 and 47671 came from Warrington Dallam and Camden sheds, followed, a few weeks later, by Nos 47270 and 47281 from Stoke. Although the number of Jintys varied thereafter, the maximum at Springs Branch at any one time was six locos and this slowly declined until the last pair, Nos 47603 and 47671, moved on to Sutton Oak shed in October 1966, the latter being the longest serving member at the shed with a stay of nearly seven years. One example of the ex-Somerset & Dorset variant, No 47314, came from Speke Junction in July 1962, leaving four years later for nearby Lostock Hall. As late as November 1965 a Jinty was booked to *Shunt 122 - The Bamfurlong South End Corner Pilot* on two shifts daily. Other regular Jinty turns were on *The Ince Moss tip shunt*, *The Incline shunt* or acting as *Wigan Bank* (the station pilot engine) although, at times, there did seem to be as many withdrawn Jintys around the shed as working ones.

Jinty 0-6-0 No 47603 stands on road 13 at the back of the site on New Years Day 1963. This is a well remembered engine which spent four years here from October 1962 until it moved, with No 47671, to Sutton Oak in October 1966. Note the sand wagons by the Kelbis Sand dryer at the bottom of Road 15.

1ST JANUARY 1963 • DANNY PRESTON

Stuck on the end of the diesel fuel road, Jinty No **47444** is going nowhere. It is out of service awaiting attention to its rear wheelset or bearings and is also captured on film undergoing this repair on page 74. The chalked headcode 1S75 is most unlikely as this is the code for the Down *Mid-day Scot* and almost certainly the result of some joke. However, it was unofficially known as *Duchess of Crawford* by the local trainspotters. Clearly visible is the oil and tool hut with all manner of cans and buckets etc.

8TH AUGUST 1965 • P. HUTCHINSON

Springs Branch's longest resident Jinty No 47671 rests at the back of the outside roads. The engine arrived here after transfer from Camden shed in January 1960 and stayed until October 1966 when, despite other Jintys being withdrawn at that time, moved on to nearby Sutton Oak shed at St Helens. This member was referred to as *City of Wigan*. **12TH JULY 1964 • ALLAN HEYES**

0-6-0 No 47395 stands on the truncated number 11 road, following the construction of the four road No 2 shed seen behind it.

2ND APRIL 1965 • ALLAN HEYES

THE 0-8-2 TANKS

Just three of these large ex-LNWR side tank shunting engines survived into the British Railways era at Wigan. Two years later, the last four remaining locos of the class (Nos 7877/81/84/96) were all now to be found at Springs Branch and these four were the only members of this class to receive the '4' prefix.

One of the quartet still retaining its LMS lettering in the very early BR period. This unidentified loco is about to come forward on to the turntable off the ash pit road.

c1950 ● N.K. HARROP

They continued to perform the same duties they always had, namely, heavy shunting work at Bamfurlong Yard for which they were most suitable, being classed 6F and basically a tank version of the Super D. Local enginemen nicknamed them 'Titanics' because they were so large and heavy, but they had no problem shifting the huge loads around the yards. Unfortunately, they were now almost 40 years old and much more modern locos were becoming available. Gradually the allocation was reduced to just one, No 47877 by July 1952. However, this lone survivor managed another 7 months' work before it was finally made redundant in February 1953, whereupon the class became extinct, leaving the Super D's to represent the former LNWR into the 1960's.

Only four of the 'Titanics' were ever allocated the BR Prefix '4' and all were Springs Branch engines. Two of these are in the old No 1 shed in this undated view, thought to be around 1950. No **47881** is nearest the camera and both may well be stored. Further employment may not have been forthcoming as it was withdrawn from the shed in July 1951.

1950 ● COLIN STACEY

THE STANIER 8F 2-8-0's

The Stanier 8F's, or 'Black Eights', as they were commonly referred to, were extremely late arrivals at Springs Branch, none being allocated until the end of 1964. With the WD 2-8-0's being gradually withdrawn, replacements were needed and progressive dieselisation in the Nottingham area resulted in Black 8's being surplus to requirements, so many were transferred to sheds in Lancashire. Initially five arrived in November 1964, followed by another one in December 1964 and then yet another batch came in January 1965, this time from Buxton and Northwich sheds, these again being surplus after new diesels took over the stone traffic those depots worked. This influx continued until the middle of 1967, by which time no fewer than 29 examples were allocated, despite some of the earlier arrivals having already been withdrawn. By this time all steam hauled freight from the shed was in the hands of either the Black 5's, Black 8's or a handful of Standard Class 4's, such was the lack of choice in these final months.

New arrival No 48678 is standing in the stabling sidings that were utilised to compensate for the loss of space caused by the new Diesel Depot construction. This loco is one of the later batches transferred here from Colwick in November 1966 and, on closure of Springs Branch to steam, moved on again to Newton Heath.

NOVEMBER 1966 • JOHN BURGESS

No 48494 stands amidst other Stanier examples outside No 1 shed. This, along with many others, had been displaced from the East Midlands coalfield in 1964 and remained until March 1967 when it was withdrawn. Of note is the unusual shedplate with the offset 'F'. The author cannot recall ever seeing the like before.

8TH AUGUST 1965 • PETER HUTCHINSON

The first six locos to arrive were still at the shed in March 1967 and No 48125 stayed until October, making it the longest resident of the class. Its other claim to fame was when it was called upon to assist a diesel failure on the Glasgow to Birmingham express in the area. No 48125 hauled the train to Crewe where it was reported that the engine was well and truly 'knackered' and so had to be left there with the men returning 'on the cushions'. When Springs Branch closed to steam in December 1967, several Black 8's were in store. Certainly No 48752 had been seen in November 1967 but disappeared, only to return in May 1968. Thereafter it went back into store until at least November 1968 and became the very last steam engine at Springs Branch. The nineteen Black 8's that were still at the shed on closure were sent to other depots in the North West with Patricroft (5) and Edge Hill (4) being the main recipients.

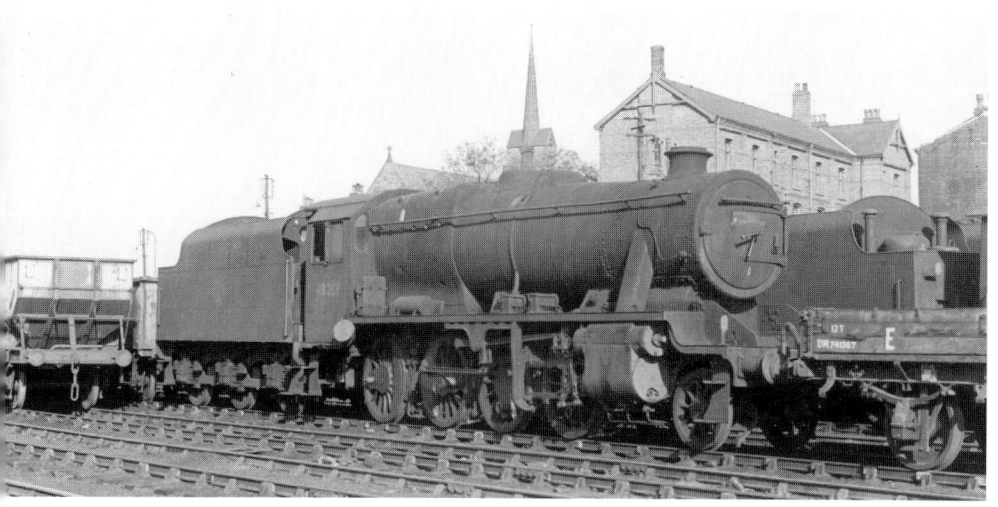

No 48261 has performed its last duty. The connecting rods are down but it was perhaps unusual to find a 'not to be moved' disc remained clamped to the running plate. Withdrawn locos and wagons stand on sidings which were once the busy Springs Branch Up yard, but from the mid 1960's saw them utilised for these purposes. Of further note is the Enginemen's Hostel above the locomotive. This 48-bed establishment lasted until the early 1970's.

1967 • LES RILEY

THE 0-8-0 'SUPER D's (G1 & G2)

If you wanted to see Super D's then Wigan was the place, as Springs Branch had the largest allocation in the country and up to 38 examples could be found at the peak of their allocation in 1945, far more than any other class at the shed until 1967, when the Black Fives surpassed this. Needless to say the Super D's dominated the freight work around the area, working everything from local freight and trip workings to yard shunts and banking duties. Footplate crews, however, complained that they were awkward for yard work, as there was very little adjustment on the regulator and the brake handle was high up.

D's or Super D's, in their various forms, had been on the Springs Branch allocation from their introduction, and they were known locally as 'Wigan Scotsmen' or 'Fat Nancys', although drivers generally called them 'D's'; either way, they considered them their top workhorses with No 49311 the pick of the bunch. Over the years they may have become elderly and tired but remained extremely reliable and surefooted and could always be guaranteed to handle whatever was thrown at them. A Super D was allowed a maximum of 90 wagons between Wigan and Warrington. Imagine that load as an unfitted freight in the hands of one 62 Ton loco!

Super D 0-8-0 No 49142 passes on the Up loop in 1961. Judging by the coal in the tender it has just been fuelled and watered and is returning to its trip, shunting or banking duty. This picture can be dated from the engine's short stay at Springs Branch, a mere three months from March 1961 to June 1961, after which it returned to Edge Hill. It's possible it was a loan but records show it as an official transfer.

MAY 1961 • JOHN BURGESS

Well remembered engines include No 49129 which had three spells at Springs Branch, including a continuous one from January 1941 until withdrawal in November 1962, and it clocked a total of over 26 years at the shed. Another 11 engines spent over 10 years here and No 49090, although withdrawn in 1950, had at least 16 years at the shed. Since standard shed allocations commenced in January 1935, no fewer than 155 different D's were allocated here with 106 of them during BR days.

Some of the Super D's had tender cabs, and these engines would usually be employed on banking duties due to the need for them to run reasonable distances tender first. Tender cabs would give the crew some protection in bad weather as opposed to the normal tender where the crew would quite literally be open to the elements.

The afternoon sun nicely highlights No 49438 trundling off shed for its next spell of work. Although the class were always well represented at Springs Branch, large numbers could also be found in the Liverpool and Birmingham areas as well as sizeable allocations at Nuneaton, Bletchley and Willesden Depots. Despite working predominantly over former LNWR metals - Swansea, Abergavenny and Pontypool Road were other unlikely outposts for this large class.

13TH APRIL 1961 • JOHN BURGESS

Even as late as the Summer of 1961, Springs Branch had 16 daily diagrams for these locomotives, 5 on banking duties and 11 on trip workings and, although they rarely ventured far, they were used constantly and most were clocking over 300 miles a week, with some doing over 500. As might be expected, opportunities for stardom were rare for these workhorses although it is reported that on one occasion a Super D came up the bank from Bamfurlong Sorting Sidings to Springs Branch carrying the Caledonian headboard. Presumably the board had fallen off the express and the crew had noticed it by the trackside and, with typical mischief, placed it proudly on the top lamp iron as they returned home. Although not quite express work, Springs Branch engine No 49451 was called upon to work a railtour organised by the RCTS on 22nd September 1962 *(see page 120)*.

In the winter of 1958, five Springs Branch Super D's were reported to have snowploughs fitted - Nos 49129, 49401/2/8/36 - but the demise of the class came in 1962 when the shed started the year with 20 engines. Just one, No 48895, was transferred away to Bushbury depot in August and fifteen worked through until November 1962 when all but one was withdrawn. The final working loco, No 49008, outlived the others by just one week being withdrawn on 4th December 1962, thus ending the shed's long association with the class.

An example of the Tender Cab version is No 49408. It is reported that the tender cab sections were created from the redundant cabs of the withdrawn Titanic 0-8-2 Tanks. The depot certainly got value for money from their members as No 49408 arrived from Rugby shed in December 1950 and lasted until the end of the class here in November 1962.

9TH AUGUST 1953 • H.C. CASSERLEY

The view across the turntable finds No 49352 stabled alongside the old No 2 shed on what was then road 17. This angle also gives a good view of the wooden sides and vents of this particular shed building

9TH AUGUST 1953 • H.C. CASSERLEY

THE EX-L&Y 0-6-0's

Of the three variants, there were ten Barton Wright 0-6-0's at Springs Branch at Nationalisation but nine months later they were down to six, and four more of these had gone by 1952, leaving just Nos 52021 and No 52051 at the shed. Loco No 52021 was withdrawn in August 1955 and No 52051 carried on a few months longer before being withdrawn in February 1956. Only three of the ex L&Y 'A' Class were allocated to the shed in 1948 but then numbers gradually built up again to a maximum of six before slowly dwindling away. The last two, Nos 52230 and 52269, both went on to do further work at Newton Heath and Lees respectively in July 1958. Only two of the superheated Hughes 3F's were allocated to the shed in BR days, namely Nos 52551 and 52598, the latter residing for a brief nine month period before withdrawal, but No 52551 did much better, with two periods at the shed from August 1952 to August 1956 when it left for Bangor only to return 2 months later and stay, until withdrawal came in March 1957.

Barton Wright No 52021 awaits its next duty in the shed yard. The loco managed over 20 years at Springs Branch after arriving from Barrow in July 1935 and was the penultimate survivor of the class at the shed, finally succumbing in August 1955.

c1953 • PHOTOMATIC

Regular turns for all these engines were the yard shunts or the less taxing trip workings and they rarely appear to have ventured far from the shed. The preserved example, No 52322, came from Nuneaton and spent four years at the shed from August 1952 before moving on to Sutton Oak in July 1956.

The No 2 shed roof looks in perfect condition as Aspinall L&Y 0-6-0 tender loco No **52098** stands outside. The engine is a mere two months away from withdrawal and is therefore unlikely to receive the new BR emblem or numbers. It was originally a Moor Row loco and came south to Springs Branch in June 1949.

9TH AUGUST 1953 • H.C. CASSERLEY

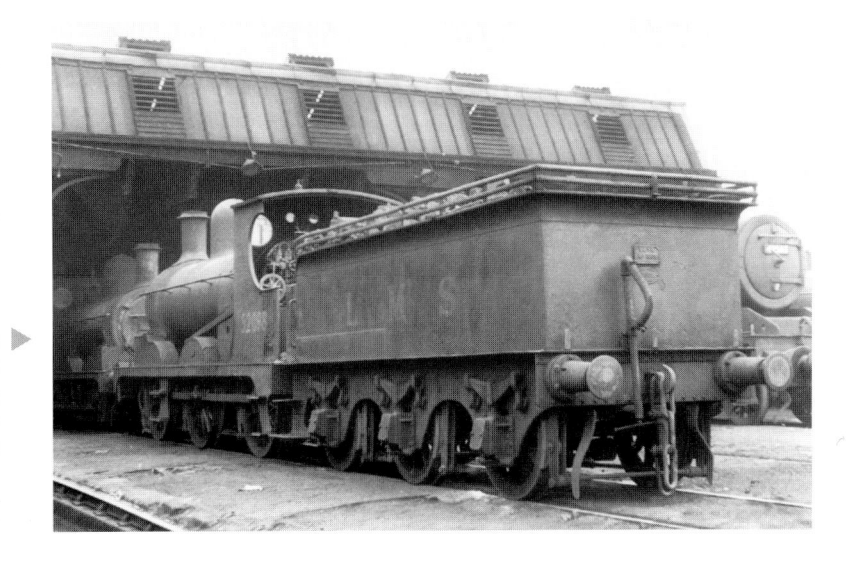

This elevated angle nicely captures the boiler profile of one of the later batch of locos, introduced in 1909 by George Hughes. A Sunday afternoon sees No **52551** standing out of steam but the engine still had much work ahead of it, for in August 1956 it left for Bangor only to return two months later to eke out its final days until withdrawal in March 1957.

23RD OCTOBER 1955 • H.K. BOULTER

THE 0-6-0 'CAULIFLOWERS' (Webb 18" GOODS)

Webb's 18" Goods Engines were an 0-6-0 Tender Engine weighing 36 ton 10cwt with 5'2" wheels and 18" cylinders. 310 of these locos were built by the LNWR between 1880 and 1902 yet only 69 made it into LMS days. Not surprisingly there were very few when British Railways was formed in 1948, but some did soldier on and Springs Branch still had four on the books in January 1948, namely Nos 28403, 28417, 28450 and 28592 and, despite some comings and goings, the shed retained a 'Cauliflower' allocation until July 1952. Some of these engines were to acquire BR numbers, the others retaining their LMS numbers until withdrawn.

There have actually been 29 different 'Cauliflowers' at Springs Branch between January 1935 and 1952, with 13 different ones during the BR period. The longest resident in BR days was No 28450, which was one of those there at Nationalisation and it stayed until March 1950 before moving on to Bangor. There wasn't really much work for these veteran engines by 1950, the only regular duties being the Wigan bank engine (Station pilot), the 'Incline Shunt' and 'Muck Link' jobs. One of the best remembered was No 58398 (28515) which had two stints at the shed in 1950 and again in 1951/2 and was a regular on the station pilot in those years along with No 58400 (28525).

The end for the Cauliflowers came in 1952 when the last three were withdrawn. The final loco to leave was No 58396 which survived until July of that year after approximately 60 years of service.

An unidentified Cauliflower 0-6-0 stands inside the old No 1 shed in the summer of 1948. At this date the shed had four 'Cauliflowers' on allocation, namely Nos 28403, 58376, 58381 and 28592. The engineman may well be studying the Notice boards which are visible on the bottom wall.

10TH AUGUST 1948 ● KRM

Seen on Shed - Sunday 18th June 1950

Fairburn 2-6-4T	42266
Stanier 2-6-4T	42442/54/4/6/65, 42539/60/3/72
Black 5	45067/73, 45141/81, 45425/49
Patriot	45542
Jubilee	45559
LNWR 0-8-2T	47881/4/96
LNWR 7F	9023/50/199, 48895/929/30, 49018/82/90/4, 49228/64/8, 49306/41/52/81, 49402
Barton Wright 2F	52053
Aspinall 3F	12341, 52098, 52126/40, 52250
LNWR 18" Gds	58398, 58400

TOTAL 47

Seen on Shed - Sunday 18th March 1962

Fairburn 2-6-4T	42235
Fowler 2-6-4T	42303
Stanier 2-6-4T	42426/56/62/5, 42572/64
LMS 4F	44069/76, 44125, 44303, 44490
Black 5	45017/24/6/92, 45135, 45372/88, 45408/25
Royal Scot	46168
Jinty	47270, 47392/5, 47517, 47671
LNWR 7F	48895, 49002/25/49, 49104/22/9/39/41
Std 4 2-6-0	76022
WD 2-8-0	90173, 90574, 90667/86
Diesel Shunters	12003/23/31
Visitors	42443 (5D), 44993 (8G), 45041 (8A), 45185 (12B), 45197 (8B), 45351 (12B), 46106 (21A), 48257 (6C), 48659 (5B), 76076 (8G), 12027 (8C)

Missing Springs Branch engines were noted at:

In Works	46161/7, 49451
Bolton	45347
Carnforth	45109, 45314, 49008, 90507
Colwick	90317
Crewe North	45521
Lostock Hall	45373, 45449
Longsight	49154
Lower Darwen	42607, 90257 (arrived on SB later)
Upperby	45019/57, 45313
Unknown	44121, 44280, 45108, 45281, 45431, 46165, 47444, 49431, 76051, 90509, 12032, 12102, D3292, D3836/7

Another unidentified member within No 1 shed stands in steam with a trusty 'Super D' bringing up the rear.

c1948 ● KRM

THE POLLITT AND ROBINSON J10 0-6-0's

When the small ex-Great Central shed at Lower Ince closed in 1952, the engines and work transferred to Springs Branch and 13 Eastern Region locos were actually allocated to the shed for the one and only time. Although the Lower Ince shed was just over a mile by road from Springs Branch, the rail journey, via Bickershaw Junction, was nearer to 4½ miles.

Initially, the J10's maintained their original roles on GC passenger and freight work but they were gradually replaced on these services by more modern power, predominantly the 2-6-4 tanks, so eventually the J10's were only to be found on local shunts and trip workings. Another 'last stand' for the class was acting as Wigan NW Station Pilot (Wigan Bank), as it was often left to one of the shed's oldest locomotives and, following the 'Cauliflowers' demise, the J10's were the obvious choice. Within 9 months of arriving, the thirteen original engines were whittled down to nine and a partial clear out in December 1956 saw five of the shed's J10's transferred to Darlington shed yet, within days, another four had arrived from Chester Northgate. After this there was a gradual reduction over the following years until, by early 1960, only Nos 65157, 65192 and 65198 remained. No 65192 was a favourite for the shed pilot duty until its demise in May 1960. The final pair were then stored for many months at the end of the loco coal wagon holding sidings and it wasn't until August 1961 when their official withdrawal took place, whereupon they were quickly removed to Gorton for cutting up.

No 65170 stands on what was to become the diesel fuel road. This engine arrived following the closure of the ex-GC shed at Lower Ince but left for Trafford Park soon after, before returning in December 1956 for a further 18 months work. Of interest are the holes in the buffer beam for the fixing of side chains - a legacy of seeing service on the 'Western Front' between March 1917 and June 1919. **1952 • J. DAVENPORT**

A fine panoramic view of the rear of the shed. Stored J10 No **65198** still has a full tender of coal but never worked again, being officially withdrawn in August 1961 having clocked up 1,120,705 miles during a lifetime of 65 years. There are at least four Jubilees on shed, all lined up behind the J10 but just two, Nos **45671** *Prince Rupert* (6G) and **45620** *North Borneo* (16A) are visible. They are being prepared for excursions to Wembley Stadium in conjunction with the Rugby League Challenge Cup Final against arch rivals St. Helens. This view also shows the original 1882 workshops behind the newly constructed four-road No 2 shed plus part of the chimney of the sand dryer on the extreme right. Although it's not possible to ascertain from this angle, there are in fact four sections of the old Northlight roof that survived together with the associated workshops, stores and sand furnaces. **13TH MAY 1961 • JOHN BURGESS**

THE BR STANDARD CLASS 4 2-6-0 and 4-6-0's

Springs Branch had both the 2-6-0 and the 4-6-0 variety allocated at different periods. First to arrive were Nos 76022 and 76051 from Lancaster in February 1962 but they left five months later. Rapid dieselisation of the Midland Division released large quantities of steam locos and, in November 1963, a batch of eight 4-6-0's arrived from Derby to replace the now dwindling numbers of WD's and 4F's. Two more followed from Southport a month later before the allocation was strengthened yet again with a further two in early 1964. All twelve stayed and were used mostly on freight workings, although they also found favour on banking duties plus occasional forays over the former GC route shortly before that service finished. They also found employment on the Rochdale - Liverpool Exchange workings. Changes in services in March 1965 saw the whole allocation of twelve transferred away, en-bloc, to Skipton shed. Finally in June 1967, just six months before the shed closed to steam, six Standard 2-6-0's arrived, following nearby Sutton Oak shed's demise. These were eventually withdrawn but four lasted until the very end in December 1967.

2-6-0's from other depots, often distant, were regular visitors either off Horwich Works after repair or on a variety of freight and parcels trains from East Lancashire.

Standard Class 4 No 75042 leaves the shed for its next turn of duty.
7TH APRIL 1964 • JOHN BURGESS

No 75017 was one of a pair which arrived from Southport in December 1963 (No 75019 was the other), following a contingent of 8 from Derby the previous month. The engine awaits its next duty and is standing on the diesel fuel road.

11TH APRIL 1964 • DANNY PRESTON

Standard Class 4's No 76084 and 76080 have only been at the shed two months following transfer from Sutton Oak, but they appear to be dead and are being pushed out of the shed yard by Black Eight No **48167**. Their official withdrawal date was December 1967 so theoretically they had another four months left in service.

26TH AUGUST 1967 • JOHN BURGESS

THE BR STANDARD CLASS 2 2-6-0's

Although the Springs Branch enginemen had experience with the LMS Ivatt 2-6-0 locos, their BR equivalent didn't appear until 1960 when Nos 78017 and 78019 arrived from Kirkby Stephen MPD. Both departed one year later and it wasn't until March 1964 when the next, No 78037, arrived from Skipton. This must have served as a trigger because, upon Wigan L&Y shed's demise one month later, another five arrived. This proved to be a very short allocation and the whole class moved on a mere two months later. Perhaps dieselisation of many of the ex-L&Y routes in the area resulted in little work for these engines - they did, however, find further work in the East Midlands.

Ivatt 2-6-0 No 78037 comes off shed for a further spell of duty. This loco had arrived from Skipton during the previous month but didn't stay long. It moved on to Derby MPD during May 1964.

16TH APRIL 1964 • JOHN BURGESS

A mere two weeks after arriving from the closed Wigan L&Y shed, Ivatt 2-6-0 No **78027** appears to be going nowhere. A swift decision with regard to its future resulted in another transfer away to Derby on the same date.

3RD MAY 1964 • JOHN LOUGHMAN

THE EX-WD 2-8-0's

Slow, plodding, methodical, uninspiring - unloved and uncared for. Whatever was thought of the somewhat bland and austere ex-War Department 2-8-0 locos, they could certainly shift loads, albeit very slowly at times. Known locally as the 'Dub Dee' and sometimes the 'Iron lung' due to the shape of their boiler, they came to replace the trusty but elderly Super D's. Their huge boilers ensured that they were rarely short of steam and performed their duties without a problem in much the same way as their predecessors had. Prior to any allocation, Springs Branch entertained the occasional visitor but in March 1959 came the first arrivals with a quartet from Woodford Halse MPD, followed a year later by a further six from North Wales and Cheshire sheds.

2-8-0 No 90686 was one of the ex-WR locos fitted with the enclosed toolbox clearly visible on the right running plate just in front of the cab. The loco spent nearly 5 years at the shed, in two periods. **17TH MAY 1964** ● **ALLAN HEYES**

Further transfers followed, both in and out, but when four more WD's were transferred in from Aintree in July 1964, the highest allocation of seventeen locos was achieved. However, withdrawals had begun in February with the loss of No 90574. This continued with a further six locos being withdrawn later that year. There was obviously still work available for them as, in September 1964, five were transferred to South Yorkshire and East Midlands sheds. Withdrawals and transfers continued in 1965 and by May they had all gone and Black 5's and 8's had taken over most of their work. The longest resident was No 90509 which stayed from March 1959 to September 1964 and escaped the cutter's torch by going to Staveley Barrow Hill. Nos 90574 and 90667 were also long term residents but both were withdrawn from the shed. The last survivor was No 90183 which arrived in December 1963 from Newton Heath and left in May 1965 for Frodingham. Some of the allocation had a final trip of less than a mile to the scrapyard as Central Wagon Works at Ince was just up the Springs Branch itself. This yard was also responsible for allegedly cutting up one it shouldn't have! *(see page 63)*

If you were passing Bamfurlong Junction on the West Coast Main Line in the early 1960's, you could almost guarantee there would be WD's standing in the banking sidings beyond the signalbox. Other regular turns were freights to Birkenhead, Northwich and Carnforth. Local trip workings around the various colliery sidings also kept them busy and often away from the shed for long periods.

WD Austerity No 90157 moves the short distance from the ash pit to the turntable. The loco came from Widnes in March 1963. **15TH AUGUST 1964** ● **DANNY PRESTON**

OTHER LOCOS ALLOCATED DURING THE BR PERIOD

LMS 2-6-2 TANKS. Both Stanier and Fowler 3P Tanks spent time at the shed with four of each showing up during the LMS period. There were none at Springs Branch at Nationalisation but Stanier Nos 40109 and 40144 both arrived in February 1949 only to be transferred away during 1950. There was one more brief visit when Fowler No 40003 arrived from Preston in February 1953 but after six months the loco moved on to Stockport Edgeley shed.

MR and LMS 2P 4-4-0's. There were a small number of these at Springs Branch and records indicate that thirteen different locos resided here between 1935 and 1949. In BR days this equated to just two locos - Nos (40)397 and (40)561 of which No 40397 was the most prominent with a stay from January 1947 until its transfer to Preston in December 1949. These engines were often used to pilot the heavy overnight trains from Wigan over Shap, a purpose for which they were well suited. One train was the combined Manchester and Liverpool sleeper to Scotland which the 2P would pilot to Carlisle, the men lodge over and return the next day. The 2P's were also used on turns on the Manchester Exchange trains. They were considered notoriously poor in starting heavy loads.

Seen on Shed - Saturday 23rd March 1957

Fairburn 2-6-4T	42235
Stanier 2-6-4T	42442/56/62/3/97, 42561/71/2
Ivatt 4 2-6-0	43001
Fowler 4F	44300
Black 5	45026/38/92, 45135, 45305/13/4
	45408/12/49/54/94
Patriot	45502
Jubilee	45563, 45633
Royal Scot	46168
Ivatt 2 2-6-0	46422/8/48
Black 8	48195, 48448, 48511, 48764
LNWR 7F	48895, 48915, 49018/23/5/34/73/93
	49129/45/54/5/60, 49203/28/62/8
	49352/81/5/93/6, 49401/2
L&Y 0-6-0T	51316
Aspinall 0-6-0	52143, 52449
LNER J10	65131/8/40/6/56/9/70/5/99
WD 2-8-0	90171, 90212/89, 90680

TOTAL 74

Standing in front of the old No 2 shed is 2P 4-4-0 No **40397**. Also of note to the left of the picture is another short-lived class at Springs Branch, Stanier 3P No **40144**.
24TH APRIL 1949 • **B.K.B. GREEN**

MIDLAND 2F 0-6-0's. No 58203's arrival from Patricroft in February 1956 was a strange and brief one month visit before being moved on to Walsall yet, just three years later, two more came from Northwich - namely Nos 58120 and 58123. Of these, No 58120 went back to Northwich in August 1960, only to return one month later and stay until April 1961 when it was transferred on to Rugby. No 58123 lasted until October 1960 before going to Monument Lane shed. One of the Midland 2F locos was involved in an incident on the wheel drop road which is described on page 159.

Pictured inside No 1 shed, Whale 19" Goods No **8834** stands in steam but has just three months left in service.
SEPTEMBER 1948 • **J.P. WILSON**

EX-LNWR 2F 0-6-2T COAL TANKS. Loco No 7703 had a few periods at the shed in LMS days and although a couple of its shedmates lasted until 1947, it was the only one of this class to survive beyond Nationalisation in January 1948, but not for long. Withdrawal came just 7 months later in July.

Ex-LNWR 4-6-0 (19" Goods). There were just two 19" Goods locos left at Springs Branch when BR took over. Although allocated BR numbers, none were ever carried. No 8834 survived until December 1948 and No 8824 continued until withdrawn in February 1950.

53

DIESEL SHUNTERS

The first diesel shunters arrived at Springs Branch in August 1957. Nos D3367 to D3371 of the BR '350hp' type were delivered brand new and were joined by Nos 13291 and 13292. No D3367 moved on to Sutton Oak after six months and in October 1958, Nos D3368/9/71 were transferred to Preston shed and replaced by the first of the similar, but older ex-LMS shunters - Nos 12071/99 and 12102. After this, the allocation fluctuated between five and six until 1965 when a further five of the ex-LMS variety arrived to replace the '08s' which departed, only to re-appear at the end of 1966. Although many of the ex-LMS diesel shunters were similar in many respects to the BR Class 08 (350hp), some of the earlier examples were fitted with a jackshaft arrangement that made them, by appearance, completely different. One of these, No 12003, was to be found at the shed from 1959 until at least 1968. As the new diesel depot was completed in 1967, a further dozen of the 'old brigade' arrived. Long term residents were Nos 12003/23/31/32.

Early in 1966 an initial batch of seven Hunslet 0-6-0 Diesel Mechanical shunters (Later class 05) arrived from East Anglia. A further exchange followed but the end result was an allocation of eight locos, and they were rarely seen in operation, spending most of their time stored in the engine shed sidings, although they lingered around until early 1968. From July 1967, a few Class 03 shunters arrived, building up to an allocation of six by October of that year. They spent most of their time working at the nearby Horwich Works and, with a few changes, lasted until at least the end of 1968. As Springs Branch was able to carry out some repair work on these locomotives in the 1960's, it was common to find other members from nearby depots undergoing maintenance, particularly those from nearby Dallam shed. Occasionally a Yorkshire Class 02 shunter from Bank Hall or Lostock Hall shed would be present for repairs and it was also possible to find a Hudswell shunter from Birkenhead receiving attention.

Going off the shed to commence its shift at Bamfurlong yard is ex-LMS diesel shunter No **12031** with its strange jackshaft arrangement.

5TH JUNE 1965 ● JOHN BURGESS

Two of the little-used Hunslet 204 hp diesel shunters No D2558 and D2568 stand in Engine Shed Sidings.

23RD APRIL 1966 ● JOHN BURGESS

LOCOMOTIVES AWAY FROM HOME

Springs Branch engines could be found on other depots for a variety of reasons. Usually they would do so as part of their normal daily turn. This might involve an engine working out one day and returning the next, such as the Carlisle runs. It also occurred locally, with Lostock Hall and Carnforth being the most regular places to find a Wigan engine stabled. On other occasions engines would be borrowed (either officially or unofficially) and used by other depots for normal turns or to work an excursion, particularly if that shed did not have sufficient motive power. Records show Springs Branch engines having appeared on Nottingham, Buxton and Eastfield sheds, to name but a few, and no doubt over the years they were observed at many other obscure places and may well have taken some time to return to Wigan. It was common practice for sheds to 'pinch' good engines and use them until their boiler washout was due, whereupon the engine would be dispatched home.

BLACKPOOL (CENTRAL) MPD

A young Peter Fitton is caught in the act of painting the smokebox numberplate of Standard Class 4 No **75041** as it rests between turns at Blackpool Central shed. The engine was earmarked for the 18:30 Blackpool Central to Manchester Victoria which would normally have a Blackpool engine. **27TH SEPTEMBER 1964** ● **PETER FITTON COLLECTION**

PRESTON MPD

Stored Tender Cab Super D No 49451 lies in the roofless remains of the closed Preston MPD which suffered from the ravages of fire. There were several of Springs Branch's Super D's stored here at the time of the photograph and in addition, between 1959 and 1961, Wigan L&Y shed was also used to store more members of the same class.

24TH FEBRUARY 1962 ● **MIKE TAYLOR**

PRESTON MPD

The shell of Preston shed remained a haven for stored locos during the early 1960's and the lack of a roof created suitable photogenic conditions to record the engines in attendance. Still carrying all her plates, Royal Scot 4-6-0 No **46168 *The Girl Guide*** stands withdrawn at the back of the building in the company of a Class 08 diesel shunter. Ironically, the loco had been on Preston's allocation prior to the fire in June 1960 which resulted in Springs Branch then aquiring the locomotive.

7TH AUGUST 1964 ● **PETER FITTON**

ROSE GROVE MPD

◀ **It may be April Fools Day,** but it's a bit early for summer excursions, so what a Springs Branch Patriot No **45531** *Sir Frederick Harrison* is doing in Rose Grove shed yard remained a mystery - unless it has been used on the Blackburn parcels. Beyond the loco, another visitor is also in evidence with an unidentified ex-LNER B1 'on shed'.

1ST APRIL 1964 ● MIKE TAYLOR

With regard to repair and periodic overhaul, and having LNWR origins, the vast majority of the Springs Branch allocation were dealt with at Crewe - although certain classes were latterly sent to nearby Horwich. The running-in turns would often be conducted over the Shrewsbury route and that particular shed witnessed a tremendous variety of ex-works engines over many years, including those from Springs Branch. Another favourite line, especially for passenger locos, was that to Manchester London Road.

CREWE WORKS

▶ **The celebrated 'Cauliflower' 0-6-0's** had a long-standing association with the shed *(see page 48)*. Although introduced as early as 1887, no fewer than 58 members survived into Nationalisation but all had gone by 1956. The penultimate member at Springs Branch, No **58377,** arrived in March 1952 from Stockport (Edgeley) having been allocated once before back in LMS days (1935). Its stay was very short, being withdrawn a mere three months later. It is seen here on the premises which were responsible for building, and then ultimately scrapping so many Springs Branch locos over the years - Crewe Works. No 58377 stands in the yard awaiting the cutter's torch. The last 'Cauli' on the books, No 58396, moved on to Widnes at this time but was also withdrawn shortly afterwards.

JULY 1952 ● STEAM IMAGE

SHREWSBURY MPD

◀ **A 'Super D' 0-8-0 in presentable external condition** such as this was a rare sight indeed. Although No **49154** is in light steam in Shrewsbury Shed yard, proudly displaying its repainted 10A shedplate, all may not be well as there is evidence of priming around the boiler. It has presumably worked in from Crewe on trial but the Shropshire town's locomotive depot regularly received ex-works locos before sending them back again. This engine had a chequered career at Springs Branch, having at least three spells there. The longest was its last - from September 1951 until withdrawal in November 1962. Shortly after its arrival, No 49154 was loaned to Northwich for trial as a bank engine.

AUGUST 1957 ● STEAM IMAGE

BLACKPOOL (CENTRAL) MPD

Early on a summer Saturday morning, the Blackpool Central shed staff made use of visiting Black Five No **45408** as acting coal stage pilot. It then proceeded light engine across to Blackpool North to work the 12:48 to Leicester.

29TH AUGUST 1964 • PETER FITTON

CARNFORTH MPD

One of the 'Royal Scots' which enjoyed a relatively short stay of 10 months was No **46161 King's Own.** The loco is seen here making use of the Carnforth turntable at about 13.00 and has probably worked the 11.40 stopping train from Wigan (NW).

29TH SEPTEMBER 1961 • PETER FITTON

NEWTON HEATH MPD

Over the years Springs Branch locos visited the Manchester area on an almost daily basis on a variety of duties. Many were serviced at the former LNWR depot at Patricroft, which, prior to 1958, had been under the jurisdiction of Springs Branch. The ex-L&Y depot at Newton Heath, on the other side of the city, received rather less and on those occasions it was often the case of a Wigan engine having been borrowed by Carlisle (Kingmoor or Upperby) or Crewe (North and South) who had regular workings. When Wigan (L&Y) shed closed in 1964, the pattern changed and they then became daily visitors. From October 1967 Class 24 diesels, often working in tandem, were also observed. The last visitor was Black Five No 44711 on 3rd December 1967, Springs Branch's penultimate day for steam, and it was subsequently transferred to Edge Hill that day. Records show that a trio of engines graced the shed together on 17th June 1967 with Nos 44679, 44962 and 45449 in attendance. Here, No **45395** stands alongside 9F No 92077.

8TH OCTOBER 1966 • STEAM IMAGE

VISITING LOCOMOTIVES

Because the Bamfurlong and Springs Branch area had a considerable amount of incoming freight workings, it was normal to find anything up to 15 foreign engines on shed at any one time. Usually these would be familiar types from the likes of Lostock Hall, Carnforth, Upperby, Dallam, Patricroft and Crewe, but other more interesting engines appeared from time to time.

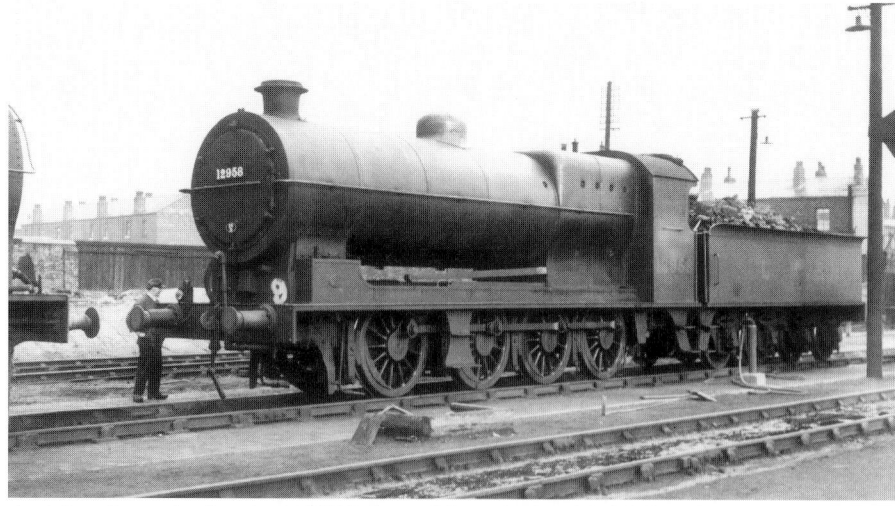

A visitor from the Lanky in LMS days. A large boilered 0-8-0 from Lower Darwen MPD, No **12958,** stands by the coaling stage. **12TH JULY 1936 ● B.K.B. GREEN COLLECTION**

Un-named Patriot No 45542 stands where the tracks have temporarily been truncated following the rebuilding of No 2 shed in 1961. The loco is a visitor from nearby Preston MPD.

20TH MAY 1961 ● RICHARD STRANGE

Caprotti Black Five No 44686 from Southport MPD stands in the shed yard.
11TH OCTOBER 1966 ● ALLAN HEYES

Apart from the brief spell after Preston shed closed, when the depot acquired the odd Rebuilt Patriot and a handful of Royal Scots, Springs Branch never had an allocation of the more glamorous passenger classes, although there would usually be one or more on the depot, generally from a local shed. Repair work brought other more interesting visitors to Springs Branch and Edge Hill's Princess Royal Pacifics have been reported undergoing repairs with, on one occasion, two in attendance at the same time.

◀ **Another un-named Patriot, No 45513** passes Cromptons Signalbox at the throat of the shed. This particular example hails from Carnforth MPD. **1961 ● JOHN BURGESS**

A local visitor from Warrington, Jubilee No 45604 *Ceylon* waits its turn for coal. This loco remained in deplorable condition up until withdrawal from Newton Heath in October 1965.

30TH AUGUST 1964 ● **ALLAN HEYES**

Crewe North locos were fairly common visitors to the shed, as Bamfurlong yard had daily freights to Basford Hall. Also, some long distance freight trains would be remarshalled at Bamfurlong and the loco would often then come on shed for fuel while this operation progressed. Jubilee, No **5694 Bellerophon** from 5A has just taken coal and stands near the ash disposal hoist during a visit.

JULY 1936 ● **AUTHOR'S COLLECTION**

A most distinguished visitor finds itself tucked away inside No 1 shed. Another Crewe North engine, Princess Royal Pacific No **46206 Princess Marie Louise** has possibly failed on the main line near Wigan. Repairs are well under way with the rods down and the vacuum pipe and associated apparatus removed.

27TH AUGUST 1956 ● **P. AVERY COLLECTION**

An unusual visitor was this 'Royal Scot', No **46140 *The King's Royal Rifle Corps.*** The engine had recently been transferred from Newton Heath over the city of Manchester to Longsight, a rather surprising move considering that the latter depot was, by this time, fast becoming dieselised. The loco retains both name and number plates but lacks a 9A shed plate. A possible explanation is that it may have been on loan, covering for Patriot No 45531 which was under repair at the time.

11TH APRIL 1964 ● **CHRIS COATES**

59

Britannia Pacific No 70031 *Byron* from Crewe North stands at the coaling plant. This photograph provides clear evidence that it had been involved in some sort of accident, showing a damaged running plate ahead of the buffer beam. Nevertheless, *Byron* survived until November 1967 but whether the damage was ever attended to remains unclear. From 1965 the 'Brits' became very regular visitors to the shed, often off the Carlisle to Bamfurlong freights and, on occasions, up to three could be found at any one time. The author has dated records of all fifty five locos being observed on shed apart from the elusive No 70027 *Rising Star*.

11TH APRIL 1965 ● ALLAN HEYES

By January 1966, the majority of the Britannia Pacifics left in service had congregated at Carlisle Kingmoor MPD. This un-named member was one such example. No **70052**, formerly named **Firth of Tay**, spent much of her time in service passing that depot whilst working out of Polmadie (Glasgow) on express passenger duties. The engine, recently transferred to 12A from Banbury, stands outside No 1 shed.

JANUARY 1966 ● FRED BANKS

The 9F 2-10-0's were rare visitors until the mid 1960's, but in the later years they became commonplace and some actually underwent considerable repair work here, often lasting weeks. Locos dealt with included a pair from Warrington, No 92053 (30th May 1965 - 3rd August 1965) and No 92116 (6th July 1965 - 9th August 1965). By 1966 it was not unusual to find three or four of these large engines on shed at any one time. After spending a lifetime in solitude at Bromsgrove, the one time Lickey Banker, No **92079** stands in the shed yard. Its final resting place, like so many others, was at Birkenhead MPD.

12TH OCTOBER 1965 ● ALLAN HEYES

The most unusual visitors appear to have arrived following failure in the area, and, over the years, many of the Coronation Pacifics were present with some having extensive repairs here. Other 'rare' engines arrived via unusual workings and in particular the Haydock Park 'Race specials' and their supporting horsebox trains.

Two days before the picture above, No 92204 from 2A -Tyseley, stands on the diesel fuel road during a short visit. Although they never had any of their own, Springs Branch men called 9F's 'Birkenhead Sulzers'!

10TH OCTOBER 1965 ● JOHN BURGESS

Some of the more unusual, confirmed and prestigious visitors recorded on shed between Nationalisation and ultimate closure to steam were:

'Princess Royal' Class	Nos 46203, 46206 (27th August 1956) and No 46207 on shed for tyre turning after accident in 1956. No 46207 re-appeared (28th January - 20th March 1962, Departed for Crewe Works the following day).
'Coronation' Class	Nos 46222/25/26/32/35/36/37/38/39/50/51/56/57 - Various dates No 46243 en-route to scrap at Central Wagon Works, Ince.
Ex-LNER V2 Class	No 60920 (64A) from 18th February 1959 until at least mid March after suffering a collapsed brick arch (see below)
Ex-LNER B1 Class	Nos 61017 *Bushbuck* (50A - 5/6th March 1966), 61031 *Reedbuck* (8th September 1963) 61122, 61189 *Sir William Gray* (56D - 17th September 1963), 61224 (4th July 1964), 61270 (27th January 1963), 61329 (3rd April 1966)
Ex-LNER K3 Class	Nos 61867 (1950's), 61889 (31B - 15th August 1952), 61921 (31B - 5th July 1952), 61947 (31B - 13th August 1952), 61960 (40A - 1st October 1952) Haydock Race traffic
Ex-LNER B16 Class	Unidentified. Newmarket horse box special
Ex-LNER K1 Class	No 62065 (29th January 1967). Photographed inside No 1 shed, probably minor repairs
Ex-LNER J39 Class	No 64745 (9G) in 1960 noted leaving shed LE after servicing (see below)
Ex-LNER N5 Class	No 69346 (6E - 8th June 1952)

The story of how this St Margarets V2 arrived on shed is worthy of mention. It started on 17th February 1959 working the 03:25 Niddrie (Edinburgh) to Oxley freight, booked engine change at Carlisle which, for reasons unknown, didn't happen. The V2 then came off at Saltney Yard near Chester (as booked) and worked the 23:05 Mold Junction to Crewe freight. Following the diagram the loco then found itself on the next day's 08:45 Oxley to Law Junction Class C freight from Crewe and seemingly heading for home. Unfortunately, No 60920 failed in the Wigan area, resulting in its arrival at Springs Branch. A remarkable event indeed! After repair the V2 returned north light engine.

Although this picture is of dubious quality, it is worthy of inclusion due to its scarcity value. A Gorton J39 0-6-0 No **64745** is caught coming off shed. 1960 • JOHN BURGESS

Another named B1, but this example is still carrying her plates. No **61189 *Sir William Gray*** from Mirfield MPD comes off shed.
17TH SEPTEMBER 1963 • JOHN BURGESS

An ex-LNER B1 visitor - No 61017 from York shed (now devoid of plates but once named *Bushbuck*) stands on the end road (no15). 6TH MARCH 1966 • P. NIGHTINGALE

Clans noted on shed

No 72001 - 29th April 1962
No 72002 - 6th July 1952 for 01:56 Carlisle freight
No 72004 - 28th March 1952 to be towed to Crewe Works
No 72005 - 8th February 1964
No 72006 - 10th May 1966
No 72007 - 29th October 1963
No 72008 - 1954/5

In the earlier years they were mainly as a result of failures but, in the later 1960's, the Kingmoor locos appeared occasionally on the Carlisle freights.

On Saturday 12th September 1964, Coronation Pacific No 46257 *City of Salford* was used in conjunction with the crowning of the British Railway Queen. That year it was Norma Corrigan, the daughter of the Newton Heath shedmaster and the ceremony took place on Platform 11 at Manchester Victoria Station. The loco was prepared for the event at Springs Branch and even had its cab interior painted white. After the ceremony it returned to Springs Branch before travelling to Preston shed for a period of storage. The loco is pictured in the yard on the evening prior to the crowning.

11TH SEPTEMBER 1964 • JOHN BURGESS

Class 6P No 72007 *Clan Mackintosh* looks impressive standing at the shed throat. There was a regular freight from Carlisle whose engine detached at Bamfurlong whilst the train was remarshalled. It refuelled on the shed, then continued on its way.

29TH OCTOBER 1963 • JOHN BURGESS

Another Kingmoor engine, No 72005 *Clan Macgregor* coming off the shed.

8TH FEBRUARY 1964 • JOHN BURGESS

EN ROUTE TO CENTRAL WAGON WORKS SCRAPYARD

From approximately 1959, withdrawn engines started to appear at Springs Branch earmarked for cutting up at the Central Wagon Works site some ½ mile up the Springs Branch itself. When the engines first started to appear they would usually be dumped on the diesel fuel road or the coal wagon storage sidings. In later years the favourite place to dump these engines was in either the Engine Shed Sidings or the Brewery sidings, both of which were on the curve at the start of the Springs Branch. Well remembered are the Pannier tanks, some still carrying their cabside plates that seemed so out of place at Wigan. Of the premier power, only the Jubilees remained at Springs Branch for any length of time, the others were quickly taken to the scrapyard.

Having just arrived, WR Pannier Tank No 7762 still retains its cabside plate whilst stored awaiting towing up to Ince scrapyard. Also visible is resident Super D No **49008** which still had four months left in service. **26TH AUGUST 1962 • JIM PEDEN**

Ex-Bank Hall Ivatt tank No 41205 awaits the ultimate fate on the storage sidings at the shed. **12TH SEPTEMBER 1964 • JOHN BURGESS**

The number plates referred to in the story below. **2010 • AUTHOR'S COLLECTION**

THE WD STORY

When WD No 90147 was withdrawn in May 1964, it was sold to the Central Wagon Works for scrap. However, in error, No 90173 was taken up to the CWW yard and was recorded there on 28th July and 8th August. When Crewe made enquires about No 90173, Springs Branch realised their mistake and tried to recover the loco, only to find that it was partly cut up and so a plot was hatched. The number plate from No 90173 was recovered and taken to the shed but, due to No 90147 having a smaller number plate and bracket, a hole had to be drilled in No 90173's plate to allow it to be fitted. No 90147's cab was then repainted and renumbered No 90173 which fortunately, by this time, was now also withdrawn. Some time later No 90173 (really No 90147) was also sold to CWW and was noted in the yard in January and February 1965. This may all sound like a typical old wives tale but, after discussions with several people involved at the time, the story is confirmed without doubt. Both plates have survived in private ownership and the photo above shows these and the extra hole inside the '9' on No 90173's plate.

CENTRAL WAGON WORKS SCRAPYARD

Over the years almost 300 engines were dealt with at the scrapyard, some lingering in the sidings at Springs Branch for months before being towed up the branch. Amongst these were engines from the Western Region including two Halls. The Eastern Region supplied B1's, K3's and O2's whilst the Midland provided several named engines in the form of one *Coronation*, one *Royal Scot*, eight *Jubilees* and one *Patriot*.

Such was the activity at the scrapyard that some engines were cut up within days of arrival whilst others could be found lying in the same spot for months. At one stage there were 35 engines within the scrapyard and many more stored at Springs Branch waiting to be brought up to the yard. By 1966 this lucrative additional business had virtually finished and the works cut up just two engines in 1967 before concentrating back on wagons.

2-6-2T No 40003, commonly known as a 'Breadvan', had a short six month stay at the shed in 1953. Some eight years later it returned to Wigan and Central Wagon for cutting up, having been withdrawn from Widnes in February 1961.

16TH SEPTEMBER 1961 ● **D. HAMPSON**

A general view of the Central Wagon Scrapyard from the elevated L&Y line with ex-GWR 2-8-0 No **3829** prominent.

1ST JULY 1964 ● **ALLAN HEYES**

STAFF AND ADMINISTRATION

Records survive from 1891 showing that 423 staff were employed at the shed. This excluded administration and management. Of these - 214 were enginemen with, surprisingly, 120 cleaners. The complete list is:

No	Title	No	Title	No	Title	No	Title
1 -	Shed Foreman's Assistant	1 -	Chief Cleaner	2 -	Storesman	3 -	Apprentice
1 -	Timekeeper + Storemaster	1 -	Chief Tubeman	1 -	Lodging House Matron	112 -	Engineman
1 -	Boiler Maker	1 -	Chief Washer-out	1 -	Stationary Engineman	1 -	Boiler Maker's Assistant
8 -	Turner	6 -	Tubeman	10 -	Labourer	1 -	Store Boy
14 -	Fitter	2 -	Loco Cleaner	2 -	Fitters Assistant	102 -	Fireman
1 -	Blacksmith	1 -	Loco Inspector	1 -	Pointsman	3 -	Fire Carrier
1 -	Coppersmith	4 -	Washer-out	120 -	Cleaner	4 -	Steam Raiser
1 -	Joiner	1 -	Brick Setter	2 -	Bar Lad	3 -	Fire Dropper
2 -	'Nightmen'	1 -	'Break' Blockman	1 -	Bricksetter's Assistant		
1 -	Assistant Storekeeper	1 -	Fuelman	4 -	Call Boy	**423**	**Total Staff**

Most of the 1891 occupations were still extant in the LMS period who created a staff structure chart in 1935. At its peak there were over 1,000 men working from the three Wigan sheds, of which Springs Branch depot would probably account for around 600 of them. This had inevitably reduced somewhat by the early 1950's when almost 400 footplate men were on the books. By 1967 there was an increase to 216 drivers and 184 secondmen/firemen, mainly due to the influx from Wigan L&Y shed. Interestingly, many Welshmen had come to the shed after the 1914-18 war rather than face redundancy at home as the original men returned from abroad. This was a common situation in the North West and due to seniority, many of these men immediately became drivers. In 1951, Springs Branch had 15 enginemen with the surname of Jones, plus plenty of others such as Williams, Jenkins, etc.

THE 1947 STAFF STRUCTURE CHART

District Motive Power Superintendant

Assistant District Motive Power Superintendant

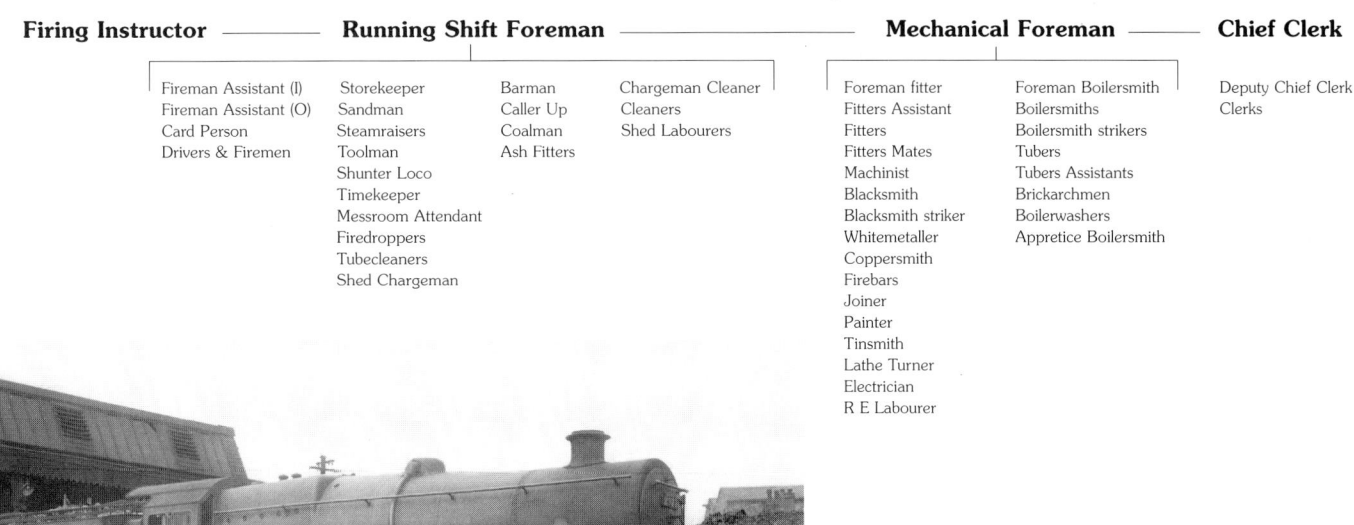

Firing Instructor ——— **Running Shift Foreman** ——————————— **Mechanical Foreman** ——— **Chief Clerk**

Fireman Assistant (I)	Storekeeper	Barman	Chargeman Cleaner	Foreman fitter	Foreman Boilersmith	Deputy Chief Clerk
Fireman Assistant (O)	Sandman	Caller Up	Cleaners	Fitters Assistant	Boilersmiths	Clerks
Card Person	Steamraisers	Coalman	Shed Labourers	Fitters	Boilersmith strikers	
Drivers & Firemen	Toolman	Ash Fitters		Fitters Mates	Tubers	
	Shunter Loco			Machinist	Tubers Assistants	
	Timekeeper			Blacksmith	Brickarchmen	
	Messroom Attendant			Blacksmith striker	Boilerwashers	
	Firedroppers			Whitemetaller	Appretice Boilersmith	
	Tubecleaners			Coppersmith		
	Shed Chargeman			Firebars		
				Joiner		
				Painter		
				Tinsmith		
				Lathe Turner		
				Electrician		
				R E Labourer		

The Shed Loco Superintendant, Mr John Henry Gaskell was also warden of the nearby St Mary's Church. He is standing in front of visiting Stanier Mogul No **2977** alongside an unidentified locoman.   c1938   COURTESY D. LONG

Wartime contingency measures brought female office staff to the shed, replacing men who were away serving in the forces. Loco Superintendent John Henry Gaskell poses in front of local Black Five **5199** with three of the new recruits.   c1938   COURTESY D. LONG

Just after the war approximately thirty men were loaned to various sheds due to a shortage of firemen. Springs Branch had plenty of passed cleaners so some went to Trafford Park, Nuneaton, Rugby, Bletchley, Willesden, Camden and Cricklewood. Staff levels at the shed were considerably reduced in the late 1960's and 70's as men signed on at Wigan Wallgate, and later at Warrington yard. During the later LMS and early British Railways period, the following offices were contained within the shed building.

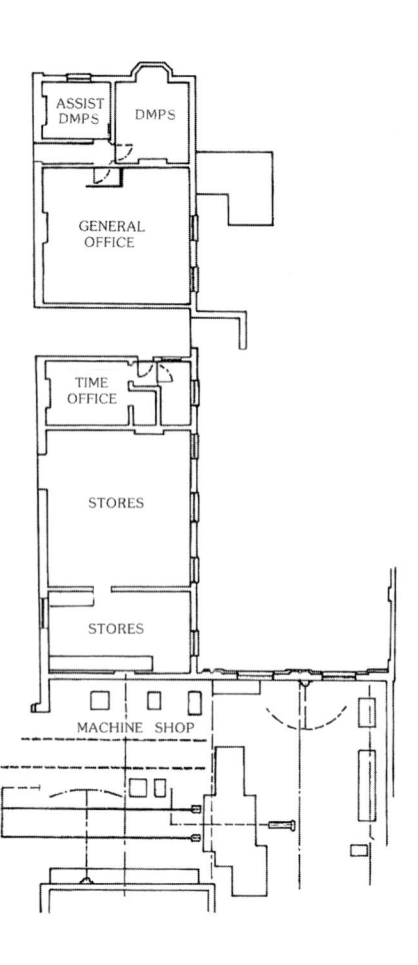

DISTRICT MOTIVE POWER SUPERINTENDENT AND ASSISTANT'S OFFICES

Housed the DMPS and his assistant, who had ultimate responsibility for the shed and sub sheds.

GENERAL OFFICE

Housed the Chief Clerk, Deputy Chief Clerk and up to six clerks dealing with time cards, wages, staff records, post, memos, any typing, special notices, report forms, ordering coal & oil. The time cards would be brought from the time office every day to be checked and updated ready for wages day. On Monday mornings, wages were collated and sent to Manchester for verifying, also the coal was ordered (little George stated what was required). Every Thursday new rosters were typed out for next week and displayed on noticeboards.

TIME OFFICE

Situated on the left of the passage into No 1 shed, this is where the footplatemen booked on/off, signed for their weekly notices, and where defects on engines would be reported. All the other staff except the clerical staff, would clock on using the machine situated just inside the corridor. The Time Office staff, would allocate engines to the various turns with due regard to availability and power requirement for the job. In the Office, on each shift, would be the Running Shift Foreman (RSF) supported by two assistants (arrangers). The inside foreman's assistant would generally sort matters with the drivers and firemen and liaise with the repair side, and do the enginemen's arrangements, whilst the outside foreman's assistant would work between the Office and the yard, instructing where engines were to be stabled. He also communicated with Control regarding the use of 'foreign' engines.

The RSF would deal with weekly roster changes relating to holiday allowances and sickness as well as recording mileages, arranging boiler washouts and generally ensuring everything ran as smoothly as possible. The following week's enginemen's rosters would be compiled with due regard to which men were available and their route knowledge, and this would then be passed to the General Office for typing up and subsequent display on the roster boards. A 'card person' would collate and file the time cards, which were kept in a box in the Office. He would also handle the 'foreign' engine book and discuss with control regarding engines away from home requiring boiler washout. The Time Office would issue and collect the drivers' work docket detailing the timings of the actual turn they were undertaking. Any defects found on the engine during this turn would be reported on a 'Repair Docket' which would be handed in to the Time Office staff who would liaise with maintenance staff to ensure the work was undertaken. The following books and documents were used in the Foremans Office:

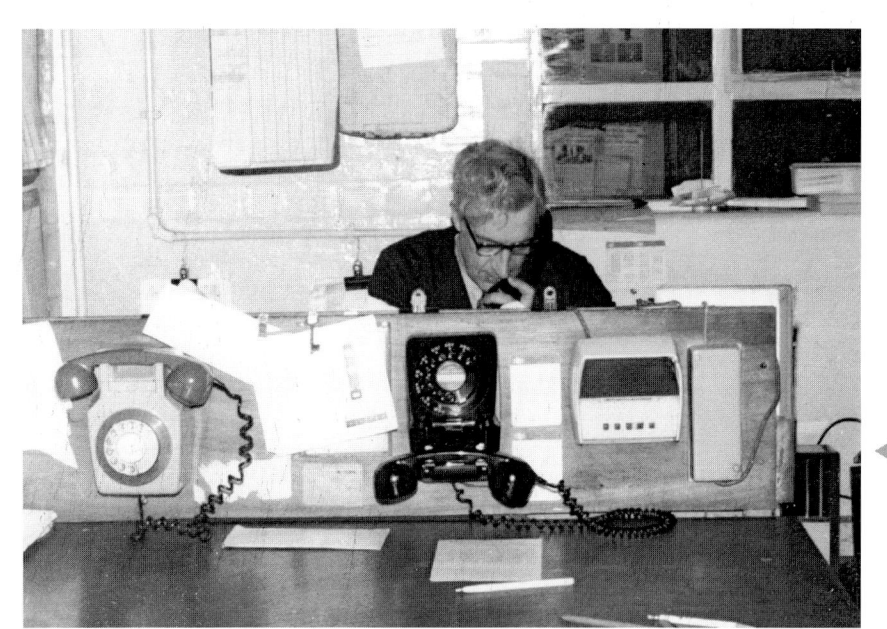

◀ **Bill Botell in the old Time Office.**

1970 ● JOHN BRETHERTON

ENGINEMEN'S TIME CARD	....	Shows work done, hours and pay due
ENGINEMEN'S ARRANGEMENTS BOOK	......	Lists men/time booked on turn and engine allocated
FOREMAN'S LOG BOOK	....	Lists availability of men/locos plus incidents
FOREIGN ENGINE BOOK	....	Lists engines from other depots and associated repairs
ENGINE DOCKETS	....	Shows exact details of individual turns
REPAIR DOCKETS	....	Driver lists faults found on last trip
REPORT FORM (explanation form)	....	Request report on incident
WEEKLY NOTICES	....	Traffic Notices, Speed Restrictions etc.

More Clerks came to the shed at the end of steam when the No 1 assistant's job was done by a clerk and the No 2 assistant's job done by a TCI (train crew inspector). Footplate staff would generally keep a diary of their turns to confirm when they qualified for possible promotion. A Passed Cleaner needed 313 turns to get fireman's rate and ensure this rate couldn't be dropped. A similar number of turns applied to Firemen who could be promoted to Passed Firemen and qualify for driving turns and subsequent promotion to driver. Most of their experience to undertake this next step up the ladder would be gained during their general day to day work and also attending the MIC meetings (mutual improvement classes) which were held on Tuesday evenings in the Barracks on Morris Street.

In the Mid 1950's, Passed Firemen Jack Armstrong and Dick Wood are well remembered as being instructors at these meetings, where all aspects of the locomotive would be discussed. Demonstrations would be given, using models to help explain all the inner workings of the valve gear, pistons, injectors, etc. plus the vital art of firing successfully. The task of controlling a large number of men was huge. There was a constant tussle between the RSF's and the footplatemen, mainly due to absence, which was common. Men 'failing to come' was a daily headache and caused a constant rearranging of rosters. (see examples) Additionally, the Time Office staff would have to be flexible to ensure that sufficient engines and men were available to cover the booked work allowing for repairs, wash outs etc. Locos would also be assigned works attention and possibly be unavailable for months on end.

Several important reporting books were used in the Time Office, one of which was the **'Foreign Engine' book.** Here is a typical page from within for Wednesday 4th June 1952. There is a wealth of information to study. The top section relates to Springs Branch (the principal depot for the area) with two more sections covering the other depots within the area that came under Springs Branch's control. Note that the BR prefix number 4 is ignored - a throwback to LMS days, whilst the Standard classes (eg No 75010) full number was recorded.

At Springs Branch itself there are sixteen engines on the depot from other sheds, and twelve are showing booked for jobs. The three Carlisle engines are all marked up for return freights to Carlisle whilst one of the Crewe South Black Fives is allocated to the 04:15 Carnforth. The other is undergoing repairs to its rocker grate. Some of the foreign engines are working the return legs of regular diagrams such as the Carnforth (11A) Super D booked on the 11:10 Oxenholme, the Speke Jn (8C) Black Eight engine on the 07:26 Fleetwood and the Lower Darwen (24D) WD on the 02:25 Blackburn. Sometimes a working produces an unusual engine such as the Rugby (2A) Black Eight on the 06:00 Birkenhead freight, a turn booked for a Birkenhead Black Eight. Rugby engines were uncommon at Springs Branch, so for two to appear is highly unusual. The other Rugby engine, No (4)4058 is booked to work a 06:00 Halliwell & Horwich turn, possibly a special working, and this loco is most likely to be in the area following overhaul at Horwich Works. Of the four engines under repair at Springs Branch, the Leeds Holbeck Royal Scot No (4)6103 *Royal Scots Fusilier* is most notable.

In the top right hand corner of the page is a list of engines 'away', which generally indicates those undergoing overhaul at the main workshops.

The four codes beneath this are:

L - Number of own engines withdrawn from traffic for washouts and exams.
M - Number of own engines under repair.
N - Number of own engines in CME shops and waiting shops.
O - Number of own engines not fit for booked class of work.

THE CONFERENCE BOOK

This gives details of engines that are the subject of repair or running trials. It also covers the staffing levels of the repair department. By 1962, Springs Branch was no longer the principal depot of the area, being re-coded 8F under Edge Hill, but because it retained considerable repair facilities, nearby sheds would still send engines for repairs that couldn't be undertaken at their home depot. The first item shows two engines away at main workshops. Note that, even at this late date, the BR prefix 4 is still not used.

Also showing are engines on trial which includes, surprisingly, a Crewe South diesel shunter, a type already allocated to the shed. This particular loco, No 12019, is shown on trials here from 31st May until this date (19/06/62) after which it presumably returned to Crewe South. Interestingly No 12006 from Speke Junction shed arrived the next day for a four week stint, so perhaps Springs Branch had a shortage of these locos at this time. No 4490 is still undergoing 'running in' almost a month after leaving workshops and Black Five No 5313, which was Ex-Works on 8th June, is also under observation. The following two lines starting 'W' denote waiting, so on this day there are no engines waiting to be accepted for workshops or CME attention.

Thirteen engines are also undergoing repairs or exams, seven of which are the depot's own locos. All manner of repair work was undertaken and at least two engines listed would have needed to use the wheel drop on road six. A number of engines involved in boiler washouts are listed, followed by the daily survey of maintenance staff, with an apparent shortage of 10 men. AL is annual leave.

Finally, the total number of loco coal wagons on site on the two roads behind the coaler is given (36) and those occupying the four storage sidings alongside the main line (62). These totals may seem high, but it should be remembered that the shed had 73 engines on allocation at this time, not to mention visitors which were regularly serviced. The coal-on-hand figure seemed to vary between a minimum of 40 and a maximum of 100.

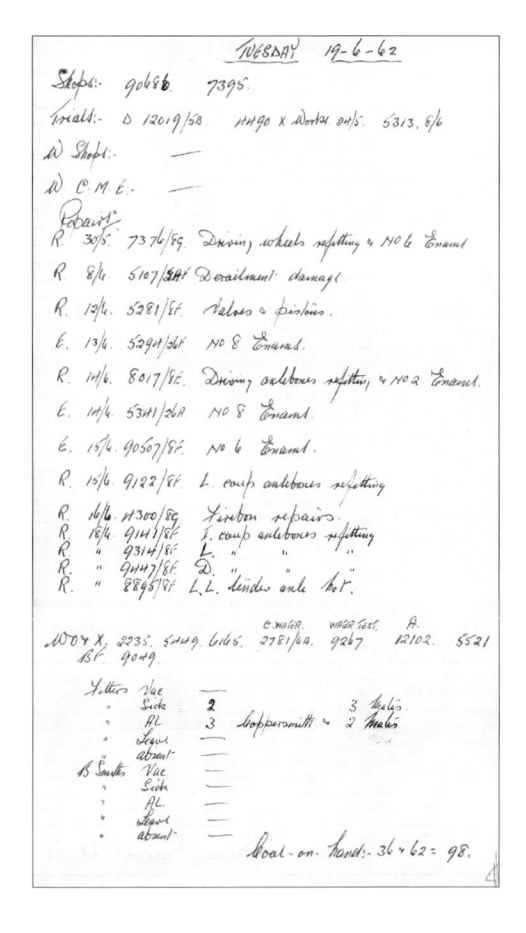

COAL CONSUMED

On 16th September 1957, The Motive Power Superintendent Costs Office sent a memo to depots requiring information on coal consumption. The depots were to calculate and report, in Tons, the following:

1 - Total issues to locomotives   2 - Less issues to other depots' engines
3 - Net issue to own engines   4 - Add coal issued to own engines at other depots
5 - Total coal consumed by engines allocated to depot

The four coal storage sidings are on the left, each of which had a name (London Road was one). To the right of the coaling stage and beyond are the two coal roads for imminent use. The short siding containing the van was known as Chain Pit Siding.

c1965 ● JOHN BRETHERTON

A pair of interesting extracts from the Running Shift Foreman's log books, exactly as written ...

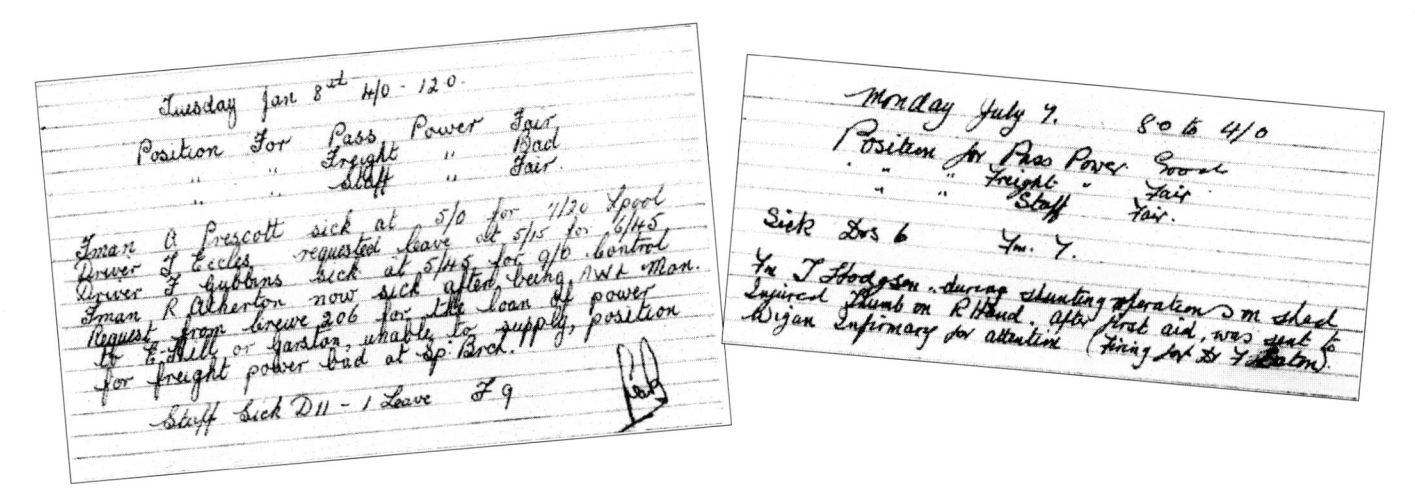

other items of interest ...

Thursday 18th October 1951. Driver E. Farren 9/0 Control called for 8/15. Refused and came own time - consequence, delay caused (57 mins) to 8/45 Ince Moss - Clock Face.

Wednesday, 5th December 1951. Complaint from Passed Fireman Ashton about his mate, Passed Cleaner D Banks not being capable of doing his work. I put another fireman with him today to instruct him further with his work. (Asst DMPS adds ... we have had many complaints about him. I shall arrange for Inspector Fry to see this lad)

Thursday 20th December 1951. Crane ordered to Bickershaw at 3/35 - two wagons derailed. Engine 9025 10A 151 shunt brought to shed at 3/45 not fit to work with (bad blows). 206 Crewe advised of pass power position for Sat. 9 Spl pass engines required between 12.22 and 12/30.

Tuesday 24th July 1951. Fireman R Stephenson unable to come for duty, sickness at home. Fireman A Grundy 2 hrs 5 min late on duty yesterday and again 1 hr 45min LOD today. 133 trip waiting on shed until his arrival. No other fireman to put on job. (Asst DMPS adds ... this lad must not be allowed to go on doing this in spite of delays).

Tuesday 7th August 1951. Passed cleaner G Bennett (406) firing for J Jones on 116 trip scalded his right foot. Coal digger pipe came uncoupled at union nut.

Thursday 10th July 1951. Please inform chargeman cleaner that we will require 3 more men on night turn. 11/0 coalman, 11/0 caller up & 11/0 firedropper, no spare shed staff on nights & difficulty is being experienced in covering this work. Serious firebox trouble will arise if Labourer Addison is persisted in on steamraising duties. Passed cleaner J Phillips AWL for 2.0 pass work.

Tuesday 14th August 1951. Engine 5439 (12A) on 6.33 ROF failed Springs Branch. Brake sticking on. Drivers' valve blowing through bad. Train worked forward by bank engine 9408. Delay one hour.

Friday 19th October 1951. Fireman C Leatherbarrow, Control Link, advised Friday for double trip Sunday. When signing off Saturday stated he would be ST Sunday. Told to work to instructions then put himself sick.

Saturday 1st December 1951. Driver J Ashurst reported Raleigh cycle missing. Railway police informed. Cycle no 529858.

Thursday 22nd November 1951. Ash elevator out of order from 7/25 until 10/15. Shortage of sand buckets. One found containing oil and one containing cement. Retained for your inspection. Crane ordered by Control at 9/30 eng no 42154 derailed at Wigan Station. Eng 2465 10A turned off to take up derailed engines working (9/45 reg pass Wigan and Blackburn) 2465 dep shed at 9/50

Friday 9th November 1951. Fireman J Melling died getting off bus at 'Old Hall' pub coming for 6.25am duty.

Sunday 11th November 1951. Youth caught by Police stealing coal from stack on plant.

Wednesday 21st November. Control demanded crane 9/50 to Springs Branch North Sidings. Engine 6428 (134 Trip) derailed 2 pairs tender wheels.

Monday 22nd October 1951. Engine 46163 failed on shed at 5.25 for 6.33 ROF. Small ejector exhaust pipe on side of smoke box uncoupled.

◀ **Arthur Gilligan (Left) Jack Heyes (Shed shunt) and Driver Jimmy Parkinson (right)** enjoy a brew and a natter in the Time Office.

1970 ● JOHN BRETHERTON

CLEANERS

The first rung on the ladder to becoming an engine driver was to become an engine cleaner. At the turn of the century Springs Branch had over 100 cleaners at the shed, such was the importance given to keeping the motive power befitting a prestige railway company. The man in charge, the Foreman Cleaner, worked 8am to 4pm only with his staff working 3 shifts, 7 days a week. Young cleaners were not allowed to work night shift. In the 1950's there would generally be around a dozen cleaners per shift, sometimes more, and these would be split into groups and allocated engines to clean. Each group would tackle an engine, two cleaners starting on the side of the boiler, another on the motion and others on the tender. Passed cleaners may be called upon to work as firemen. Many of the Bamfurlong shunt turns signed on at 5.30am, 1.30pm and 9.30pm, and so did the cleaners, so that if any of the shunt firemen were required for other turns, the passed cleaners could replace them on the shunts.

Passed Cleaner Walter Meadows on a visiting Standard Class Five No **73097** from Patricroft. **1965** ● **TOM SUTCH**

Passed Cleaners Alan Dickinson and Brian Mills. c1965 ● JOHN DANIELS

The system of engine cleaning, as officially given by the Chief Mechanical Engineer in May 1908 was:

1 - All brass parts to be scoured with Bath Brick and Rape Oil and polished up with a new sponge cloth.

2 - Boiler, Cab Panels, Tank and Smoke-box. Remove dirt with a dry cloth from the these parts, which must then be well washed with hot water, a washed cloth being used for the purpose, then wipe off dry and polish with a new cloth. On side tanks and tender bodies a little cleaning oil should be used when the engines are dirty through bad weather.

3 - Smoke-boxes and Fire-boxes. When engines are not cleaned daily and the smoke-boxes become discoloured or if they have been burnt, they must be washed with a mixture of yellow grease and hot water and then wiped dry. Fire-boxes can be treated in the same manner. Under no circumstances must oil or paraffin be used upon smoke-boxes or fire-boxes. Yellow grease must not be used upon any part of the engine which is painted and varnished as it will destroy the varnish. The issue of yellow grease to be left to the discretion of the foreman cleaner.

4 - Buffer Blank, Cylinder Covers, Main Framing, Engine Wheels, Motion, Brake Gearing, Foot Framing, Brake Gear and Tender Wheels. The thick grease should be removed from these parts with a cloth or scraper according to the conditions, then cleaning oil should be used and wiped off dry.

5 - Newly-painted engine. When a newly painted engine arrives at the shed from the Works, the dirt should be wiped off the boiler, cab, panels and smoke-box with a damp cloth and the parts named must then be washed with hot water. If the grease cannot be got off owing to the varnish being sticky, a little soap should be used. Under no circumstances should gease or paraffin be used on the above parts.

6 - Bright Work. Hand rails, angle iron round tank tops, hand pillars, coupling rods, spindle rods and weigh bars. These parts to be greased over with cleaning oil then scoured over with no 1 emery or bath brick and oil and a little tallow rubbed over them.

A young John Daniels poses in front of No **47395** - one of the shed's Jinty 0-6-0's.

MAY 1964 ● **JOHN DANIELS**

Passed Cleaner Tom Pye's Time Card for January 1950. This would be a most acceptable working week for Tom with a 9.55am start and a teatime finish with no weekend working. He was obviously firing this week and seems to have been on a different ex-L&Y 0-6-0 tender engine each day yet his turn no 517 should have put him on a 6.50am start on Trip 123. Often local workings would be changed, at short notice, to fit in with available men, engines or changes in traffic requirements.

A Group of Springs Branch cleaners pose in front of 'Prince of Wales' 4-6-0 No 2249 *Thomas Campbell*. c.1920 • WIGAN ARCHIVES SERVICE (WLCT)

Sponge cloths were obviously an important part of the engine cleaning process and were generally issued by the Stores, but some were kept in the Time Office to help when the Stores was closed. On Tuesday 18th December 1951, things had become so bad as to warrant an entry in the Foreman's log book with the added note 'Crewe asked' suggesting the shed were completely out of new sponge cloths and a request had gone to Crewe to provide replacement supplies. *(below)*

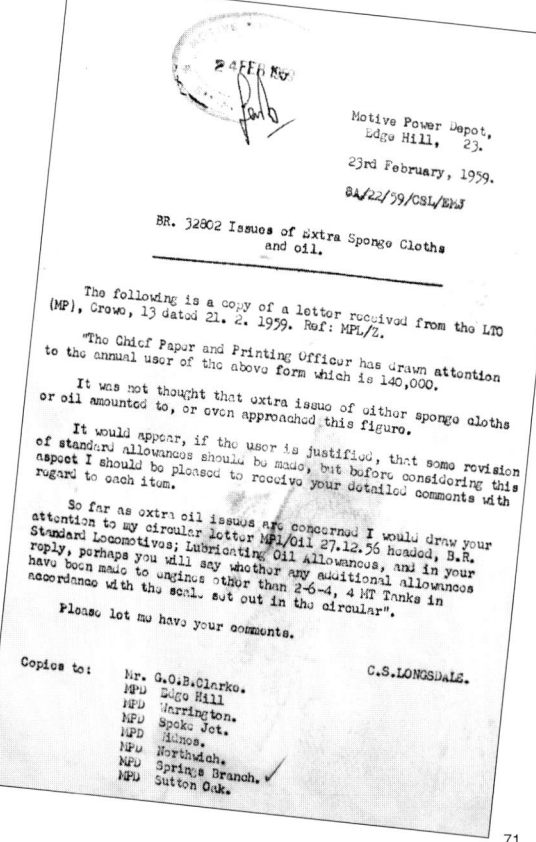

Engine Record Card. Each loco had two cards - An 'Engine History Card' which was kept at the main Works (in this case Horwich) and the 'Engine Record Card' kept at the depot. Details on the reverse of the Engine Record Card show Tender details, Allocation and Shopping histories.

The standard LMS uniform card still in use throughout the 1960's and 1970's. Mr Jones's personal sizes are all noted and further study reveals that he seems to get a new jacket and cap each year plus two jean jackets and trousers. An overcoat is occasional and a mackintosh every 5 - 10 years.

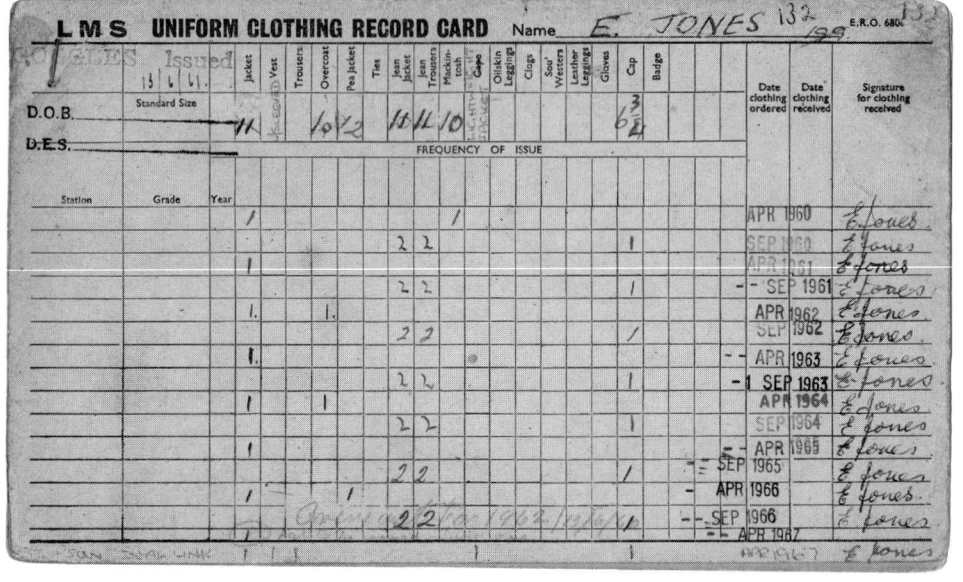

MAINTENANCE SECTION AND FITTERS OFFICE (inside No1 shed building)

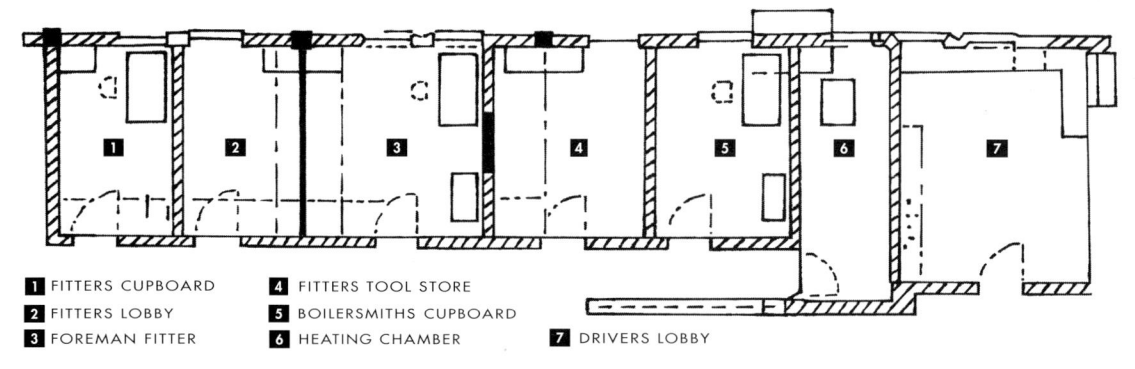

1. FITTERS CUPBOARD
2. FITTERS LOBBY
3. FOREMAN FITTER
4. FITTERS TOOL STORE
5. BOILERSMITHS CUPBOARD
6. HEATING CHAMBER
7. DRIVERS LOBBY

Two clerks worked in conjunction with the Time Office regarding engine repair notes and organised repairs. They also dealt with matters regarding the fitters, their tools, engine record cards and the ordering of parts etc. Working out of these offices were:

Foreman Fitter and a Chargehand Fitter
Fitters and mates - Approx 15 pairs starting 8am then 1 pair starting afternoons and 2 pairs on nights.
Examining Fitter who liaised to see what repairs were necessary.
Firebars and bricks One pair of men per shift.
Tube cleaner - 2 men each day.
Washout men - 4 on days, one on nights.
Night man - swill out boilers ready for washout on following day turn. Boiler inspections would be done to coincide with the washouts.

The following would normally be day shift only
Blacksmith plus one striker.
Foreman Boilersmith plus 3 to 4 boilersmiths, one of which would be the chargehand boilersmith.
Tinsmith - attended to oil lamps, etc.
Coppersmith - attended to copper pipework, brazing, axleboxes and journals.
Lathe turner possibly with mate.
Apprentices The shed was allowed up to 10 of these.

Repair work included retubing, wheel turning, axleboxes, motion & bearings, firebricks and baffleplates. In the later years an electrician was a permanent feature on the payroll. In 1944, repairs were done in No 2 shed on roads Nos 10 to 16. Road Nos 14 and 15 were used for washout and No 17 for the sand wagons. No 10 also contained the original wheel drop. After No 1 shed was rebuilt in 1951, repairs were transferred here and the drop road became No 6 road with its new electrical wheel drop. There was also a hoist (5 ton) just outside of the shed on No 6 road which was used to lift wheelsets to/from wagons, should these have needed to be sent away.

Ivatt 2-6-0 No 46429 undergoes attention to its left hand cylinder within No 2 shed. This is a Preston loco under repair at its principal depot.

25TH JUNE 1950
AUTHOR'S COLLECTION

The connecting rods of Super D No 49129.

25TH JULY 1962 • TONY GILLETT

In March 1964 just prior to Wigan L&Y shed's closure and the work being taken over by Springs Branch, the non-footplate staff at both sheds was:

	8F	8P
Apprentice Boilersmith	1	
Fitter	3	
Boilersmith	3	2
Brickarch & Asst	1	
Joiner	1	
Coppersmith	1	
Electrician	1	
Fitter Grade 1	1	6
Fitter Temp	1	1
Fitter's Mate	13	5
Fitter Chargehand	1	
Blacksmith	1	
Smiths Striker	1	
Tuber	3	1
Turner	1	

Things look surprisingly tidy around Fowler 2-6-4T No 42374 as it stands in the repair section at the bottom of Road No 4.

20TH JUNE 1965 • JOHN BURGESS

Inside No 1 shed and No 75041 has its rods down, probably for attention to the bearings. **20TH JUNE 1965** ● **ALLAN HEYES**

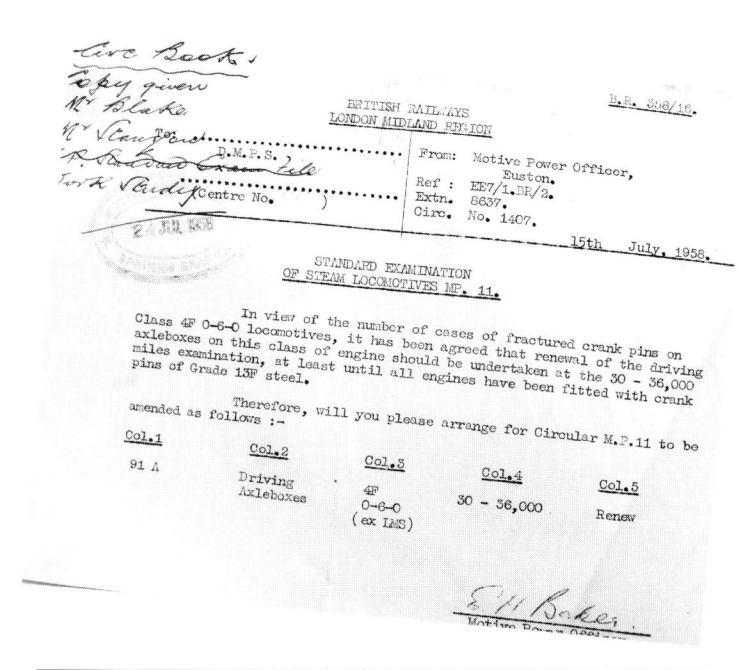

Dumped outside nine days earlier *(see P11)* **Jinty No 47444** is now receiving attention to its trailing wheelset and is temporarily a 0-4-4 thanks to a small rail truck used to ensure there is no tilting. **17TH AUGUST 1965** ● **PETER FITTON**

Ivatt No 46470 has its RH cylinder stripped down for repair. The fitters have dragged a work bench arrangement across to assist for convenience. Note the cylinder covers placed at the front of the smokebox saddle. **10TH AUGUST 1961** ● **TONY GILLETT**

Repairs to the boiler tubes are well underway with visiting 9F No **92018** from Birkenhead. **23RD MARCH 1967** ● **ALLAN HEYES**

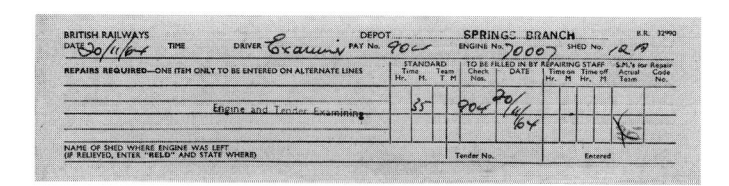

A visitor from Sutton Oak, 0-6-0 No 47298 stands where the boiler washouts are normally undertaken. **3RD JULY 1966** ● **ROBIN LUSH**

Standing proudly by the wheel lathe are Ronnie Sharrock (wheel lathe operator) and Bert Richards (Coppersmith).

1964 ● FRED BANKS

The wheel lathe was situated at the bottom of the second road in no 2 shed (road 8). All repairs had originally been done in No 2 shed until the new No 1 was built in 1951 which then became the repair shed. The workshops, originally built in 1881, remained at the rear of the old No 2 shed and even survived the demolition of that shed in 1961 when a further four road shed was built.

1964 ● FRED BANKS

Ronnie Sharrock at work on one of the workshop lathes. Note the neat rack on the wall for storage of spanners and the pulley block in the corner.

1964 ● FRED BANKS

4F 0-6-0 No 44303 stands at the bottom of Road 15 (the old 17). Part of the old workshops and the sand dryer chimney are clearly seen.

22ND MARCH 1963 ● AUTHOR'S COLLECTION

Tommy Green hard at work on a fuel injector probably belonging to one of the many diesel shunters 'on shed'.

c1966 ● FRED BANKS

A couple of the newly arrived Hunslet 0-6-0 shunters (later Class 05) are being inspected by the maintenance staff.

c1966 ● FRED BANKS

Posing at the front of No 1 shed are (Left to Right) an unknown apprentice, Bill Shufflebottom *Mechanical Foreman*, Tony Rigby *Apprentice* and Roy Lancaster *Fitter's Mate*.

c1964 ● FRED BANKS

WAGES

In the 1860's, footplatemen were considered well paid workers and a driver in 1867 would earn from 5/6 to 7/- per day. Firemen would get 3/6 to 4/- yet the chart for wages in 1891 shows, 24 years later, these had hardly changed. One significant item earned by the Unions in 1919 was the reduction of the working day to 10 hours. As can be seen no real changes occurred until after 1938 and it was around 1947/8 when the working week was reduced from 48 hours to 44 hours. More progress was made in the 1960's when the working week became 42 hours but it was a decade later before the 40 hour week was established. Drivers could also boost their wages slightly with the mileage allowance scheme which paid a supplement once a footplateman had done over 70 miles a shift. Thereafter the bonus rate would increase, in stages, at set mileages. This scheme still existed in 1968.

WEEKLY WAGES In 1891

Shed Foreman's Assistant	42/-	Fuelman	20/-
Timekeeper/Storemaster	39/-	Storesman	20/-
Boiler Maker	36/-	Lodging House Matron	20/-
Turner	33/-	Stationary Engineman	20/-
Fitter	32/- to 34/-	Labourer	18/- to 20/-
Blacksmith	32/-	Fitters Assistant	18/-
Coppersmith	30/-	Pointsman	15/-
Joiner	30/-	Cleaners	8/- to 15/-
Nightman	30/- & 27/-	Bar Lad	11/-
Assistant Storekeeper	27/-	Bricksetters Assistant	10/-
Chief Cleaner	25/-	Call Boy	6/- to 8/-
Chief Tubeman	24/-	Apprentice	8/-
Chief Washer-out	24/-	Engineman	5/6 to 7/6
Tubeman	22/-	Boiler Makers Assistant	7/-
Tube Cleaner	21/-	Store Boy	7/-
Loco Inspector	21/-	Fireman	3/9 to 4/6
Washer-out	21/-	Fire Carrier	3/3
Brick Setter	21/-	Steam Raiser	3/3
Break Blockman	21/-	Firedropper	3/3

WEEKLY WAGES In 1957/58

Eng Cleaner	£7.14/- to £7.16/-	Shed Chargeman	£9.9/6d to £10.4/-
Fireman	£8.8/- to £9.10/-	Foreman's Assistant CL3	£8.13/6d
Driver	£10.4/- to £11.9/-	Foreman's Asst CL2	£9.1/-
Shed engineman	£10.4/-	Foreman's Asst CL1	£9.8/6d
Engineman's mate	£8.8/-	Junior Clerk	£3.13/8d to £4.04d
Shedman	£7.11/6d to £7.16/-	Senior Clerk	£6.2/- to £10.04d
Coalman	£8.2/-	Boilersmith	£11.12/4d
Leading Shedman	£8.2/-	Coppersmith	£10.2/2d
Coalman/Plant Attendant	£8.4/6d	Brickarchman	£11.10/8d
Firedropper	£8.4/6d	Chargehand	£14.0/1d
Machinery Attendant	£8.4/6d	Fitter	£13.0/11d
Boilerwasher	£8.5/6d	Apprentice	£5.3s/6d
Craneman	£8.5/6d	Fitters Mate	£12.3/2d
Steamraiser	£8.5/6d	Blacksmith	£13.19/10d
Water Soft Attendant	£8.9/-	Striker	£9.16/11d
Storekeeper	£8.12/6d	Tubers	£10.13/7d
Timekeeper (N.C.)	£8.12/6d	Joiner	£10.15/5d
Changeman Cleaner	£9.2/-		
Shed Shunter	£8.11/6d		

During the period 1919 to 1938 there was no wage increase at all. For 6day/48hr week, rates were:
Cleaner .... 28/-   Fireman .... £3.12/-   Driver (Engineman) £4.10/-

The basic for footplatemen in October 1965:   Cleaner .... £10.18/- to £12.5/-
Fireman .... £12.5/- to £16.3/-   Driver .... £14.8/- to £16.19/-

Springs Branch (25) Pay Tally

UNIONS

As with all Motive Power Depots, there was a strong union representation and the two principal railway unions, the NUR and ASLEF, were very active in the Wigan area. The then new Wigan branch of ASLEF (Associated Society of Locomotive Engineers & Firemen) opened on Sunday 4th November 1888, made up of 19 enginemen & firemen working on the L&Y and LNWR and was the 11th branch to be opened that year. Branch meetings were held in the Rock Hotel, Ince and the very first meeting was on Sunday 18th November. Then, in 1906, the Ince Branch was formed with 32 members and this had risen to 150 members by 1912. Generally the union representation was strong and in 1909, when the railways employed 530,000 people, 21,000 were ASLEF members. The strength of the Union continued to grow and, in 1915 ASLEF claimed to have 36,000 members and the NUR had 29,000 although the NUR dispute this as they claim to have 50,000. In 1932 the Ince Branch was split into two sections, returning to one circa 1956. Finally, in 1977, the Wigan and Ince Branches of ASLEF merged. In 1924, when there was a major strike lasting 8 1/2 days, the support of the ladies justified the creation of a ladies' section from that year.

The Amalgamated Society of Railway Servants (ASRS) was formed in 1871, merging with the General Railway Workers' Union and the United Pointsmen and Signalmen's Society in 1913 to form the NUR. This union then represented most railway workers apart from those in ASLEF or the RCA (Railway Clerks' Association). At its peak in 1947 the NUR had 462,205 members. Several years after the major 1982 strike, the NUR joined with the National Union of Seamen to form the RMT (National Union of Rail, Maritime and Transport Workers). There was also a Steam Engine Makers' Society in existence in 1908 with a Wigan Branch and another union known as TESA, mainly for the administration staff.

The ASLEF and NUR boards on the wall inside No 1 shed. 1970 • JOHN BRETHERTON

The notorious strike of 1955 caused serious bad feeling amongst fellow footplatemen. At this time there were 77,000 ASLEF members and 17,000 NUR members on the footplate. At Springs Branch, about 20 NUR men were told or forced to work. Some worked normally but some benefited from lots of overtime and these latter men were never forgiven by their colleagues.

On a social basis, various events were organised by the Unions. For example the Ince ASLEF branch held its first smoking concert on Nov 23rd 1908 at Ince Hall Inn, and the Wigan Branch held an annual knife and fork tea and social at the Raven Hotel, Wallgate, Wigan on Thursday 2nd Jan 1908, when it was reported that 55 members and their wives sat down to a magnificent repast provided by their worthy host and hostess Mr and Mrs W Parkinson. After all had satisfied their wants, the party adjourned to the club room where the rest of the evening was spent in harmony - the vocal and musical items being given in a praiseworthy manner. The following year it was noted that justice had been done to the tempting viands and again they adjourned to the club rooms for the social entertainment. In LMS days there had been various annual events, such as whist drive dances and tea & social evenings, often raising money for the orphans' fund.

In the early 1950's, retirement funds were started with associated meetings and these continue to this day. Another mediating body, the Local Development Committee, existed from at least 1928 and dealt with local disputes and proposed changes.

Has a union meeting been called at the banking cabin at Bamfurlong Junction. From L to R Jimmy Melling (NUR Sec) Fireman Bernard Lowe and John Sloan (ASLEF Sec). c1964 • BERNARD LOWE

SOCIAL

In addition to the social activities organised by the Union branches, Springs Branch had a St John's Ambulance section at the shed plus a Bowling Club, Cricket team, Rugby League team and a Football team.

Members of the Springs Branch Bowling Club proudly display their trophies. The club was in the Wigan Workshops league and based at the 'Buck' at Abram, moving later to the Colliers Arms, Orrell until 1967.

AUTHOR'S COLLECTION

Springs Branch had a football Club from at least the 1940's, playing in the Sunday School League at the Carrington Forge ground and later at Foster Playing Fields at Ince. Local derby matches with the Prescott Street L&Y shed were always a highlight. When L&Y shed closed in 1964, their team (Wigan BR) combined with Springs Branch's to form Springs Branch FC which then existed for about 5 years. They played league and cup games in the Wigan & District Sunday League. At this time the team was managed by Donald Hodson with Jack Edwards as the Chairman. Ron Davies was Captain and later became Secretary. An inspiration for both the football and rugby teams was their coach Len McIntyre, an ex-Great Britain Rugby League hooker. Plans for a dedicated football ground on railway allotment land at Buckley Street never materialised, the land later being used for the new BR social club building. A cricket team also existed, the organiser being Harold Spencer who arranged local friendly matches.

The football team is seen outside the famous Old Trafford Ground in the late 1960's. Sadly this was not their venue, that being the MUFC training ground. The match against Trafford Park Loco was a close one but they eventually lost 4-3. They also played games in Blackpool, Barrow, Dublin and London.

COURTESY R. DAVIES

The Rugby League team originally played at St Mary's, Lower Ince in the Amateur League and took part in the occasional cup competition. A later venue was the playing grounds at Carrington Forge and even as late as 1992, shortly before the depot closed, the team is reported to have been sponsored by Railfreight who provided new kit.

The local watering hole was initially the *Old Hall Inn* on Cemetery Road. The bowling green here later made way for the replacement *Old Hall Hotel* in 1895. The new building was situated on the corner of Warrington Road and was the favourite with shed men until an encounter with one of the Depot Superintendents, which resulted in the *Walmsley Arms* on Warrington Road becoming their new regular. All sheds had their Bookies runner and in the 1960's it was the job of one of the fitters (Bill Fairclough). His apprentice covered for him whilst he was performing his Bookies activities and was suitably reimbursed for his efforts. A most lucrative position by all accounts!

BR opened a railway club just after the war, which was situated in the old stationmaster's office above the booking offices at Wigan Wallgate station. This was very much an L&Y establishment and not often frequented by the Springs Branch men who tended to live towards Ince. It was replaced in September 1966 by a brand new club built on railway allotment land off Buckley Street, about a mile north of Wigan NW, and this proved a very popular venue. The club took £800 a week in its first year but then, after the breathaliser, subsequent takings fell to £450. Despite this setback it served the railwaymen, their families and the local population for 33 years until its closure on 28th October 1999.

SIGNING ON/OFF & DISPOSAL

Enginemen could book on at any time of the day (or night) depending on the turn. Walking through the passage, the men would sign on at the window on the left and then continue through to the corridor where, in front of them, would be the huge Enginemen's Arrangements board. This would confirm the men's turn, which locomotive they would have, and where it was located in the shed. Also in the corridor was the late notice board which would also be perused. The footplate crew had 10 minutes to read notices and further time to prepare their engine. Sometimes the engine would have been prepared by another crew. Similarly a crew may prepare engines other than their own. They would be allowed 45 minutes to prepare a Black 5 and 30 minutes for a small engine such as a 2-6-0 Ivatt, a 2-6-4 tank or a 0-6-0 Jinty.

There would also be a 'walking time' allowance if the turn didn't start from the depot. For example, 20 minutes was allowed to walk to Bamfurlong North End, Pemberton Corner or Ince Moss and 25 min to Bamfurlong South End. The bank engine siding beyond Bamfurlong Yard was 35 minutes and 45 minutes to Bamfurlong Junction. Other allowances were 45 minutes to Wigan NW Station and 25 minutes to Ince Station. Relieving (taking over a footplate from another crew) was mainly done at Bamfurlong Yard, Platt Bridge, Springs Branch No 2, Ince Moss Junction, Wigan NW Station and in the vicinity of the shed.

Also booking on at the time office were Loco turners (tank & coal men) plus a set of men for the shed shunt. In 1951 the general (Mon - Sat) arrangement for these was for 2 sets of turners to book on at 6am with a set of shed men at 7am. The late shift also had two sets of men booking on at 2pm with shed shunt at 3pm and the night shift had a set of men booking on at 10pm and the shed shunt at 11pm. The outside arranger worked with these men and sorted which road particular engines had to go on. He also started, on each shift, at 7am, 3pm and 11pm.

This is the view that would present itself to the enginemen as they came into the passageway from the pathway leading down to the shed from Morris Street. The windows and speaking grille on the left communicate with the men inside the Time Office and this is where the men would sign on/off duty. A strategically placed desk allowed the men to jot down anything relevant. One wonders whether the proliferation of hanging notices and memos was to impart information or merely to give the Time Office some privacy! c1968 ● JOHN BRETHERTON

The windows and desk previously featured are now on the left. The 'Late Notice' boards are on the wall in the centre whilst out of sight to the extreme left would be the 'Roster' boards. The 'Enginemen's Arrangements Board' (*page 94*) is situated behind the photographer. c1968 ● JOHN BRETHERTON

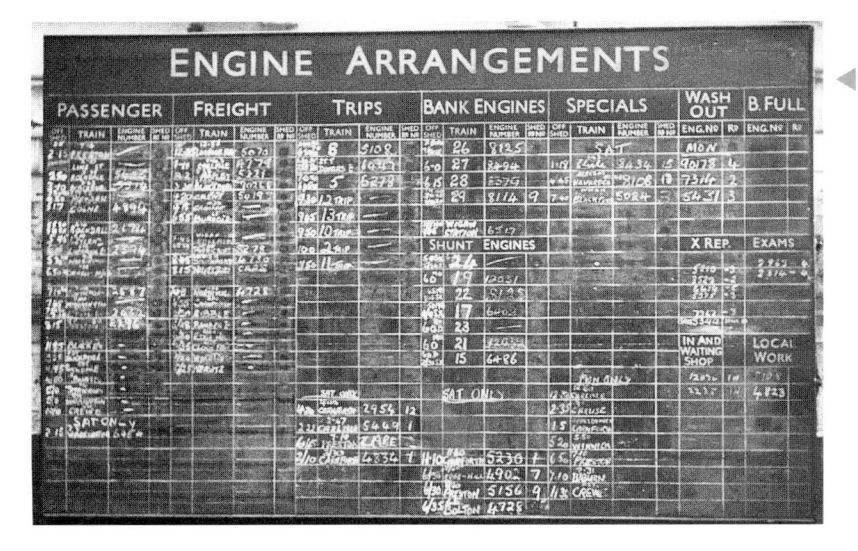

The Enginemens' Arrangements Board. After signing on and reading the notices, the footplatemen would turn and consult this board. It would confirm their turn and time off shed and where their engine was stabled. A detailed description of this board and full explanation of a day's activity in 1965 can be found on page 94.

29TH MAY 1965 ● B. MAGILTON

TIMING OF ENGINES FROM SHEDS.

Engine for all Passenger, Freight etc. trains in the Wigan area must arrive at the Springs Branch M.P.D. Disc at the times laid down below:

M.P.D.	Train from	Minutes before train is due to leave
	TRAIN ENGINES	
SPRINGS BRANCH	Springs Branch Up Sidings Engine Shed Sidings	10
	Passenger Station	30
	Ince Moss Springs Branch North Sidings Wigan Goods Yard	20
	Bamfurlong Sidings	25
	Bickershaw Branch Sidings Chanters Siding Golborne	45
	Bamfurlong Screens	30
	Sidings on Whelley Line Coppull Hall Blainscough Adlington Junction	60
	SHUNTING AND BANK ENGINES	
	Springs Branch North Sidings Springs Branch Up Sidings Engine Shed Sidings, Ince Moss Bamfurlong Platt Bridge	10

A popular activity were games of cards played in the mess room between duties. This room was originally the General Office. A favourite game was a made up one called 'Blob'. It involved money and there were many losers.

1970 ● TOM SUTCH COLLECTION

Gathered in the mess room are *(left to right)* Eric Titley, Bill Sudworth, Tommy Moorfield, Bill Frodsham, Jack Jolley and Colin Hewitt.

29TH MAY 1965 ● TOM SUTCH COLLECTION

Enginemen's Rosters sheet would be filled in and displayed in the cabinet in the main corridor.

ENGINEMENS' LINKS

The depot's work would be split into turns (diagrams) based on the following:

Engine Only turns ……….. the shed provided the loco but not the crew.
Enginemen Only turns ….. the shed provided the crew but not the loco.
Engine and Men turns ….. the shed provided both the loco and the crew.

These turns would then be put into LINKS, usually around 16 to 18 of them at Springs Branch, and these would maximise the use of both the men and the engines. A set of turns would be collated into a Link with a corresponding quantity of drivers and firemen, typically 8 to 10 sets of men. The pairs of men would generally only work the jobs in that link, and would progress through the jobs, changing to another turn (or set of turns) each week. If there were, for instance, 10 sets of men in the link, then, after 10 weeks, the men would have worked each turn and so would start again on the first turn, and so on. The complexity of these turns is better explained by the examples shown below.

Over the years, the men could progress through the links to more desirable work in the higher links, which usually involved less night work. The links also allowed the office staff to collate 'sets of men' to cover each type of work and allocate the jobs accordingly. Some older men or those with an ailment might request a lower link to ease the work load and the ultimate turn for this was 'Wigan Bank' Link (Wigan NW Station Pilot) which would normally be comprised of about 6 enginemen. The jobs within each link sometimes changed over the years but this was often of a minor variety, nevertheless, the links were a complicated mix as will be seen. If we take the winter of 1951 when the men worked 48 hour weeks, we find the following situation:

PASSENGER LINKS (8 or 10 sets of men in most links)

W1951	Passenger Link 1	R - Reman job	AP - As Passenger				
	Sun	Mon	Tue	Wed	Thu	Fri	Sat
1		06:43 Lime St	06:43 Lime St	06:43 Lime St	06:43 Lime St	06:43 Lime St	06:43 Lime St
2		02:00 Lime St	02:00 Lime St	02:00 Lime St	02:00 Lime St	02:00 Lime St	02:00 Lime St
3		R 14:23 Crewe	R 14:23 Crewe	R 14:23 Crewe	R 14:23 Crewe	R 14:23 Crewe	R 14:23 Crewe
4		09:05 Lime St	06:39 Tebay	06:39 Tebay	06:39 Tebay	06:39 Tebay	06:39 Tebay
5		AP 16:17 Ordsall Ln	AP 16:17 Ordsall Ln	AP 16:17 Ordsall Ln	AP 16:17 Ordsall Ln	AP 16:17 Ordsall Ln	AP 16:17 Ordsall Ln
6		06:30 Newton	06:30 Newton	06:30 Newton	06:30 Newton	06:30 Newton	06:30 Newton
7			R 09:28 Preston	R 09:28 Preston	R 09:28 Preston	R 09:28 Preston	08:06 Man Ex
8		R 13:55 Lime St	R 13:55 Lime St	R 13:55 Lime St	R 13:55 Lime St	R 13:55 Lime St	12:18 Man Ex
9			R 09:25 Lime St Pcls	R 09:25 Lime St Pcls	R 09:25 Lime St Pcls	R 09:25 Lime St Pcls	09:05 Lime St
10		R 15:40 Lime St	R 15:40 Lime St	R 15:40 Lime St	R 15:40 Lime St	R 15:40 Lime St	R 15:40 Lime St

W1951	Passenger Link 2					
1			05:20 Preston	05:20 Preston	05:20 Preston	05:20 Preston	05:20 Preston
2		12:35 Earlestown	12:35 Earlestown	12:35 Earlestown	12:35 Earlestown	12:35 Earlestown	13:00 Blackburn
3		05:20 Preston		06:15 Lime St	06:15 Lime St	06:15 Lime St	07:10 Blackburn
4		16:17 Huddersfield	16:17 Huddersfield	16:17 Huddersfield	16:17 Huddersfield	16:17 Huddersfield	16:30 Preston
5		05:47 Tyldesley	09:05 Lime St	09:05 Lime St	09:05 Lime St	09:05 Lime St	
6		16:37 Preston	16:37 Preston	16:37 Preston	16:37 Preston	16:37 Preston	
7		04:52 Newton	04:52 Newton	04:52 Newton	04:52 Newton	04:52 Newton	
8		16:30 Preston	16:30 Preston	16:30 Preston	17:11 Chester	17:11 Chester	18:44 Warrington

W1951	Passenger Link 3					
1		09:28 Preston	R 06:16 Crewe	R 06:16 Crewe	R 06:16 Crewe	R 06:16 Crewe	R 06:16 Crewe
2		07:10 Blackburn	07:10 Blackburn	07:10 Blackburn	07:10 Blackburn	07:10 Blackburn	
3		12:18 Manchester Ex	12:18 Manchester Ex	12:18 Manchester Ex	12:18 Manchester Ex	12:18 Manchester Ex	
4		06:33 Chorley ROF	06:33 Chorley ROF	06:33 Chorley ROF		06:33 Chorley ROF	06:15 Lime St
5	06:42 Bank	17:11 Chester	17:11 Chester	17:11 Chester	16:30 Preston	17:40 Warrington	12:55 Earlestown
6		06:15 Lime St	06:15 Lime St	06:43 Lime St	06:33 Chorley ROF		06:45 Tyldesley
7		R 17:40 Warrington	R 17:40 Warrington	R 17:40 Warrington	R 17:40 Warrington	16:30 Preston	18:25 Manchester Ex
8			R 02:07 Warrington	R 02:07 Warrington	R 02:07 Warrington	R 02:07 Warrington	R 02:07 Warrington
9		R 12:45 Preston	R 12:45 Preston	R 12:45 Preston	R 12:45 Preston	R 12:45 Preston	
10		R 14:42 Preston Pcls	R 14:42 Preston Pcls	R 14:42 Preston Pcls	R 14:42 Preston Pcls	R 14:42 Preston Pcls	

W1951	Wigan Bank Link					
	06:42 Bank	05:50 Bank	06:30 Bank	05:50 Bank	06:20 Bank	06:20 Bank	06:20 Bank
	11:15 Bank		12:30 Bank	12:50 Bank	12:30 Bank	12:30 Bank	12:30 Bank
	16:25 Bank						
	22:45 Bank	23:30 Bank	23:30 Bank	23:30 Bank	23:15 Bank	23:30 Bank	00:00 Bank

Notes See how certain trains don't always stay in a particular link. For example the 09:05 Lime St is worked by Link 1 (MO) but Link 2 (Tue - Fri). Similarly, the 17:11 Chester is in Link 3 Mon - Wed and Link 2 Thu/Fri. The 06:33 ROF has the same men Mon - Wed and on Friday, but a different crew from the same Link on Thursday (prob rest day for other men). Passenger work wasn't totally confined to their links and vice versa. For example, the 05:47 Tyldesley was worked by freight men (Tues to Fri). With re-man jobs, the trains are not always obvious such as the 02:07 Warrington which is actually the 19:40 Carlisle - Rugby Parcels. There are sometimes slight differences in the times shown in the book compared to the actual WTT as old timings were commonly just reused.

FREIGHT LINKS

There were 6 freight links with 10 sets of men in each link during the winter of 1951. This is by far the most complex set of links as the men worked a complicated series of freight workings, banking duties and the odd trip working.

W1951 FREIGHT LINK 1 R - Reman job   AP - As Passenger

	Sun	Mon	Tue	Wed	Thu	Fri	Sat
1		11:10 Oxenholme	11:10 Oxenholme	11:10 Oxenholme	11:10 Oxenholme	11:10 Oxenholme	08:25 Astley Green
2		R 07:37 Crewe	R 06:04 Carnforth	R 06:04 Carnforth	R 06:04 Carnforth	R 06:04 Carnforth	
3	09:40 Bank 163	R 11:50 160 Bank	R 11:50 160 Bank	R 11:50 160 Bank	R 11:50 160 Bank	R 11:50 160 Bank	09:30 161 Bank
4		05:05 Crewe	05:05 Crewe	05:05 Crewe	05:05 Crewe	05:05 Crewe	
5		R 22:53 Preston	R 22:53 Carnforth	R 22:53 Carnforth	20:45 Clock Face	20:45 Clock Face	
6		R 13:30 163 Bank	R 13:30 163 Bank	R 13:30 163 Bank		R 13:30 163 Bank	R 13:30 163 Bank
7		R 04:27 Carnforth	04:15 Carnforth	04:15 Carnforth	04:15 Carnforth	04:15 Carnforth	04:15 Carnforth
8	R 01:02 Crewe	R 19:41 Liverpool	R 19:41 Liverpool	R 19:41 Liverpool	R 19:41 Liverpool		R 11:50 160 Bank
9		08:25 Astley Green	08:25 Astley Green	08:25 Astley Green	08:25 Astley Green	08:25 Astley Green	
10			AP 18:10 Monton Green	AP 18:10 Monton Green	AP 18:10 Monton Green	AP 18:45 Monton Green	R 22:16 Warrington

W1951 FREIGHT LINK 2

	Sun	Mon	Tue	Wed	Thu	Fri	Sat
1		09:30 Edge Hill	06:30 163 Bank	09:55 Kearsley		R 07:55 162 Bank	05:05 Crewe
2		17:40 Preston	17:40 Preston	17:40 Preston	17:40 Preston	17:40 Preston	17:45 Crewe
3			04:30 Canada Dock	04:30 Canada Dock	04:30 Canada Dock	04:30 Canada Dock	04:30 Canada Dock
4		17:30 164 Bank	17:30 164 Bank	17:30 164 Bank	17:30 164 Bank	17:30 164 Bank	R 18:50 160 Bank
5		06:00 164 Bank	06:00 Birkenhead	06:00 Birkenhead	06:00 Birkenhead	06:00 Birkenhead	
6		20:35 Crewe	20:35 Crewe	20:35 Crewe	20:35 Crewe	20:35 Crewe	20:00 Crewe
7				R 03:20 161 Bank	07:00 Spare	07:00 Spare	06:00 Birkenhead
8	R 10:30 161 Bank	R 20:30 163 Bank	R 18:50 160 Bank	R 18:50 160 Bank	AP 21:27 Longsight	AP 21:27 Longsight	AP 21:27 Longsight
9		R 07:27 Edge Hill	07:00 Spare	10:00 Spare	10:30 Special	10:30 Special	
10		AP 18:10 Monton Green	20:50 Clock Face		R 22:53 Carnforth	R 22:53 Carnforth	R 20:47 Carnforth

W1951 FREIGHT LINK 3

	Sun	Mon	Tue	Wed	Thu	Fri	Sat
1		AP 21:29 Longsight	AP 21:27 Longsight	AP 21:27 Longsight	R 18:30 160 Bank	R 18:50 160 Bank	
2	(00:30 Mon 161 Bank)	R 22:58 Carnforth	R 22:58 Carnforth		R 00:25 162 Bank	R 00:20 162 Bank	R 00:55 162 Bank
3	R 03:30 161 Bank	07:20 Blackburn	Spare	Spare	Spare	08:00 Spare	
4		22:15 Patricroft	22:15 Patricroft	22:15 Patricroft	22:15 Patricroft	22:15 Patricroft	
5		06:00 Birkenhead	R 05:16 Crewe	09:05 Preston		05:30 Special	07:26 Fleetwood
6			(23:30 spare)	R 00:00 164 Bank	R 00:00 164 Bank	00:10 (Sat) Farington	22:45 Carnforth
7			05:00 Spare	05:00 Spare	05:00 Spare	05:00 Spare	R 06:04 Carlisle
8		R 13:20 161 Bank	R 14:55 162 Bank	R 14:55 162 Bank	R 14:55 162 Bank	R 14:55 162 Bank	R 14:55 162 Bank
9		08:45 138 Trip	08:45 138 Trip	08:45 138 Trip	08:45 138 Trip	08:45 138 Trip	08:45 138 Trip
10		R 08:00 163 Bank	R 03:30 163 Bank	R 05:30 163 Bank	R 03:30 163 Bank	R 03:30 163 Bank	R 01:03 Crewe

W1951 FREIGHT LINK 4

	Sun	Mon	Tue	Wed	Thu	Fri	Sat
1		R 16:25 Bank	17:55 Bullfield	17:55 Bullfield	17:55 Bullfield	17:55 Bullfield	
2		05:15 Blackburn	R 01:50 160 Bank	R 01:50 160 Bank	R 01:50 160 Bank	R 02:50 160 Bank	R 01:50 160 Bank
3		R 07:45 161 Bank	09:55 Kearsley		09:55 Kearsley	09:55 Kearsley	09:55 Kearsley
4		03:00 Bushbury	R 01:03 Crewe		R 01:03 Crewe	R 03:20 161 Bank	R 00:00 164 Bank
5	R 04:36 Carlisle	Return Carlisle?	01:56 Carlisle	01:56 Carlisle	01:56 Carlisle	01:56 Carlisle	
6		R 14:50 ROF		R 14:50 ROF			R 13:04 Warrington
7		R 03:45 Crewe	R 03:20 161 Bank	R 03:20 161 Bank	R 03:20 161 Bank		
8			R 00:55 162 Bank	R 00:55 162 Bank	R 22:58 Carnforth	R 22:58 Carnforth	R 22:58 Carnforth
9			R 06:30 163 Bank	R 06:30 163 Bank	R 06:30 163 Bank	06:20 Wigan Bank	
10	R 02:40 163 Bank	R 12:50 Warrington	R 13:04 Warrington	R 13:04 Warrington	R 13:04 Warrington		R 09:37 Carnforth

W1951 FREIGHT LINK 5

	Sun	Mon	Tue	Wed	Thu	Fri	Sat
1			02:25 Blackburn	02:25 Blackburn	02:25 Blackburn	02:25 Blackburn	02:25 Blackburn
2	08:50 160 Bank	19:36 Kearsley	R 20:50 161 Bank	R 20:20 161 Bank	R 20:20 161 Bank	R 20:20 161 Bank	R 20:20 161 Bank
3		06:10 Carlisle	09:05 Preston		09:05 Preston	09:05 Preston	07:40 Lime St
4	R 08:40 Liverpl Rd	R 00:03 Carnforth?		R 00:20 Carnforth	R 00:20 Carnforth		R 21:55 162 Bank
5		08:50 Clock Face	08:50 Clock Face	08:50 Clock Face	08:50 Clock Face	08:50 Clock Face	
6		R 11:46 Crewe	R 11:46 Crewe	R 11:46 Crewe	R 11:46 Crewe	R 11:46 Crewe	R 07:50 162 Bank
7		01:45 163 Bank	00:10 Farington	00:10 Farington	00:10 Farington	00:10 Farington	
8		R 23:17 Fleetwood	R 23:17 Fleetwood	R 23:12 Fleetwood	R 23:27 Fleetwood	R 23:17 Fleetwood	R 21:51 Crewe
9			R 09:00 161 Bank	R 09:30 161 Bank	R 09:30 161 Bank	R 09:45 161 Bank	08:50 Clock Face
10			19:36 Kearsley	19:36 Kearsley	19:36 Kearsley	19:36 Kearsley	17:35 Bullfield

W1951 FREIGHT LINK 6

	Sun	Mon	Tue	Wed	Thu	Fri	Sat
1		R 21:02 Carnforth	R 21:02 Carnforth	R 21:19 Carnforth	R 21:19 Carnforth	R 21:19 Preston	R 00:35 Carnforth
2		R 11:45 162 Bank	R 07:55 162 Bank	R 07:55 162 Bank	R 07:55 162 Bank	08:45 138 Trip	
3		R 06:46 Carlisle	R 07:50 Carnforth	R 07:50 Carnforth	R 07:51 Carnforth	R 07:57 Carnforth	
4			R 02:25 Carnforth	R 02:25 Carnforth	R 02:25 Carnforth	R 02:26 Carnforth	R 02:26 Carnforth
5	R 06:46 Carlisle	AP 20:25 Birkenhead	AP 19:33 Birkenhead	AP 19:38 Birkenhead		AP 20:25 Birkenhead	19:00 Carnforth
6		07:26 Fleetwood	07:26 Fleetwood	07:26 Fleetwood	07:26 Fleetwood	07:26 Fleetwood	
7		R 18:40 162 Bank	R 18:40 162 Bank	R 18:45 162 Bank	R 18:45 162 Bank	R 18:45 162 Bank	R 19:41 Liverpool
8			02:45 Colne	02:45 Colne	02:45 Colne	02:45 Colne	02:45 Colne
9		R 19:05 Carlisle	return?	19:20 Liverpool	19:20 Liverpool	19:20 Liverpool	19:20 Liverpool
10		07:00 Spare		R 05:16 Crewe	R 05:16 Crewe	R 05:16 Crewe	R 05:16 Crewe

Notes: Once again a particular job can all be in the same link (08:25 Astley Green) or in two different links (09:55 Kearsley). The bank turns are totally distributed throughout the whole of the freight links, there being no separate bank link in 1951. There is one Trip working in the Freight Link, the 08:45 138 Trip. Note that the shed shows Fleetwood, but the trains would actually go to Wyre Dock. Often the departing times seem to vary by a few minutes on the same train but this was how the Time Office noted it.

OTHER LINKS

TRIP LINKS Link 1 was 10 weeks work, Link 2 was 14 weeks work.

SHUNT LINKS Shunt Link 1 was 20 weeks work covering most of the shunt workings. Shunt Link 2 was 3 weeks work. Incline shunt and Long Drag only. Shunt Link 3 was 2 weeks work involving Wigan Canal Sidings shunt only.

CONTROL LINK was 25 sets of men under the orders of Control. The RSF would have to request permission to use these men.

SPARE LINK was provided to cover for holidays/sickness plus any additional jobs that needed men. About a dozen men in this link. Some links were known as 'Muck Links' and these were usually the bottom freight or trip links. The *young muck link* would contain the new firemen and the *old muck link* the elderly and 'not to go mainline' footplatemen and usually involved the easier local work, particularly trip workings. They did contain a little passenger work such as the Summer SO Wigan to Llandudno train. The closure of Lower Ince MPD in 1952 not only brought a transfer of engines but an additional 19 turns came to Springs Branch. As a result, a couple of new mixed links were formed including a GC static link (mainly freight) for men who didn't want to progress. In later BR days a 'Wigan Link' was formed, mainly of older ex-L&Y men. They were principally involved with DMU's and earned the nickname 'Mothercare'. Another link that came later was the 'Bank link'. From 1964 all the links changed considerably as the Beeching plan came into force and flexiwork was introduced.

W1951 TRIP LINK 1 R - Reman job

	Sun	Mon	Tue	Wed	Thu	Fri	Sat
1		18:00 134 Trip	18:00 134 Trip	18:00 134 Trip	18:00 134 Trip	18:00 134 Trip	16:30 134 Trip
2		R 11:10 133 Trip	R 11:40 133 Trip	R 11:30 133 Trip		R 11:30 133 Trip	R 11:00 133 Trip
3	R 106 Trip?	13:40 109 Trip	R 15:30 101 Trip	R 15:30 101 Trip	(Job in Trip link 2)	R 15:10 101 Trip	
4		06:50 101 Trip	06:50 101 Trip	06:50 101 Trip		06:50 101 Trip	06:50 101 Trip
5		R 14:00 137 Trip	R 14:00 137 Trip	R 14:00 137 Trip	R 14:00 137 Trip	R 15:30 137 Trip	R 14:58 112 Trip
6			R 13:30 132 Trip	R 13:30 132 Trip	R 13:20 132 Trip	R 13:20 132 Trip	R 15:30 132 Trip
7		05:00 133 Trip	05:00 133 Trip	05:00 133 Trip	04:30 133 Trip	04:30 133 Trip	05:00 133 Trip
8	R 07:00 102 Trip	13:00 126 Trip		13:00 126 Trip	13:35 124 Trip	13:40 124 Trip	
9		R 15:00 101 Trip	13:30 126 Trip	13:00 116 Trip	R 11:10 133 Trip	13:40 109 Trip	R 14:00 145 Shunt
10		07:40 122 Trip	07:40 122 Trip	07:40 122 Trip	07:40 122 Trip	07:40 122 Trip	

W1951 TRIP LINK 2

	Sun	Mon	Tue	Wed	Thu	Fri	Sat
1		(Job In Trip Link 1)	R 13:20 109 Trip	R 13:00 109 Trip	R 13:40 109 Trip	11:00 Special	08:15 132 Trip
2		09:30 123 Trip	09:30 123 Trip	09:30 123 Trip	09:30 123 Trip		06:50 123 Trip
3		17:10 112 Trip	16:30 112 Trip	17:15 112 Trip	17:15 112 Trip	17:30 112 Trip	
4		20:45 Clock Face	R 20:30 163 Bank	R 20:30 163 Bank	R 20:30 163 Bank	R 20:30 163 Bank	00:30 Clock Face
5		13:30 116 Trip	13:00 116 Trip		13:00 116 Trip	13:00 116 Trip	11:00 109 Trip
6		R 18:30 133 Trip	R 18:30 133 Trip	R 18:35 133 Trip	R 18:50 133 Trip	R 18:30 133 Trip	R 18:30 133 Trip
7		R 10:25 151 Shunt	07:15 154 Shunt		08:50 101 Trip	R 06:00 147 Shunt	R 05:00 163 Bank
8		R 23:45 112 Trip	R 23:45 112 Trip	R 00:00 112 Trip	R 23:45 112 Trip	R 00:00 112 Trip	23:00 134 Trip
9		13:40 124 Trip	13:40 124 Trip	13:40 124 Trip	13:30 126 Trip	13:40 126 Trip	
10		06:00 151 Shunt	R 00:45 134 Trip	R 00:45 134 Trip	R 00:45 134 Trip	R 00:45 134 Trip	R 00:45 134 Trip
11			05:30 Special	Spare	Spare	Spare	Spare
12		18:25 140 Trip	18:25 140 Trip	18:25 140 Trip	18:25 140 Trip	18:25 140 Trip	R 14:50 132 Trip
13		06:50 132 Trip	06:50 132 Trip	06:50 132 Trip	06:50 132 Trip	06:50 132 Trip	
14		17:20 Preston	R 16:30 161 Bank	R 16:30 161 Bank	R 16:30 161 Bank	R 16:30 161 Bank	R 16:30 161 Bank

W1951 SHUNT LINK 1

	Sun	Mon	Tue	Wed	Thu	Fri	Sat
1		06:00 145 Shunt	R 06:00 145 Shunt	R 06:00 145 Shunt	R 06:00 145 Shunt	R 06:00 145 Shunt	R 06:00 145 Shunt
2	R 06:00 145 Shunt	R 14:00 145 Shunt	R 14:00 145 Shunt	R 14:00 145 Shunt	R 14:00 145 Shunt	R 14:00 145 Shunt	
3		R 22:00 145 Shunt	R 22:00 145 Shunt	R 22:00 145 Shunt	R 22:00 145 Shunt	R 22:00 145 Shunt	R 22:45 145 Shunt
4		06:00 147 Shunt	R 06:00 147 Shunt	R 06:00 147 Shunt			R 06:00 147 Shunt
5	R 06:00 147 Shunt	R 14:00 147 Shunt	R 14:00 147 Shunt	R 14:00 147 Shunt	R 14:00 147 Shunt	R 14:00 147 Shunt	R 14:00 147 Shunt
6			R 22:00 147 Shunt	R 22:00 147 Shunt	R 22:00 147 Shunt	R 22:00 147 Shunt	R 22:00 147 Shunt
7		06:00 148 Shunt	R 06:00 148 Shunt	R 06:00 148 Shunt	R 06:00 148 Shunt	R 06:00 148 Shunt	R 06:00 148 Shunt
8	R 06:00 148 Shunt	R 14:00 148 Shunt		R 14:00 148 Shunt	R 14:00 148 Shunt	R 14:00 148 Shunt	
9		R 22:00 148 Shunt	R 22:00 148 Shunt	R 22:00 148 Shunt	R 22:00 148 Shunt	R 22:00 148 Shunt	R 22:00 148 Shunt
10		(Job in trip link)	R 06:00 151 Shunt	R 06:00 151 Shunt	R 06:00 151 Shunt	R 06:00 151 Shunt	R 06:00 151 Shunt
11		R 00:20 (Tu) 151 Shunt	R 00:20 (We) 151 Shunt	R 23:40 151 Shunt	R 23:45 151 Shunt	R 23:30 151 Shunt	R 23:20 151 Shunt
12		R 16:40 151 Shunt	R 14:00 151 Shunt		R 13:40 151 Shunt	R 13:40 151 Shunt	R 14:00 151 Shunt
13		06:00 150 Shunt	R 06:00 150 Shunt	R 06:00 150 Shunt	R 06:00 150 Shunt	R 06:00 150 Shunt	R 06:00 150 Shunt
14		R 14:00 150 Shunt	R 14:00 150 Shunt	R 14:00 150 Shunt	R 14:00 150 Shunt	R 14:00 150 Shunt	
15		R 22:00 150 Shunt	R 22:00 150 Shunt	R 22:00 150 Shunt	R 22:00 150 Shunt	R 22:00 150 Shunt	R 22:00 150 Shunt
16		07:30 154 Shunt	(Job in trip link)	07:30 154 Shunt	07:30 154 Shunt	07:15 154 Shunt	06:00 154 Shunt
17		R 14:05 154 Shunt	R 14:45 154 Shnt	R 14:45 154 Shunt	R 14:45 154 Shunt	R 14:45 154 Shunt	
18		06:00 149 Shunt	06:00 149 Shunt	06:00 149 Shunt	06:00 149 Shunt		06:00 149 Shunt
19			16:00 152 Shunt	16:00 152 Shunt	16:00 152 Shunt	16:00 152 Shunt	14:00 152 Shunt
20		R 22:00 152 Shunt	R 00:10(W) 152 Shunt	R 23:58 152 Shunt	R 23:45 152 Shunt	R 23:55 152 Shunt	

W1951 SHUNT LINK 2

	Sun	Mon	Tue	Wed	Thu	Fri	Sat
1		06:00 141 Shunt	06:00 141 Shunt	06:00 141 Shunt	06:00 141 Shunt	06:00 141 Shunt	
2		R 23:00 149 Shnt	R 23:00 149 Shunt	R 23:00 149 Shunt	R 23:00 149 Shunt	R 23:00 149 Shunt	
3		R 13:30 141 Shnt	R 12:40 141 Shunt	R 12:40 141 Shunt	R 12:40 141 Shunt	R 12:40 141 Shunt	

W1951 SHUNT LINK 3

	Sun	Mon	Tue	Wed	Thu	Fri	Sat
1		05:00 156 Shunt	06:00 156 Shunt	06:00 156 Shunt	06:00 156 Shunt	06:00 156 Shunt	06:00 156 Shunt
2		16:40 156 Shunt	16:00 156 Shunt	16:30 156 Shunt	16:30 156 Shunt	16:30 156 Shunt	

A complete description of each Trip, Shunt and Bank working is given in the WORKINGS section of the book. Shunt Link 2 was normally the preserve of the elderly crews.

GETTING READY FOR THE ROAD

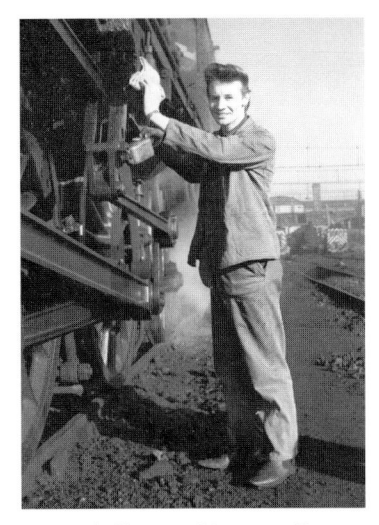

Passed Cleaner Norman Barton oils around. c.1965 • TOM SUTCH

The crew of ex-L&Y 0-6-0 No 12030 attend to their loco as it stands on the old road 16. c1935 • AUTHOR'S COLLECTION

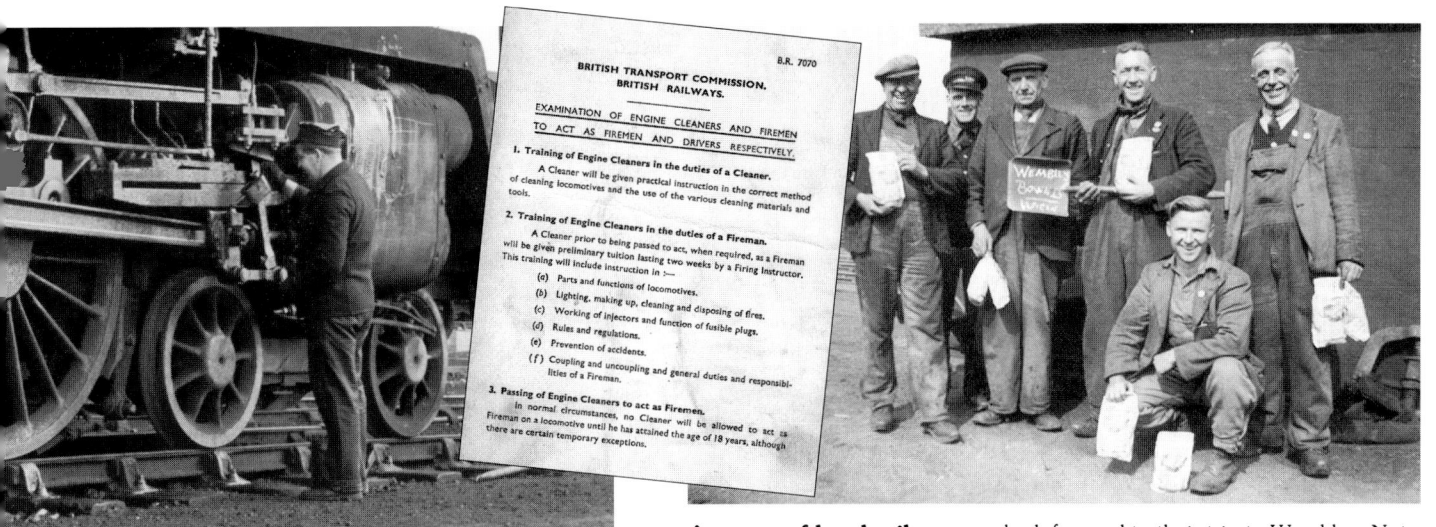

Alan Box is dwarfed by the BR Standard loco as he oils around its Caprotti valve gear. 1967 • LES RILEY

A group of local railwaymen look forward to their trip to Wembley. Note the pre-prepared food bags and the 'Wembley bownd Wigan' in typical Wigan speak chalked on the shovel. Second from the left is Bert Birchall and fifth left is George Meadows. c1948 • COURTESY P. GRATTON

Whoever was on shed at the time of the photograph appears to have congregated in front of Jubilee No **5668** *Madden* before its journey south with a Wembley Rugby League special *(see also page 116)*. 8TH MAY 1948 • COURTESY S. PRICE

85

Renowned Springs Branch Driver Israel Hewitt, born 1846, is on the footplate of Special DX Class 2-4-0 No **1581**.

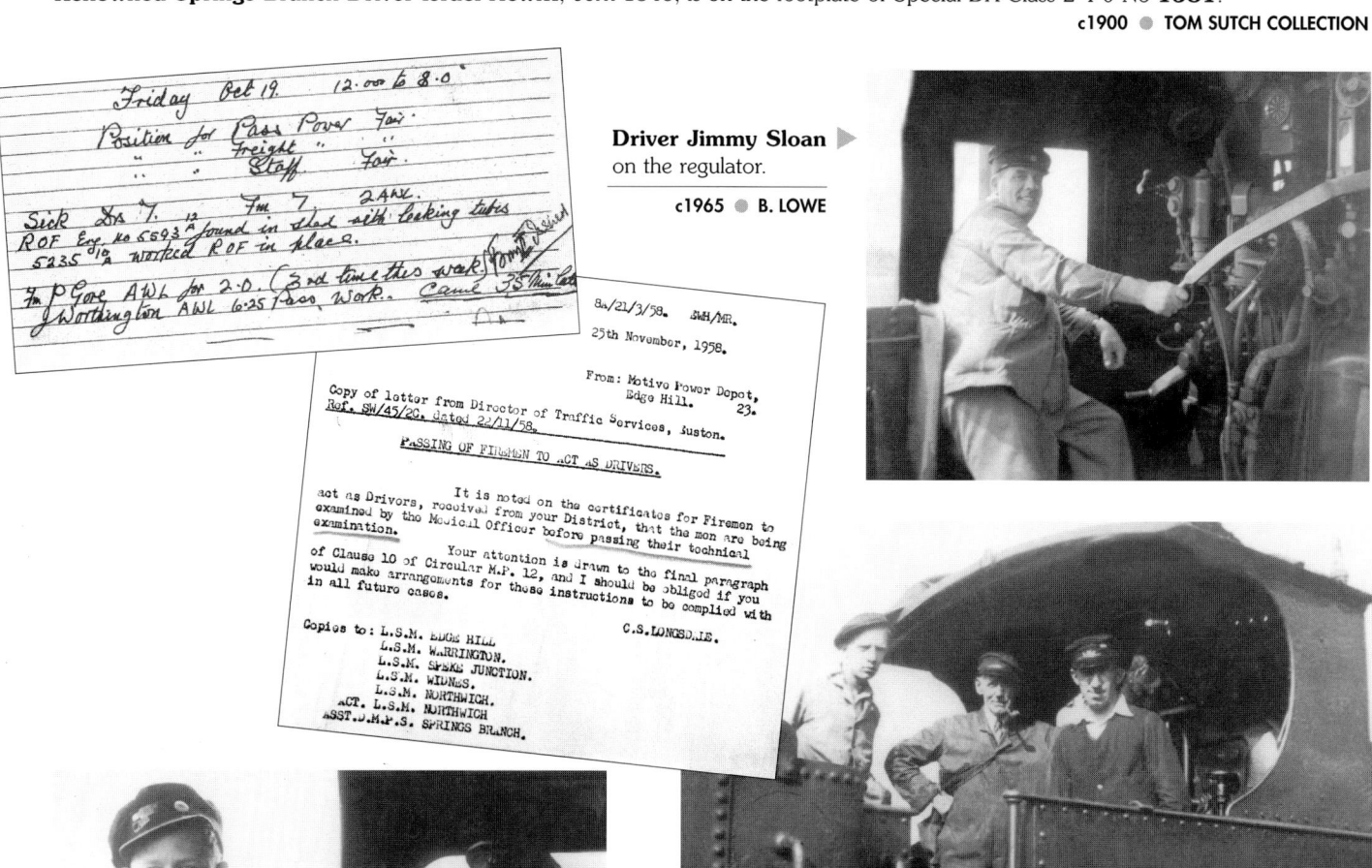

c1900 ● TOM SUTCH COLLECTION

Driver Jimmy Sloan ▶
on the regulator.

c1965 ● B. LOWE

Fireman Alan Edwards and Driver Jimmy Frears.

c1956 ● ALAN EDWARDS

Driver Tommy Hart and Fireman Alf Jones on the footplate of Cauliflower 0-6-0 No **28343** in the Blackburn bay at Wigan NW station. This engine was allocated to the shed from March 1944 to December 1947.

c1946 ● AUTHOR'S COLLECTION

TOM TAYLOR'S DIARY

Most footplatemen had diaries in which they recorded their work. There were several benefits from this practice, one of the most important being to keep track of the hours worked and the pay due. It also created a written record of the number of turns they had worked should they be eligible for promotion. It is most fortunate that the diary of Mr Tom Taylor (Fireman then Driver) has survived and gives a glimpse of work on the footplate at Springs Branch in the 1920's. The diary starts in September 1920 and at that time Tom is mainly engaged in engine turning, shunting and preparation, with a little firing. Shortly after this he seems to have had quite a spell doing 'shed turning', but a note in January 1921 states 'put back to firing from 8th January 1921'. This starts with local freight work but by the end of the year Taylor is mainly firing on passenger trains with just a little freight work. The mention of 'Day of Trial' in November 1922 may actually be when Tom was passing out for driving as he has his first driving turn in January 1923. There followed a long and happy career on the footplate at Springs Branch.

Here is a sample of the diary from his firing days. By way of explanation, the left columns show the time on/off, then the actual train time and destination, followed by the hours/minutes worked. The final column on the right shows the loco number. Some of the turns can be cross referenced with the 1920 trip and shunt information shown in the ENGINES AT WORK sections.

		ON	OFF		hrs claim	Loco/Class
Thur	07/04/21	06:35	13:31	08:05 Liverpool	08:55	1932 Renown
Fri	08/04/21	06:35	09:35	On shed	08:00	
Sat	09/04/21	05:00	12:00	06:45 Preston	08:00	897 1P
Mon	11/04/21	11:30	19:20	13:50 Liverpool	08:00	1930 Renown
Tue	12/04/21	11:30	15:40	On shed	08:00	
Wed	13/04/21	11:30	19:20	3:50 Liverpool	08:00	1932 Renown
Thur	14/04/21	11:30	14:00	On shed	08:00	
Fri	15/04/21	11:30	19:30	13:50 Liverpool	08:00	2112/1618 Experiment
Sat	16/04/21	07:30	11:30	On shed	08:00	
Mon	18/04/21	04:00	11:20	LE to Crewe, home pass	08:00	2602 19" Goods
Tue	19/04/21	02:00		Wigan Bank	08:30	3225 DX
Wed	20/04/21	02:00	07:45	Wigan Bank	08:30	3430 DX
Thur	21/04/21	02:00	07:45	Wigan Bank	08:30	3430 DX
Fri	22/04/21	02:00	08:05	Spl frt..xx Bamfurlong	08:30	
Sat	23/04/21	02:00	07:30	Ince Moss Bank	08:30	2321 18" Goods

21st April - 8th July - MINERS STRIKE - 3 day working

Worthy of mention is the DX on the Wigan Bank (NW Station Pilot). This turn was notable for its use of the eldest engines on allocation, which was obviously the situation in 1921. The Ince Moss bank (as it was then known) was using a Cauliflower 18" Goods and probably continued to do so for most of the LMS period.

A later table *(below)* when Tom was driving which is obviously a passenger link. Most of these turns are local workings, using a Webb 5' 6" tank, although the 'Cauliflower' on the Blackburn is interesting and possibly presented a bit of a challenge for the crew. The Cauliflowers appear elsewhere in the diary on Blackburn locals so perhaps nothing is out of the ordinary. 'Experiments' and 19" Goods also featured on the local Blackburn service around this time. Elsewhere within the diary, the Manchester locals were in the hands of 'Alfred the Great' and 'Renown' engines, whilst the Liverpools tended to have 'Experiments' and '19" Goods'.

		ON	OFF		Hrs claim	Loco/Class
Thur	20/04/22	14:35	23:00	16:07 Manchester	08:25	897 W 1P
Fri	21/04/22	14:35	22:30	16:07 Manchester	08:15	787
Sat	22/04/22	15:20	00:30	16:07 Manchester	10:05	1575
Mon	24/04/22	09:15	17:00	10:45 Blackburn	08:00	2300 Prince of Wales
Tue	25/04/22	09:15	16:00	10:45 Blackburn	08:00	1798 18" Goods
Wed	26/04/22	09:15	17:00	10:45 Blackburn	08:00	1575
Thur	27/04/22	10:30	18:30	No 8 Trip	08:00	2467
Fri	28/04/22	09:15	17:00	10:45 Blackburn	08:00	2192
Sat	29/04/22	09:15	16:00	10:45 Blackburn	08:00	1798 18" Goods
Mon	01/05/22	13:00	21:30	Garswood & St Helens	08:30	897 W 1P
Tue	02/05/22	13:00	21:25	Garswood & St Helens	08:25	408 W 1P
Wed	03/05/22	13:00	21:35	Garswood & St Helens	08:35	408 W 1P

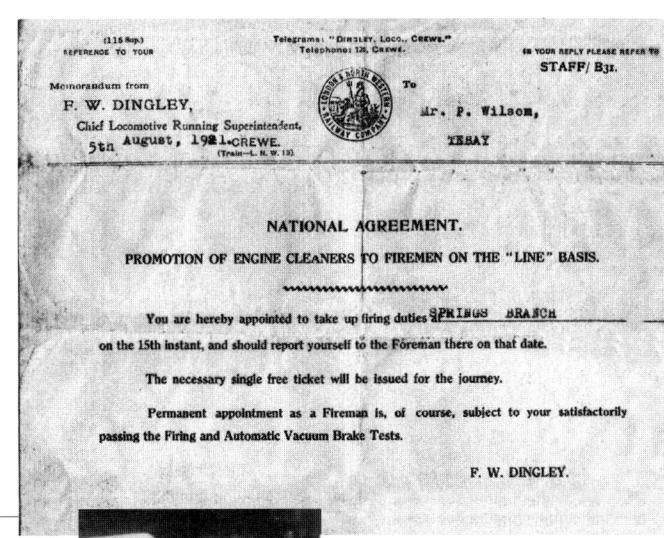

Promotion Certificate awarded to Percy Wilson, a long standing driver at Springs Branch.

Driver Percy Wilson on the footplate.

c1960 • PERCY WILSON COLLECTION

SPRINGS BRANCH CHARACTERS

(Left to right) **Harold Yates** (Coalman), **Fred Cox** (Firedropper), **Alf Hall** (Firedropper), **Fred Hilton** (Shed Shunt) **and Jimmy Brown** (Fireman) in the shed yard. The Britannia Pacific in view is No **70025** *Western Star*. c1965 ● J. DANIELS

Shed Labourer Bert Grimes in front of the shed's own Ivatt 2-6-0 No **46506**. 1964 ● TOM SUTCH

Apprentice Fitters (L-R) Alan Mason, Roy Truman, Peter Lucas, Eric Sharples and Brian Appleton (crouched) gather in front of Aspinall Loco No **52250** in front of No 1 shed. c1950 ● AUTHOR'S COLLECTION

Driver Bill Boulton in the cab of Class 25 No **D5291**. 1965 ● TOM SUTCH

Driver Tommy Crook. 25TH FEBRUARY 1983 ● TOM SUTCH

ENGINEMEN'S ARRANGEMENTS

The large 'engine arrangements' board was situated on the screen wall inside the shed, showing all engines and the turns they were allocated to. It also listed engines on repair/wash out or waiting works but not those stored or withdrawn. One section listed any locos restricted to local work due to faults (see page 94 for picture of this board). A similar listing was kept in book form in the Time Office (enginemen's arrangements book) but, unlike the board, the book copy had a passenger section and a freight section where the trips, shunts and banks were all mixed together based on their time on duty.

PASSENGER

FREIGHT

The actual turns would commence with one of the following:

1 - Engine and Men off shed with an engine to commence diagram.
2 - 'Relieving' an existing crew on a train which could be your own depot's working or another depot's working.
3 - 'As Passenger'. This would involve a journey 'on the cushions' to a convenient point to relieve another train.

Therefore, No 2442 is booked to work the 02:00 passenger train from Wigan NW to Liverpool Lime St with a fresh engine off shed with Driver J W Jones and Fireman J Robinson. The men were booked to sign on at 01:15 allowing time to read notices, prepare engine (if necessary) and run down to Wigan NW Station. The turn number was 24. The office staff who allocated this work had details of every driver's 'route knowledge' and would ensure the men didn't get booked for any route they had not signed for. Should this happen, then a pilotman would be needed for the sections the driver had not signed for.

Part of the Route Knowledge Card. Each driver would sign the appropriate section to confirm he was conversant with that particular route. It was a simple but effective method that protected both men and management.

Unlike the board, all the freight workings were mixed together and booked goods trains, trip working, shunt engines and banking engines appear together, generally in the order the men/loco left the shed. Where 'R' shows in the engine column, this indicates the crew will be relieving an existing train. The time shown would be the relieving time, or the time of departing on 'cushions' (as passenger) to relieving place. The driver and firemen's names would sometimes be altered to accommodate late changes/absentees/etc.

The rostered time on duty (signing on time) may allow for the crew to prepare other engines, plus any walking time to a relieving or starting place. Another section of the book covered the workings of the Control men, a pair of which booked on every hour from midnight. These were Springs Branch men under the command of (Crewe) Control who would allocate their work. This could literally be anything from additional trains or covering for absent men. The Time Office would issue the driver with a docket detailing all the timings for the turn that he was about to undertake.

Note that the BR '4' prefix never appeared.

A typical docket is for Turn 48, Saturday only, involving a couple of local passenger trains on the ex-L&Y route. Total time for turn 7 hours 22 minutes. This is a straightforward out and back run. Others could be very complex!

```
                                          a.m.    p.m.
                                          6. 0    1.22    7.22
Turn 48
              Springs Branch MPD          6.45am  LE      SO
              Wigan W.                    7.25am  ECS     SO
  7.38am      Orrell                      8. 0    2J57    SO
  8.55        Manchester Vic.             9. 2    ECS     SO
  9.14        Red Bank                    9.20    LE      SO
  9.30        Newton Heath MPD COAL       11.24   LE      SO
              Red Bank                    11.42   ECS     SO
 11.46        Manchester Vic.             12. 8pm 2F51    SO
 12.53pm      Ince
              RELIEF 12.53 for Wigan by Turn 49           SO
```

OTHER STAFF AND THEIR DUTIES

If the enginemen's shift finished back at the shed, the men would take the engine onto the coaling road, observing the 5 mph speed limit in the shed yard, where they would be relieved by the 'tank & coal' men. Their system of working was for one pair of men to 'tank' (top up water) and coal, then move engine to the ash pit. When the ash pit men had finished, the other pair of men turned the loco on the turntable (if required) and stabled it. There was a third set of men known as 'shed shunt' who would move engines and coal around the yard as required. The outside arranger (Clerk) would walk in the disposal area, chalking the designated road/direction on the tender of the loco (ie S9 - facing South, 9 road). Sometimes he would chalk AL for 'fire all out' or WO for 'wash out' when prearranged maintenance was due. Wash outs were done every 21 to 30 days at the south end of road Nos 2 to 5 and occasionally No 6. Approximately 40 locos would be coaled on night shift with slightly less on others.

ASH PIT   There were 3 firedroppers per shift who handled approx 36 locos each. Some engines went straight on and off without stabling. In later years there were 2 firedroppers on early and late shift with 3 on nights. After each had done 8 locos per shift they got a bonus thereafter. 3 Locos could be tackled at once, one at the ash pit skip and two over the other pits. There was also an ash pit cleaner, sometimes 2, despite the shed having a mechanical ash pit skip. This was fickle and hardly used, as the pump would seize up, so most work was done manually by initially shovelling the ash from the pit to the surrounding ground and then into mineral wagons, a very labour intensive task!

STEAMRAISERS   3 men started at 4pm on Sunday and were relieved at midnight by another 3 men. Thereafter it was 2 men during the day (6 - 2) and late (2 -10) shifts. They would do 16 - 17 engines each per shift. In the Mid 60's, in an attempt to reduce the smoke problem, coke was used for the Sunday light up.

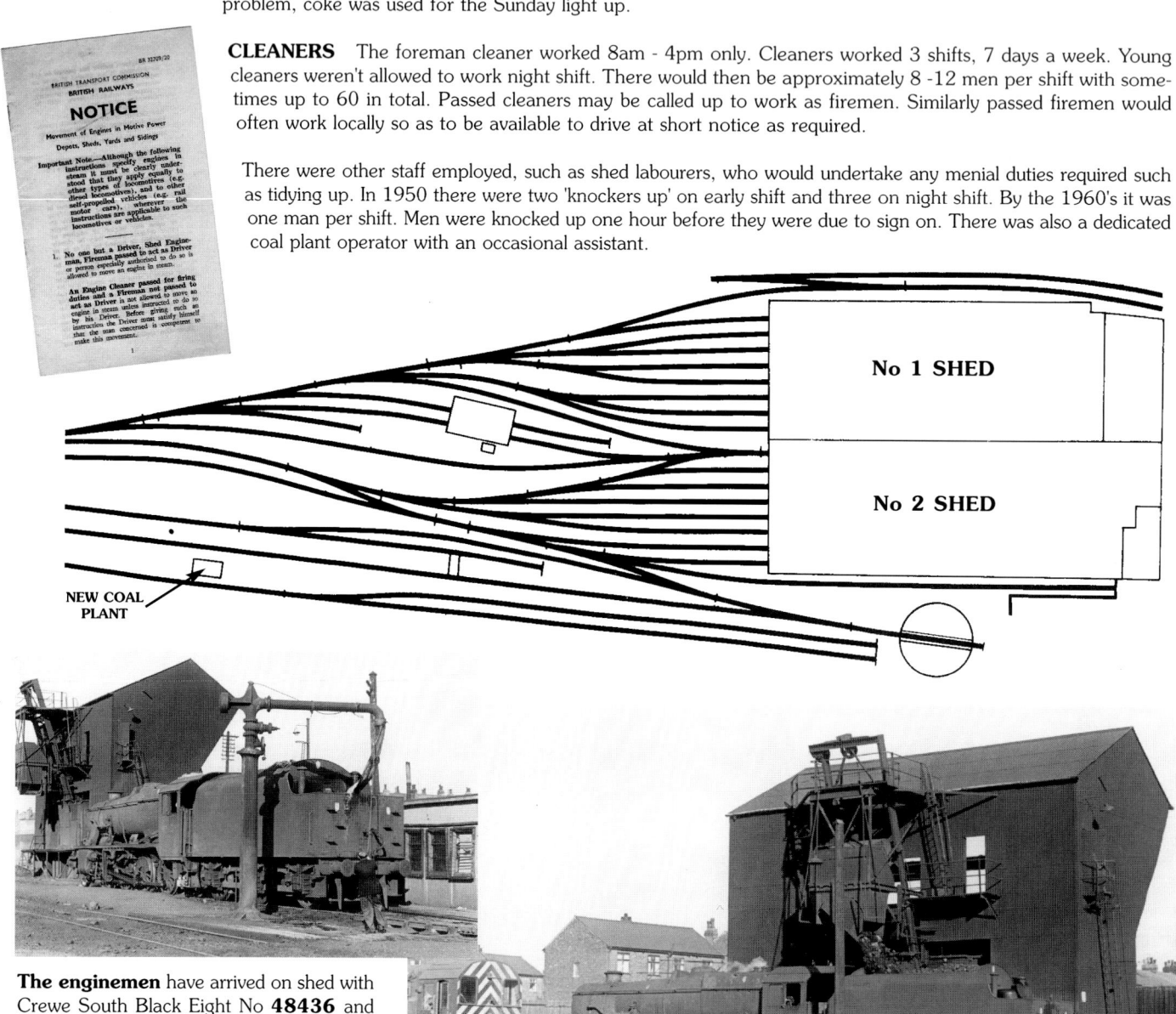

CLEANERS   The foreman cleaner worked 8am - 4pm only. Cleaners worked 3 shifts, 7 days a week. Young cleaners weren't allowed to work night shift. There would then be approximately 8 -12 men per shift with sometimes up to 60 in total. Passed cleaners may be called up to work as firemen. Similarly passed firemen would often work locally so as to be available to drive at short notice as required.

There were other staff employed, such as shed labourers, who would undertake any menial duties required such as tidying up. In 1950 there were two 'knockers up' on early shift and three on night shift. By the 1960's it was one man per shift. Men were knocked up one hour before they were due to sign on. There was also a dedicated coal plant operator with an occasional assistant.

The enginemen have arrived on shed with Crewe South Black Eight No **48436** and the replenishing of water and coal has commenced. Firstly, the tank is filled from the water column. To the right of the tender is the hut used by footplate staff as well as the tank and coal men. The latter appear to be suspiciously absent on this occasion as it's the crew who are attending to the loco's needs.   c1967   ● LES RILEY

No 48436 has moved forward to the coaling stage, revealing the coalmen and firedroppers' cabin, situated left of the previously mentioned hut. After coaling, the loco will move on to the ash pit and then the turntable if necessary.
c1967   ● LES RILEY

LOCO PROGRAMMES AND TRAIN CREW PROGRAMMES

By 1967 the old steam terminology for 'engine' or 'mens' turns became known as Loco Programmes (for engine workings) and Train Crew Programmes (for the men) although the documentation and layout of the actual diagrams remained unaltered.

Here is an example of a 4-6-0 Class 5 diagram

By way of explanation, looking at the loco programme for Turn 140 (which shows what the engine does) the work differs depending on the day. On Mondays the turn commences off the shed at 06:55, running light engine to Bamfurlong Sidings and works 6L70 Class 6 freight to Blackburn. Next the engine works back to Bamfurlong on 6F27 then light engine onto the shed.

The next part of the diagram may well be with another crew and takes the loco light engine to Chester to work 6M81 (ex Abercumboi) from Chester to Bamfurlong Sidings, where the loco again goes onto the shed.

On Tuesday to Friday the engine works a completely different diagram starting light engine off the shed to Bamfurlong and then 8K09 freight to Crewe Basford Hall. Here the loco goes light engine across to Crewe Gresty Lane yard and works 7F58 freight to Bamfurlong and goes light onto the shed. The final leg of the diagram runs Monday to Friday and takes the loco light engine to Wigan NW station to work 3K13 parcels to Crewe, whereupon the loco will either return home light engine or work home 'as required' if there is a job available.

The following day this loco works diagram 148.

The 'Train Crew programme' involving this loco is shown left. On Tuesday to Friday the men on Turn 804 book on at 03:20 and take the loco to Crewe and back, booking off at 10:10. The men on Turn 782, booking on at 20:05 then work the loco to Crewe on 3K13 parcels but they return with a different (12A Kingmoor) engine on 3F03 (ex Curzon St) and are relieved at Springs Branch by Turn 761.

The loco arrangements can be very complex and it is difficult to sum up any single day's turns if the engine and the men do not stay with each other throughout, and this happens much of the time. Some turns involve the loco being left at a foreign shed, sometimes by that depot's men and the diagram being picked up from there the following day.

A DAY IN THE LIFE - FRIDAY 16TH NOVEMBER 1951

These tables represent Friday 16th November 1951, a typical day in the life of Springs Branch, showing all the booked engines on their trains exactly as it happened.

PASSENGER SECTION

Engine	Time	Working	On duty	What the working actually is
2442	02:00	Lime St	01:05	02:00 Wigan NW - Liv Lime St Mails
2454	05:18	Preston	04:20	05:20 Wigan NW to Preston local
2456	05:47	Tyldesley	01:50	05:45 Wigan NW - Tyldesley local
2465	07:04	Preston	02:15	05:50 Man Ex - Preston local
2453	04:52	Newton	04:37	To work 06:02 Newton Le W - Lime St
5593 12A	06:33	ROF	04:42	Wigan NW - Chorley ROF Workers train
R	06:20	Bank	05:25	Wigan NW Station Pilot
2539	06:15	Lime St	03:20	06:18 Wigan NW - Liv Lime St local
R	06:16	Crewe	05:19	05:30 Preston - Crewe
R	06:39	Tebay	05:40	06:00 Warr BQ - Carlisle
5289	06:30	Newton	06:15	To work 07:15 Newton Le W - Lime St
2266	06:43	Lime St	05:58	06:43 Wigan NW - Liv Lime St local
2563	07:10	Blackburn	06:25	06:00 Liverpool - Blackburn
5235	09:08	Lime St	05:55	09:05 Wigan NW - Liv Lime St local
R	09:25	Preston	06:55	08:10 Liverpool - Preston
R	09:28	Lime St	08:25	09:25 Wigan NW - Liv Lime St Parcels
2442	12:18	Manchester	11:03	12:18 Wigan NW - Man Ex local
R	12:30	Bank	11:35	Wigan NW station pilot
2266	12:35	Earlestown	11:08	12:37 Wigan NW - Earlestown local
R	12:45	Preston	11:00	12:45 Wigan NW - Preston local
R	13:55	Lime St	12:55	13:53 Wigan NW - Liv Lime St local
R	14:42	Preston	13:23	12:45 Crewe - Carlisle parcels
R	14:53	Crewe	13:31	Carlisle - Crewe parcels
R	15:40	Lime St	13:55	15:40 Wigan NW - Liv Lime St local
2453	16:17	Huddersfield	15:51	16:20 Wigan NW - Leeds City South
R	16:17	Eccles	14:45	travel passenger on above to relieve
R	16:20	Preston	15:26	15:20 Liverpool - Preston
R	16:37	Preston	16:05	15:58 Man Ex - Barrow
2456	17:11	Chester	15:59	17:14 Wigan NW - Chester local
2539	17:40	Earlestown	16:20	17:52 Wigan NW - Warr BQ via Earlestown
cape	20:35	Crewe	19:05	Re-engine 19:05 W Dock - Broad St
28398	23:30	Bank	23:15	Wigan NW Station Pilot

FREIGHT SECTION

Engine	Time	Working	On duty	What the working actually is
5258	00:10	Farington	00:45	00:15 Spr Bch - Farington 'H' Freight
R	00:45	134	00:45	TRIP 134 Bamfurlong Sidings
R	00:20	162	00:25	BANK ENGINE
9449 11A	01:56	Carlisle	00:36	01:56 Bamfurlong - Carlisle 'E'
R	02:07	Warrington	01:12	(prob 21:05 Carlisle - Crewe 'E')
90112 24D	02:25	Blackburn	01:05	02:25 Spr Branch - Blackburn 'H'
9659 24D	02:45	Colne	01:25	02:45 Bamfurlong - Colne 'E'
R	02:50	160	01:20	BANK ENGINE
R	02:26	Carnforth	01:50	(prob 00:35 Gresty Lane - Carlisle 'F')
R	03:20	161	02:00	BANK ENGINE
R	03:30	163	03:00	BANK ENGINE
90313 8G	05:05	Crewe	03:35	05:05 Bamfurlong NE - Gresty Lane 'H'
4708 5B	04:15	Carnforth	03:40	04:15 Spr Branch - Carnforth 'J'
9311	04:30	Canada Dk	03:55	04:30 Ince Moss Jn - Canada Dock 'K'
52098	04:30	133	03:55	TRIP 133 Bamfurlong Sidings/Wigan
52107	05:00	156	04:00	SHUNT Wigan Canal Goods
R	05:16	Crewe	03:56	03:10 Carnforth - Bushbury 'H'
52021	06:00	141	05:15	SHUNT (Incline/Bridge Hole)
8764 6C	06:00	Birkenhead	05:25	06:00 Bam NE - Birkenhead 'J'
	05:30	special	05:30	
R	06:00	145	05:35	SHUNT Springs Branch North Sidings
R	06:00	147	05:30	SHUNT Ince Moss
	05:00	special	05:00	
R	06:00	148	05:30	SHUNT Bamfurlong Sidings N. End
R	06:00	149	05:45	SHUNT Bamfurlong Long Drag
R	06:00	150	05:30	SHUNT Bamfurlong Pem Corner
R	06:00	151	05:55	SHUNT Bamfurlong Sidings S. End
R	06:04	Carnforth	05:20	22:05 Willesden - Carlisle Viaduct
5026	06:50	132	05:50	TRIP 132 Rylands & Howe Bridge
9268	06:50	101	05:50	07:15 Spr Branch - Bam NE
R	06:30	163	06:00	BANK ENGINE
9153 8C	07:26	Fleetwood	06:45	07:26 Springs Branch - Wyre Dock 'J'
9393	07:15	154	06:40	SHUNT (Ince Moss Tip)
9306	07:40	122	07:06	TRIP 122 Coppull
R	07:57	Carnforth	07:20	04:40 Harlescott - Carlisle Vdct 'E'
3968 20A	08:50	Clock Face	07:25	08:50 Ince Moss Jn - Clock Face 'K'
90267	08:45	138	07:25	TRIP 138 Bolton, Halliwell
R	07:55	162	07:45	BANK ENGINE
9163	08:25	Astley Gn	07:45	08:25 Bamfurlong NE - Patricroft
5258 12A	09:05	Preston	07:38	09:05 Springs Branch - Ribble Sidings 'H'
2954 5D	09:55	Kearsley	08:40	08:48 EBV to Bickershaw Colliery
52341	09:30	123	09:30	TRIP 123 Victoria Colliery
5296 12A	09:55	Carlisle	09:00	09:55 Bamf - Carlisle Vdct 'H'
R	09:45	161	09:50	BANK ENGINE
9438 11A	11:10	Oxenholme		11:10 Springs Branch - Oxenholme 'H'
8017 6C	11:55	Crewe	10:51	11:55 Bamf NE - Basford Hall 'F'
R	11:46	Crewe	11:00	05:30 Carlisle - Basford Hall 'H' (6 days)
R9025	11:30	133	11:20	TRIP 133 Bamfurlong Sidings/Wigan
R	11:50	160	12:25	BANK ENGINE
R	12:40	141	12:25	SHUNT (incline/bridge hole)
R	13:41	Warrington	12:45	10:40 Carnforth - Warrington 'J'
5449	13:00	116	12:45	TRIP 116 Ravenhead Col & Garswood
5414 11A	13:40	124	12:20	TRIP 124 Rylands Siding
9311	13:40	109	13:20	TRIP 109 Kenyon Jn & Bickershaw
R	15:30	137	13:00	TRIP 137 Moss Hall/Chanters
R	13:30	163	13:00	BANK ENGINE
R	15:30	132	13:05	TRIP 132 Rylands & Howe Bridge
R	13:40	151	13:40	SHUNT Bamfurlong Sidings S. End
R	15:10	101	13:35	TRIP 101 Golborne/Earlestown
R	14:00	145	13:30	SHUNT Springs Branch North Sidings
R	14:00	147	13:30	SHUNT Ince Moss
R	14:00	148	13:30	SHUNT Bamfurlong Sidings N. End
2854	14:00	126	13:53	TRIP 126 Darlington Sidings
R	14:50	ROF	13:30	Freight to ROF Chorley
R	14:00	150	14:00	SHUNT Bamfurlong Pem Corner
9381	14:55	162	13:30	BANK ENGINE
R	14:45	154	15:00	SHUNT (Ince Moss Tip)
2610	16:00	152	15:30	SHUNT Bamf Sidings S. End (Lanky)
8895	16:30	156	16:00	SHUNT Wigan Canal Goods
R	16:30	161	16:20	BANK ENGINE
8520	17:20	112	16:15	TRIP 112 Kenyon & Bickershaw
90267	19:36	Kearsley	16:30	17:24 EBV Spr Branch - Bickershaw
9163	17:30	164	17:10	BANK ENGINE
9007	17:40	Preston	16:35	17:45 Spr Branch - Farington Jn
Cape	17:55	Bullfield	17:25	poss to Rylands Sidings
R	18:45	162	17:35	BANK ENGINE
R	18:40	Monton Gn	17:25	as passenger for (Liv Rd - Kingmoor)
52107	18:00	134	17:15	TRIP 134 Bamfurlong Sidings
9023	18:25	140	18:05	TRIP 140 Atherton B. Ln & Moss Hall
R	18:30	133	18:20	TRIP 133 Bamfurlong Sidings/Wigan
R	18:50	160	19:09	BANK ENGINE
5413	19:41	Liverpool	19:30	19:20 Ince Moss Jn - Edge Hill 'J'
R	20:25	Birkenhead	19:25	crew travel as passenger
9311	20:45	Clock Face	19:50	20:45 Ince Moss Jn - Clock Face 'H'
R	20:20	161	20:00	BANK ENGINE
R	20:30	163	20:50	BANK ENGINE
R	21:19	Preston	20:29	19:45 Basford Hall - Carlisle Vdct 'D'
R	21:27	Longsight	22:25	(rel 21:30 Liv Rd - Kingmoor)
R	22:53	Preston	21:05	09:30 Liverpool Road - Carnforth 'E'
9306	22:15	Patricroft	21:35	22:15 Garswood Hall - Weaste 'K'
R	22:00	145	21:30	SHUNT Spr Branch North Sdgs
R	22:00	147	21:30	SHUNT Ince Moss
R	22:00	148	21:30	SHUNT Bamfurlong Sdgs N. End
R	22:00	150	22:00	SHUNT Bamfurlong Pem Corner
R	23:00	149	23:00	SHUNT Bamfurlong Long Drag
R	22:58	Carnforth	22:30	22:35 Basford Hall - Carnforth 'F'
R	23:17	Fleetwood	23:05	21:35 Basford Hall - Wyre Dock 'E'
R	23:30	151	23:15	SHUNT Bamfurlong Sidings S. End
R	23:55	152	22:15	SHUNT Bamf Sidings S. End (Lanky)
R	00:00	112	23:30	TRIP 112 Kenyon & Bickershaw
R	00:00	164	23:36	BANK ENGINE
R	00:20	Carnforth	00:05	(prob 00:03 Spr Br - Carnforth 'J')
Driped	03:00	IM - Garston		(Ince Moss - Garston)
			05:00	(Scowcrofts - Ditton sleepers)
Driped			06:00	(Crompton Sdgs - Springs Branch)
Driped			07:00	(Ince Moss - Edge Hill)
		Parkside	08:00	Parkside - Barrow
Driped			09:00	Springs Bch to Crewe. 5:30 x Carl
Driped				(Springs Branch - Horwich)
			10:00	LE Monument Lane
Driped		Platt Br rel	11:00	(Abram - Warrington)
			12:00	Rel 11:30 Crewe. Blong frt K Aintree
Driped		Platt Br rel	13:00	7:15 x Carl
Driped		Fir Tree rel	13:00	
	08:35		14:00	Carlisle - Ince Moss
Driped			15:00	Fir Tree - Ince Moss
Driped			17:00	Fir Tree - xxx greens
			18:00	
Eger			19:00	Cam St - Howe Br
job 700			21:00	Ince Moss - Edge Hill

FREIGHT SECTION *Continued*

Engine	Time	Working	On duty	What the working actually is
spl	23:00	Bullfield	22:00	
Driped		Platt Bridge	03:00	
90649 8C	05:00		05:00	Scowcrofts Sidings - DittonSleeper
Driped	special	Bal rel 134	23:00	
9393	07:00	Crane (Ince Moss)	07:30	
9023	08:30	EBV Spr B - Abram	07:45	
cape	09:00	Abram Ballast	05:30	
Driped			06:15	Springs Branch - Crewe
	07:10	R/ Blackburn	09:00	(reman Blackburn)

Engine	Time	Working	On duty	What the working actually is
			09:30	xxx Rd - Earlstown MC
5299 12A	11:00	Parkside - Barrow		
4827 5B	LE	Crewe	20:09?	
Eger	21:24	XXX - MC	17:00?	
5196	12:00	LE Sutton Oak	21:00	
9253	23:45	Bamf - Bullfield		

Men booking on from 03:00 (in italics) are control and could be given any job. 'Driped' seems to indicate change of crew, conducted or train changed enroute. EBV - Engine and brake van   R - Reman job   Cape - Cancelled

ENGINES ALLOCATED AND BOOKED WORKINGS - 16TH NOVEMBER 1951

Engine	Booked working	Engine	Booked working	Engine	Booked working	Engine	Booked working
42266	Lime St	45313	-	49163	Astley Green/B164	49401	-
42442	Lime St	45413	19:41 Liverpool	49228		49402	-
42453	Newton	45449	Trip 116	49253	Bamfurlong - Bullfield	49408	- Prev day worked 12:10 Farington
42454	Preston	45454	-	49268	Trip 101	49436	- Prev day worked Trip 122
42456	Tyldesley	46430	-	49306	Trip 122/22:15 Patricroft	52021	Shunt 141
42465	Preston	47877	-	49311	Canada Dock/T109	52045	-
42539	Lime St	48895	Shunt Wigan canal	49322		52051	- Prev day worked Shunt 141
42563	Blackburn	49007	17:40 Preston	49341		52053	-
42572	-	49018		49352	-	52098	Trip 133
42610	Shunt 152	49023	Trip 140	49378	-	52107	Shunt 156/T134
45026	Trip 132	49025	Trip 133	49381	Bank 162	52341	Trip 123
45235	Lime St	49129	-	49385	-	58398	Wigan Bank
45289	Newton	49154	- Prev day worked 05:05 Crewe	49393	Shunt 154/crane		

Looking at the locos booked to work from the shed, Springs Branch has provided 11 engines for passenger work including one foreign engine whose turn would usually be part of another shed's diagram.

Some of the depot's Black 5's would be away at places like Carnforth, Carlisle and Crewe after working out on a previous job. Additionally some of the Super D's would already be out in the yards, as 6 shunt diagrams are not allocated engines, just relief crews. These engines left the shed on Monday mornings and didn't return until the end of the week. Similarly, Bank engines Nos 160, 161 and 163 would be on duty, so that out of the missing 13 Super D's, nine are accounted for on local work. Relevant engines on workings the previous day are shown. Whether the depot was short of power is not known but this is quite likely to have been the case. The shed has obviously made use of other depot's engines on their jobs namely:

No 42854 (Crewe South) on Trip 126.   No 42954 (Stoke) on local colliery work.   No 45414 (Upperby) on Trip 124.
No 48520 (Speke Junction) on Trip 112.   No 49153 (Speke Junction) on 07:26 Wyre Dock.   No 90267 (Accrington) on 19:36 Kearsley.
An interesting visitor on the 05:15 Crewe was No 90313 which was in the process of transfer from Eastfield (Glasgow) to Shrewsbury.

ENGINEMEN - 16TH NOVEMBER 1951 (**Bold** - Passenger Link Men)

Tommy (T)	Abbott	Driver	Jack (J)	Beardsmore	Driver	Edward (E)	Crook	Driver	Sammy (SA)	Foster	Fireman
Harry (HC)	Ackers	Fireman	George (G)	Bennett	Passed Cleaner	Tom (T)	Crooke	Driver	Harry (HC)	Fox	Fireman
Bert (H)	Acton	Driver	Arthur (A)	Bennett	Fireman	Bill (W)	Davenport	Driver	Tommy (T)	France	Driver
Hughie (H)	Aitken	Arranger	Jack (J)	Bennett	Passed Cleaner	Ken (K)	Davenport	Fireman	**Freddie (FD)**	**France**	Passed Fireman
Tommy (T)	Allsopp	Driver	**Sid (S)**	**Bentley**	Passed Fireman	**Jack (J)**	**Davenport**	Driver	Bob (R)	Francis	Driver
Gordon (G)	Anders	Fireman	Edward (E)	Berry	Driver	**Harold (H)**	**Davenport**	Driver	Jimmy (J)	Frears	Driver
Bob (R)	Anderson	Driver	**R (R)**	**Berry**	Driver	**Jimmy (J)**	**Davenport**	Fireman	D (D)	Gallagher	Passed Cleaner
Gordon (G)	Anderton	Fireman	Harry (H)	Birchall	Driver	Dickie (R)	Davies	Fireman	**Les (L)**	**Gaskell**	Fireman
Jimmy (J)	Anderton	Driver	Harry (HC)	Birchall	Fireman	**Thomas (T)**	**Dawber**	Passed Fireman	Fred (F)	Gibson	Driver
Harry (H)	Appleton	Driver	Dickie (R)	Blackledge	Fireman	Sid (S)	Darbyshire	Fireman	Norman (N)	Gibson	Driver
Ken (K)	Appleton	Fireman	Teddy (E)	Blackledge	Driver	Bill (W)	Darbyshire	Fireman	Percy (P)	Gibson	Driver
Bob (R)	Armstrong	Driver	Dickie (R)	Blackledge	Fireman	Bill? (W)	Dickinson	Driver	Harry (HC)	Gibson	Fireman
Tommy (T)	**Armstrong**	Driver	Teddy (E)	Blackledge	Fireman	JG (JG)	Dickinson	Passed Cleaner	Jack (J)	Gilbert	Driver
Jack (J)	**Armstrong**	Passed Fireman	Tommy (T)	Bloomer	Driver	Bert (H)	Dixon (D)	Driver	George (G)	Glover	Driver
Frank (FD)	Arnold	Fireman	Frank (F)	Bragg	Driver	**Bert (HC)**	**Dixon**	Fireman	Peter (P)	Gore	Fireman
Bob (R)	Ashton	Passed Fireman	Ken (K)	Brooks	Fireman	Len (L)	Duckworth	Driver	Stanley (S)	Gray	Fireman
Walter (W)	Ashton	Passed Fireman	Bob (R)	Brooks	Fireman	T (T)	Durnian	Fireman	Harry (H)	Green	Driver
Arthur (A)	Ashurst	Driver	Alf (HK)	Brown	Driver	**Frank (F)**	**Dutton**	Fireman	Harry (HC)	Green	Fireman
Jimmy (J)	Ashurst	Driver	Frank (F)	Bryne	Fireman	Frank (F)	Eaton	Driver	Alan (AD)	Green	Driver
Bill (JW)	**Ashurst**	Driver	Ronnie (R)	Burrows	Fireman	Tommy (T)	Eccles	Driver	Alec (A)	Green	Fireman
Freddie (F)	Ashwin	Driver	**Tommy (T)**	**Butler**	Passed Fireman	Jackie (J)	Edwards	Driver	**William (W)**	**Gregory**	Driver
R (R)	Aspinall	Passed Cleaner	H (H)	Butler	Passed Cleaner	**Jimmy (JE)**	**Edwards 1**	Fireman	Grom Owen (GO)	Griffiths	Driver
Teddie (EJ)	Aston	Fireman	Steve (S)	Cannon	Passed Cleaner	Jack (J)	Edwards 2	Passed Cleaner	Alan (A)	Grundy	Fireman
R (R)	Atherton	Fireman	Sid (S)	Carrington	Fireman	WD (WD)	Evans	Fireman	Fred (F)	Gubbins	Driver
Ronnie (RC)	Atherton	Fireman	Frank (F)	Carter	Passed Cleaner	P (P)	Fallon?	Fireman	**George (G)**	**Gubbins**	Driver
Frank (F)	Bache	Driver	Jim/Jack? (J)	Cartwright	Passed Fireman	E (E)	Farren	Driver	Jack (J)	Halliwell	Driver
Ben (B)	**Bainbridge**	Driver	Jim (J)	Catterall	Driver	**Donald (D)**	**Farrar**	Fireman	Frank (F)	Halliwell	Driver
W (W)	Balderson	Fireman	Bill (W)	Catterall	Driver	Arthur (A)	Fazackerley	Driver	Norman (N)	Halliwell	Driver
Emmanual (E)	Ball	Turner/Driver	Sid (S)	Catterall	Driver	Ken (K)	Fazackerley	Fireman	Freddie (F)	Harding	Driver
Jonti (J)	Banks	Fireman	Bill (W)	Catterall	Fireman	Harold (HC)	Finch	Passed Fireman	Bob (R)	Hardman1	Fireman
Tommy (T)	Banks	Passed Cleaner	**John (J)**	**Chamberlain**	Fireman	George (G)	Finney	Driver	Ronnie (R)	Hardman2	Fireman
D (D)	Banks	Passed Cleaner	Jackie (J)	Cheers	Fireman	Arthur (A)	Fisher	Fireman	Billy (WE)	Harrison	Driver
Jimmy (J)	Barker	Fireman	Alf (A)	Cherrington	Driver	Jack (J)	Fisher	Fireman	Tommy (T)	Harrison	Fireman
Sid (S)	Barker	Passed Fireman	Bert (T)	Cherrington	Driver	Derek (D)	Fisher	Fireman	William (W)	Harrison	Passed Cleaner
Tommy (T)	Barnes	Driver	Walter (W)	Clarke	Driver	Albert (R)	Fisher	Passed Cleaner	Bill (W)	Hart	Turner
Edward (E)	Berry	Driver	Eric (E)	Clayton	Driver	Albert (R)	Fisher	Passed Cleaner	**Tom (T)**	**Hart**	Driver
Jack (J)	Barton	Fireman	William (W)	Clough	Driver	R (R)	Fletcher	Turner/Fireman	Jimmy (J)	Hattersley	Fireman
Percy (P)	Barton	Driver	Walter (W)	Clarke	Driver	A (A)	Ford	Turner	Harry (H)	Hayes	Driver
Joe (J)	Bates	Driver	Eric (E)	Clayton	Fireman	John Willie (JW)	Foster	Fireman	**Jack (J)**	**Hayes**	Driver
Harold (HC)	Bates	Passed Firemanm	William (W)	Clough	Driver	Jimmy (J)	Foster (D)	Driver	S (S)	Heaton	Fireman
Eric (E)	Baxter	Fireman	Joe (J)	Collins	Driver	John (Jack) (J)	Foster (F)	Fireman	Bill (W)	Heppenstall	Fireman
Bob (R)	Baxter	Passed Cleaner	Eddie (E)	Coyne	Fireman	E (Willy?) (E)	Foster	Passed Fireman	Sammy (S)	Hewitt	Driver
Freddie (FD)	**Beachy**	Fireman	George (G)	Crompton	Fireman	Richard (R)	Foster	Passed Fireman	Jack (J)	Heyes	Fireman

93

Name	Surname	Role
George (GP)	Hill	Driver
Jack (J)	Hill	Fireman
CF (CF)	Hilton	Passed cleaner
George	Hodgkinson	Driver
William (W)	Hodgson	Driver
Donald (D)	Hodgson	Fireman
Tommy (T)	Hodgson	Fireman
Stan?	Hodgson	
William (W)	Hodgson	Fireman
Albert (A)	Hogarth	Driver
G (A)	Holding	Driver
Albert (A)	Holgate	Fireman
William? (W)	Holland(s)	Turner
Jimmy (J)	Holt	Driver
Jimmy (J)	**Howarth**	Driver
Harry (HC)	Hulse	Fireman
Harry (H)	Humphrieson	Turner
Jack (J)	Humphreys	Driver
Steve (S)	Hurst	Driver
Albert (A)	Hurst	Driver
FD (FD)	Hurst	Fireman
W (W)	Hurst	Turner
Tommy (T)	Ingram	Driver
Wilf (W)	Jenkins	Driver
Norman (N)	Jenkins	Fireman
S (S)	Johnson	Driver
S (S)	Johnson	Passed Fireman
Jack (J)	**Jolley 1**	Fireman
Jack (J)	Jolley 2	Fireman
Cecil (C)	Jones	Driver
Glyn? (GW)	Jones	Driver
Howell (H)	Jones	Driver
Val (TV)	Jones	Driver
Jack (J)	Jones	Driver
Jeff (J)	Jones	Driver
Alan? (AR)	Jones	Passed Cleaner
George (GE)	Jones	Fireman
Alf (A)	Jones	Fireman
Robert (R)	Jones	Driver
George (RG)	Jones	Fireman
RA (RA)	Jones	Fireman
John Willie (JW)	**Jones**	Driver
Howell? (H)	**Jones**	Driver
Percy (P)	**Jones**	Driver
George (G)	Kellett	Driver
S (S)	Killinger	Turner
Ernie (E)	Kniveton	Driver
Tommy (T)	**King**	Passed Cleaner
Eric (E)	**Lancaster**	Driver
Eric (E)	Lancaster	Fireman
Harold (H)	Latham	Passed Fireman
Charlie (C)	Leatherbarrow	Fireman
Jimmy (J)	Lewis	Driver
Jack (J)	Leyland	Passed Fireman
Jimmy (J)	Lincoln	Fireman
C (C)	Litchfield	Fireman
Tommy (T)	**Littler**	Driver
A? (A)	Lord	Fireman
Archie (A)	Lord	Turner
Bill (W)	Lowe	Fireman
Bill (W)	Lowe	Turner
Walter (W)	Lunn	Driver
Bob (R)	Makin	Driver
Harry (H)	Marriott	Driver
Tommy (T)	Marrow	Fireman
Herbert (H)	**Martland**	Driver
George (G)	Mason	Fireman
Jimmy (J)	McClure	Driver
Jimmy (J)	McGuirk	Driver
Norman (N)	McQuade	Shed Arranger
Jimmy (J)	Melling	Driver
Jack (J)	**Mills**	Driver
Alf (A)	Mitchinson	Fireman
Vince (T)	Monks	Fireman
Wilf (W)	Monks	Fireman
Amos (A)	**Moore**	Driver
Harold (H)	Morrell	Driver
B (B)	Morris	Passed cleaner
Hughie (H)	Morris	Driver
Thomas (T)	Morris	Fireman
Jimmy (J)	Mosley	Driver
Sid (S)	Mosley	Fireman
Tommy (T)	Muir	Driver
Bill (W)	Norburn	Fireman
Jack (J)	**Oates**	Driver
Tommy (T)	O'Neill	Driver
Jimmy (J)	Parkinson	Fireman
FD (FD)	Parry	Passed Cleaner
Jack (J)	Patterson	Fireman
Harold (HC)	**Pearson**	Fireman
Joe (J)	Peglar	Driver
Ken (K)	Pendergast	Fireman
Jerry (J)	**Pendlebury**	Passed Fireman
William (W)	**Peters**	Driver
Tim (T)	Pey	Driver
S (S)	Philips	Turner
Ken? (K)	Phillips	Passed Cleaner
Joe (J)	Pollitt	Driver
Joe (J)	Pollitt	Fireman
Harold (H)	Porter	Driver
Peter (P)	Porter	Driver
Cliff (C)	Porter	Fireman
A (A)	Prescott	Fireman
Gryff (G)	Price	Driver
M (M)	Price	Passed cleaner
Tony? (T)	Price	Fireman
Charlie (C)	**Priestley**	Passed Fireman
Charlie (C)	Prudham	Driver
Freddie (F)	Pye	Fireman
Bill (W)	Pye	Passed Fireman
Arthur (A)	Railton	Driver
Albert (A)	**Ramsdale**	Fireman
J (J)	Ramsdale	Passed Cleaner
Jack (J)	Rigby 1	Driver
Jack (J)	Rigby 2	Driver
Jackie (J)	Rigby	Fireman
Len (L)	**Riley**	Fireman
Ken (K)	Rimmer	Passed Cleaner
Jackie (J)	Roberts	Fireman
Len (L)	Roberts	Turner
Tommy (T)	Robinson	Driver
J (J)	Robinson	Driver
George (G)	**Robinson**	Driver
Freddie (FD)	**Robinson**	Fireman
Jack (J)	Rogers	Driver
Bert (J)	Roscoe	Fireman
Heath (E)	**Rowlands**	Driver
David (D)	Rowles	Driver
Jack (JH)	Rowles	Driver
Freddie (FD)	Rutter	Fireman
Harry (H)	Rutter	Arranger
Jack (J)	**Rutter**	Fireman
Wilf (W)	**Sanson**	Passed Fireman
Jack (J)	**Sedgewick**	Driver
Bill (W)	Sharples	Fireman
George (G)	Sharratt	Fireman
Tommy (T)	Sharrock	Driver
Alf (A)	Sherrington	Driver
R (R)	**Sherrington**	Passed Cleaner
Elias (E)	**Shufflebottom**	Driver
Richard (R)	Simm	Fireman
Jimmy (J)	Sloan	Fireman
J (J)	Smart	Driver
Evan (E)	Smith	Driver
John (J)	Smith	Driver
Tom (T)	Smith	Passed Fireman
Bernard?(TB)	Smith	Turner
Alan (A)	Southworth	Fireman
Harry (H)	**Southworth**	Driver
J (J)	Stafford	Fireman
Stanley (S)	Stainton	Fireman
Bob (RJ)	Stephenson	Fireman
Harry (H)	Swarbrick	Driver
Jimmy (J)	Tattersall	Passed Fireman
J (J)	Taylor	Passed Fireman
Andrew (A)	Taylor	Driver
Gilbert (G)	Taylor	Passed Fireman
George? (G)	Taylor	Driver
Jack (JW)	**Taylor**	Driver
Tommy (T)	**Taylor**	Driver
Sammy (S)	**Taylor**	Driver
Gilbert? (G)	**Taylor**	
Stan (S)	Thompson	Driver
S (S)	Thompson	Turner
Tommy (T)	Thornborough	Driver
Reg (R)	Tierney	Driver
William (W)	Tinsley	Driver
Joe (J)	Tinsley	Fireman
Harry (H)	Toleman	Driver
Harold (H)	Tomlinson	Driver
Harry (H)	Topping	Driver
Bill (W)	Topping	Driver
Joe (J)	Townsend	Driver
H (H)	Trezise	Fireman
George (G)	**Upton**	Driver
Stan (S)	Vernal	Passed Cleaner
Joe (J)	Waite	Driver
Alan (A)	Waite	Fireman
Len (L)	Walls	Passed cleaner
Cliff (C)	Ward	Passed cleaner
Ken (K)	Westhead	Fireman
Jack (J)	Weston	Driver
Albert (A)	Whittaker	Driver
Jack (J)	Wigan	Passed Fireman
Freddie (FD)	**Wilcocks**	Passed Fireman
George (G)	Wilkinson	Driver
Clive (C)	Wilkinson	Fireman
Billy (W)	Williams	Driver
Jack (J)	Williams	Fireman
Cliff (C)	Williams	Fireman
A (A)	Williams	Fireman
Percy (P)	Wilson	Driver
Billy (W)	**Winstanley**	Passed Fireman
Jack (J)	Winter	Turner
Sammy (S)	Wood	Driver
Albert (TA)	Wood	Driver
Richard (R)	**Wood**	Fireman
(F) J	Wood	Passed Cleaner
Tommy (T)	Worthington	Fireman
Johnny (J)	**Worthington**	Passed Fireman
Joe (J)	Wright	Driver
Bob (R)	Wright	Driver
Tommy (T)	Wych	Fireman
Bill (W)	Yates	Driver

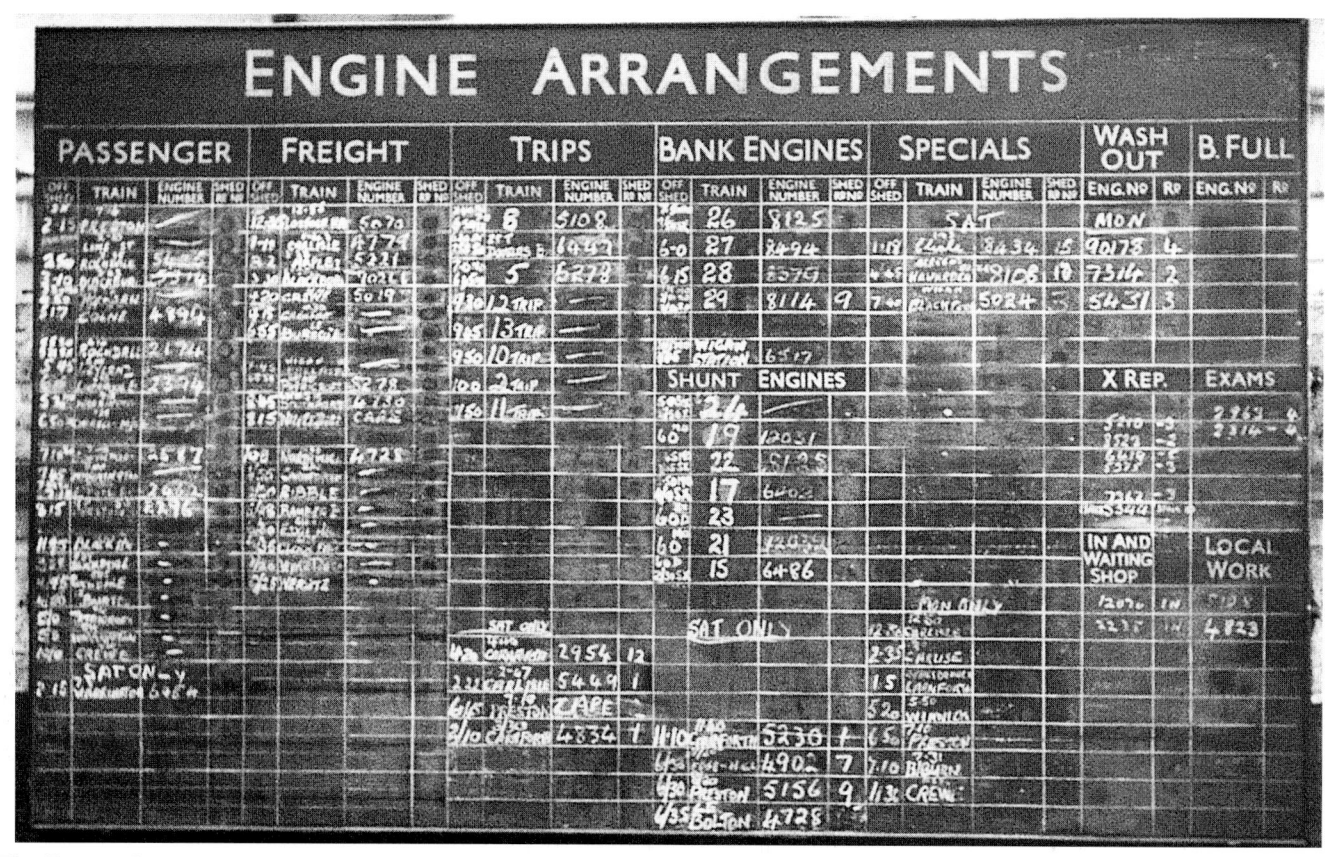

The Engine Arrangements Board for Saturday 29th May 1965. The tables opposite are a more legible version and although some writing proved impossible to read, most has been deciphered. Note the prefix train number was omitted - eg 126 is shown as 26.

29TH MAY 1965 ● B. MAGILTON

A DAY IN THE LIFE - SATURDAY 29TH MAY 1965

	Off shed	Train	Eng No	The actual working is	Notes
PASSENGER	2.15	7:04 Preston	----	07:04 Wigan NW - Preston (ex Man X) 6 days	9H loco on Saturdays so nothing allocated
		2:10 Lime St	----	1F51 02:10 Wigan NW - Lime St (6 days)	does run so should be allocated loco
	2.50	3:35 Rochdale	5425	1J97 03:35 Parcels WNW to Rochdale (6 days)	
	3.10	3:42 Blackburn	5314	1P27 03:42 Parcels WNW to Blackburn (6 days)	
	4.50	5 :20 Preston	----	2P65 05:20 Wigan to Preston (SX)	Saturdays Excepted
	5.17	5:47 Colne	4894 10A	3P05 Parcels Wigan WNW to Colne (MX)	"Loco to Rose Grove, men return passenger"
	5:05? SO				
	5:11? SX	6:14 Rochdale	2174	2J58 06:14 WW - Rochdale	
	5.45	6:48 Leyland	----	2P65 06:48 Wigan to Leyland (SX)	Saturdays Excepted
	6.00	6:55 Liv Ex 6d	2374	2J59 06:55 Liv Ex - Rochdale	"Loco returns 17:00 Liv Ex - Pr,19:10 PR-Wigan NW"
	5.30	7:08 Warrington	----	2F74 07:08 Wigan NW - Warrington (6 days)	
	6.50	7:25 Orrell	----	07:25 Orrell - Man Vic (SX)	Saturdays Excepted
	7.10	Orrell-Man V	2587	crew relieves 07:18 Orrell - Man Vic (SO)	Change footplate Wigan. Loco works Pcls to Southport
	7.45	8:40 Warrington?	----	2F73 08:40 Wigan NW - Warr BQ (SX)	
	7.10?	Liverpool Ex	2462	(08:20 WW - Liv Ex 6 days)	returns on 12:03 SO Liv Ex - Wigan W
	8.15	(9:30) Preston	2296 10D	2P65 09:30 Wigan to Preston (6 days)	booked Lostock Hall engine
	11:15	Blackburn	----	12:18 Blackburn Parcels (SX)	Saturdays Excepted
	3/29	Blackpool	----	prob 16:35 to Blackpool N (SX)	Saturdays Excepted
	4/45	5/15. Rochdale	----	2J58 17:15 Wigan W - Rochdale	
	(4/50)	Bursco	----	LE to Burscough Bridge	For 18:14 Parcels to Normanton
	5/00	Patricroft	----	19:00 Wigan Cen Gds - Leeds,	Men to Patricroft
	5/05.	Normanton?	----	poss 17:26 Bursco Br - Normanton Pcls	Engine & Men to ?
	10/00	Crewe	----	3K17 23:30 Wigan NW - Crewe Pcls	Saturdays Excepted
Saturday Only	2.15	7:08 Warrington	6484?	07:08 Wigan NW - Warr BQ	also show on sx ?
FREIGHT	12.35	12.55 Lostock Hall	5070	8P02 00:55 Spr Branch - Lostock Hall (MX)	Via Ince Moss & Whelley Line
	1.10	1.43 Carlisle	4779	8L03 01:43 Blong - Carlisle (SX) (01:35 MO)	
	3.02	3.22 Arpley	5221	8F45 03:22 Bamfurlong NE - Arpley (MX)	
	3.30	3:35 Blackburn	90261(LD)	7P60 03:10 Spr Branch - Blackburn (MX)	"Not Wigan Loco, Via Wigan NW, 6F30 back"
	4.20	4:45 Crewe	5019	8K09 04:45 Bamfurlong NE - Crewe	MX turn 306
	4.15	04:38 Carnforth	----	6P03 04:40 Spr Branch - Carnforth (MX)	Via WNW
	6.55	LE Burscough	----	LE To Burscough Br for 07:40 Bursc Jn	
	3.02	Wigan Ballast	----		
	?	8:40 Patricroft	5278	8J87 08:40 Bamfurlong NE - Weaste (6d)	Via Golborne
	3.30	9:15 Southport	4730	9K98 09:15 Bamfurlong - Southport (6d)	returns 7F10
	4.20	Whitebirk	cape	8P11 09:00 Parkside - Whitebirk (6d)	Coal
	10.00	10:33 Northwich	4728	8F24 10:33 Bamfurlong NE - Northwich (6d)	7K67 back (so 6P54 back)
	1/55	2/30 Carnforth	----	6P13 14:30 Spr Branch - Carnforth (6d)	Via WNW,turn 307, then 6K03 to Crewe
	2/20	2/40 Ribble	----	9P04 14:40 Spr B N Sdgs - Ribble Sdgs (SX)	Via Wigan NW
	5/48	6/08 Bamber Br	----	9P06 18:08 Spr Branch - Bamber Br (SX)	Via Wigan NW, back on 7K28
	6/20	6/50 Edge Hill	----	8F15 18:50 Ince Moss - Edge Hill (SX)	calls St H, back on 8F86
	(4)/35	6/55 Clock Face	----	9F08 18:55 Ince Moss - Clock Face (SX)	calls collieries, 8F16 back
	7/20	Wyre Dock	----	8P01 21:55 Spr Branch - Wyre Dock? (SX)	
	9/25	Weaste	----	9J93 SX 22:45 Ince Moss - Ordsall Lane	LE ex shed
TRIPS	(04:40 fo)				
	06:50 MX	8	5108	Bamfurlong, Wigan NW, later CWS, Roundhouse	Turns 337/8/9/40
	06:20 SX				
	06:50 SO	Douglas B	6447	125 trip, Blong, Douglas Bank, Gas Wks, Canal Sdg	Turns 392/3/4
	7:00 SO				
	6:45 xx	5	5278	Bamfurlong, Ravenhead, Ince Moss	Turn 483
	09:30	12 Trip	----	Blong, Golborne, Parkside, Bamfurlong (SX)	Turn 333
	09:45	13 Trip	----	Pem Corner, Bolton C St, Bamfurlong (SX)	Turn 331
	09:50	10 Trip	----	Eng Shed Sdgs, Canal Sdgs, Blamfurong	Turns 401/2/3
	10:00	2 Trip	----	Bickershaw, Abram North	Turns (540/1/2)
	11:50	11 Trip	----	Pem Corner, trips Bamfurlong to Bickershaw (SX)	335 (does E Hill first MO) Weaste later
Saturday Only	4.20	4:40 Carnforth	2954	6P03 04:40 Springs Br - Carnforth (mx)	
"	2.22	2:47 Carlisle	5449	6L19 00:55 E Port - Carlisle (SO) ?	
"	6.45	7:10 Preston cape		8P06 07:19 Springs Branch - Ribble Sidings (SO)	
"	2.10	3/30 Carnforth	4834	8L14 15:23 Bamfurlong - Carlisle (SO)	
BANK	07:50 MO				
	xxxxxx	26 Bank	8125	Bamfurlong Banker	Turns 408 - 412
	6.00	27 Bank	8494	Bamfurlong Banker	Turns 436 - 442
	6.15	28 Bank	8379	Bamfurlong Banker	Turns 416 - 420
		29 Bank	8114	Ince Moss Banker	Turn 514
		Wigan Sta	6517	Wigan Bank (NW Station)	
SHUNT	5:00 SX				
	x/50 xx	24 Shunt	----	124 Trip is Wigan Goods Yard Shunt	512/3
	6:00 MO	19 Shunt	12031	119 Shunt is Bamfurlong North End Shunt	312/3/4/5
	9:45 (MO)				
	xx:45 SX	22 Shunt	8125	122 Trip is Bamfurlong South End Shunt	09:15 Bamf - Southport(SX), 22:45 IMJ - Weaste
	5:50 MO				
	4pm SX	17 Shunt	6402	117 Shunt is Springs Branch North Sidings	Turn 18
	6:00 D	23 Shunt	----	123 Trip is Ince Moss P S Shunt	Turns 481 - 483
	06:00	21 Shunt	12032	121 Shunt is Bamfurlong Pemberton Corner	Turns 317/8/9/20
	6:00 D				
	2/30 SX	15 Shunt	6486	115 Shunt is Incline Shunt	Turns 504/5/6

	Off shed	Train	Eng No	The actual working is	Notes
Saturday Only 11:10	11:40 Carnforth	2954	11:40 Wigan NW - Carnforth (SO)	
" 6/30	19:20 Edge Hill	4902	9F16 19:20 Ince Moss - Edge Hill (SO)	calls St Helens
" 6/30	8/20 Preston	5156	2P65 20:20 Wigan NW - Preston 6d	
" 6/35	Bolton	4728	LE to Bolton	Bolton engine
SPECIALS Saturday 01:19	01:55 Carlisle	8434		
" 04:45	xxx Hawarden	8108		
" 07:40	Blackpool	5024		
Monday Only 00:30	00:50 Carlisle		6L07 00:50 Bamfurlong - Carlisle (MO)	
" 02:35	xxx Carlisle		poss 00:55 E Pt - Carl (normally MX)	Turn 306
" 01:05	Springs Branch - Carnforth		7P24 02:15 Springs Branch - Carnforth (MO) Q	
" 05:20	05:50 Winwick		7F44 05:50 Bamfurlong screens - Winwick (MO)	formed off 17:27 from Carlisle
" 06:50	07:10 Preston		8P00 07:10 Springs Branch - Wyre Dock (SX)	
" 07:10	07:31 Blackburn		6P70 07:31 MO Springs Branch - Blackburn (MO)	Returns LE
" 11:30	xxx Crewe		??	

PLANAGRAM

The planagram below shows the position of all locomotives on shed on Sunday 30th May 1965 which was, by coincidence, the day after the photo of the engine arrangements board was taken overleaf. Some engines shown on the board have departed on trains that were not seen. Of the 76 engines on shed, 11 are withdrawn and at least 3 stored, and there are 16 visiting engines, of which half were noted around the shed the previous day. Springs Branch's own WD's are stored but members are still appearing on shed as visitors, with four showing over the weekend. Although sheds didn't normally do boiler washouts on other depots' locos, WD No 90178 from Sutton Oak is so favoured.

Interesting to see all the shunt, trip and bank engines have arrived back on shed for a Sunday rest. Britannia Pacific No 70032 *Tennyson* and the two 9F's are interesting visitors. Bolton engine No 44728 worked the 08:17 Bolton to Wigan passenger but must then have been borrowed for the Northwich freight (as shown), returning on the northbound working, then going light engine to Bolton shed.

15		48434	42948					coaler	46517	
14	44500	47671	48261	48187				avoider	70032	92086
13	44490	42465	42601	42369	45221	90563				
12	90585	42954	48125	45019	48114	45108				
11			42558	45341	92053					
10	42295	42462	42296	42587	42374	45449	45024			
9	44823	48675	44658	48494	45425					
8	47603 47395	42456	45314	45372	45278					
7		73140	45242			fuel road				
6	44918		48379	48278	45455					
5	46419		42959	46484	46486	46447				
4	42814	42963	90178	47367	45296	45385				
3	45210	45375	45431	42647	42174	46402				
2	48523		47314	45140						
1	12003	12031	12032	45376				scrap line	90317	90686	90561	90399

SPRINGS BRANCH OBSERVATIONS FROM ENGINE ARRANGEMENTS BOARD & ACTUAL VISITS (Bold type indicates visiting engine from another depot)

	Sat 29/05/65	Sun 30/05/65		Sat 29/05/65	Sun 30/05/65		Sat 29/05/65	Sun 30/05/65
12003	On shed	On shed	44918	On shed	On shed	47367	Repair	Repair
12031	19 Shunt	On shed	45019	04:45 Crewe	On shed	47395	Withdrawn	Withdrawn
12032	21 Shunt	On shed	45024	Spl 07:40 Blackpl	On shed	47444	-	-
12074	Workshops	Workshops	45070	00:55 L. Hall (unseen)	Wkg off 10D	47493	-	-
42174	06:14 Rochdale	On shed	45108	8 Trip	On shed	47603	On shed	On shed
42235	Workshops	Workshops	45140	On shed	On shed	47671	On shed	On shed
42295	Stored	Stored	45156	20:20 Preston	-	48108	Spl Hawarden Br (unseen)	-
42296	09:30 Preston	Visitor	45210	Repair	Repair	48114	29 Bank	mpd
42343	On shed	-	45221	03:22 Arpley	On shed	48125	26 Bank/22 shunt	mpd
42369	Withdrawn	Withdrawn	45230	Carnfth (unseen)	-	48187	On shed	On shed
42374	06:55 Liverpool Ex	On shed	45242	-	Visitor	48261	On shed	On shed
42456	Withdrawn	Withdrawn	45278	5 Trip/22:45 Weaste	On shed	48275	On shed	-
42462	Liverpool Ex	On shed	45281	-	-	48278	-	On shed
42465	Withdrawn	Withdrawn	45296	On shed	On shed	48379	28 Bank	mpd
42558	Withdrawn	Withdrawn	45314	03:42 Blackburn	On shed	**48434**	Spl Carlisle	Visitor
42587	07:10 Orrell	On shed	**45341**	-	Visitor	48494	27 Bank	mpd
42601	Withdrawn	Withdrawn	45344	Exam	-	48511	On shed	-
42647	On shed	On shed	45372	-	On shed	48523	Repair	Repair
42814	Exam	Exam	45375	Repair	Repair	48675	On shed	On shed
42948	On Shed	On Shed	**45376**	-	Visitor	**70032**	-	Visitor
42953	On shed	-	45385	-	On shed	**73137**	On shed	-
42954	04:40 Carnforth	On shed	45408	-	-	**73140**	-	Visitor
42959	On shed	On shed	45425	03:35 Rochdale	On shed	90178	Wash Out	Wash Out
42963	Exam	On shed	45431	washout	washout	90261	03:35 Blackburn	-
44490	Stored	Stored	45449	02:47 Carlisle	On shed	90317	Withdrawn	Withdrawn
44500	Stored	Stored	**45455**	Visitor	Visitor	90361	On shed	-
44658	-	Visitor	46402	17 Shunt	On shed	90399	Withdrawn	Withdrawn
44728	10:33 Northwich (unseen)	Bolton	46419	Repair	Repair	90561	Withdrawn	Withdrawn
44730	09:15	Southport	46447	125 Trip Douglas Bnk	On shed	**90563**	Visitor	Visitor
44779	01:43 Carlisle	At Carlisle	46484	07:08 Warrington	On shed	90585	Withdrawn	Withdrawn
44823	On shed	On shed	46486	15 Shunt	On shed	90686	Withdrawn	Withdrawn
44834	15:30 Carnfth (unseen)	-	46487	On shed	-	**92053**	Visitor	Visitor
44894	05:47 Colne (unseen)	-	46517	Wigan NW pilot	On shed	**92086**	-	Visitor
44902	19:20 Edge Hill	-	47314	Wash Out	Wash Out			

96

PASSENGER WORKINGS

Although about 75% of Springs Branch locomotive working had always been freight orientated, there was still a reasonable number of local passenger turns to Blackburn, Liverpool Lime St, Manchester Exchange, Preston and Warrington. In the years following Nationalisation, the passenger work gradually declined. When the ex-Great Central shed at Lower Ince closed in 1952, Springs Branch took over their engines and workings and continued to run the Wigan Central to Lowton St Marys, Glazebrook and Manchester Central services until they ceased in November 1964. The Wigan NW - Liverpool Lime St service went over to DMUs in 1959 and the Wigan NW to Blackburn trains ceased in 1960. Many of the Preston locals were shared initially with Preston MPD and later with Lostock Hall but most of these had also become DMUs by 1966. The Manchester Exchange route stayed loco hauled until March 1965 when the service was reduced to a single DMU turn and, similarly, the Warrington Bank Quay locals had been reduced to three by the early 1960's before petering out in the late 60's.

Another route - the Blackburn line via Chorley, had a decent service in the 1930's with 8 trains each way, some of them being through trains from Liverpool, but by the mid 1940's the service was down to just four each way. 1950 saw the closure of many intermediate stations such as Boar's Head and Red Rock and the service was further reduced to just three trains, finally finishing in 1960. This left the ROF train as the only booked passenger working over the route, although parcels trains did continue for many more years. The Boar's Head Junction to Adlington Junction section was also used by certain summer Saturday trains such as the Llandudno to Colne as well as the many excursions that ran from the East Lancashire towns to North Wales and points further south. It was also used at weekends as a diversionary route when the improvements to the West Coast main line were being undertaken in the late 1960's. Springs Branch also supplied engines for the Manchester Exchange portion of the overnight Liverpool to Glasgow service for many years.

Passenger work slightly increased after 16th April 1964 when Wigan (L&Y) MPD closed. Springs Branch then supplied locomotives for services between Liverpool Exchange and Rochdale and some parcels trains over the former ex-L&Y routes, but ultimately these became DMUs or diesel hauled. And so, as steam ended, there were hardly any passenger duties and, like so many other MPD's, the duties became almost exclusively parcels and freight. Although the crews still manned many passenger trains, they were, in railway jargon, *enginemen turns* only. Over the years there were some non advertised 'Workers' or 'Colliers' trains and, going back to LMS days, they served Tyldesley, Bickershaw, Garswood, Leyland and Chorley ROF. Of these, the Bickershaw and Garswood trains had ceased by BR days although there were Tyldesley locals still running. The Leyland workers' train continued until at least 1967. In the latter LMS period, Chorley ROF was served by 3 trains via Wigan NW (one each weekday shift and one on Sunday) originating from the Liverpool area. These were later cut back to become Wigan NW to ROF trains and by Nationalisation there was just the morning 06:33 to ROF and the evening return. This was a 12 coach formation routed over the challenging Boar's Head to Adlington Junction line to the private platforms of the Royal Ordnance Factory's own station. In the late 1950's it was a Camden loco turn, with Preston and Springs Branch men on the footplate and later a Preston turn before finally becoming exclusively a Springs Branch operation, but it appears to have ceased at the end of 1964.

Springs Branch allocated Cauliflower No 539 stands at Wigan North Western Station whilst hauling an unidentified local train, probably from Preston to either Liverpool Lime Street or Manchester Exchange. c.1905 ● LNWR SOCIETY

Other workings over the years include a Springs Branch diagram involved with the up *Lakes Express*, bringing the Workington coaches into Preston. There was a little more work in the summer months and Springs Branch engines hauled the dated Saturday trains from St Helens and Eccles to Blackpool, and the 07:08 Wigan NW to Llandudno plus various 'extras' or excursions in the area.

The *Enginemens' Arrangements for the Winter of 1951* show that the shed supplied 13 locomotives on a daily basis for passenger work. Of these, the vast majority were 2-6-4 tanks with the odd Black Five also appearing. The *Wigan Bank* job came under the passenger turns but this would invariably be an elderly engine (and crew!) and would often be a 'Cauliflower' at this time. This turn is covered in the 'Shunt' section on pages 153 and 154.

PASSENGER TURNS - WINTER 1951

LOCO	TIME	TURN	DESCRIPTION OF THIS TURN
Tank A	02:00	Lime St	
Tank B	04:52	Newton	to work 06:02 Newton le Willows - Lime St
Tank	05:20	Preston	Local Passenger
Tank	05:47	Tyldesley	Local Passenger
Tank	06:15	Lime St	Local Passenger
R	06:16	Crewe	05:30 Preston - Crewe
R	06:20	BANK	Wigan Station Pilot & Bank engine
Black 5	06:30	Newton	to work 07:15 Newton Le Willows - Lime St
12A loco	06:33	Chorley ROF	Local Passenger
R	06:39	Tebay	6am Warrington - Carlisle
Tank C	06:43	Lime St	Local Passenger
Tank	07:04	Preston	05:50 Man Ex - Preston
Tank	07:10	Blackburn	06:00 Liverpool - Blackburn
Tank	09:05	Lime St	Local Passenger
R	09:25	Preston	08:10 Liverpool - Preston
R	09:28	Lime St	Parcels
Tank A	12:18	Manchester	Local Passenger

LOCO	TIME	TURN	DESCRIPTION OF THIS TURN
R	12:30	BANK	Wigan Station Pilot & Bank engine
Tank C	12:35	Earlestown	Local Passenger
R	12:45	Preston	Local Passenger
R	13:55	Lime St	Local Passenger
R	14:42	Preston	12:45 Crewe-Carlisle parcels
R	14:53	Crewe	Carlisle-Crewe parcels
R	15:40	Lime St	Local Passenger
Tank B	16:17	Huddersfield	Passenger to Leeds
R	16:17	Eccles	as passenger on 16:17 and relieve another at Eccles
R	16:20	Preston	15:20 Liverpool - Preston
R	16:37	Preston (FO)	15:58 Man Ex - Barrow
Tank	17:11	Chester	Local Passenger
R	17:21	Preston (FX)	16:45 Man Ex - Carlisle
	17:40	Warrington	Local Passenger
Black 5	20:35	Crewe	19:20 Wyre Dock to Broad St Fish (as far as Crewe)
Various	23:30	BANK	Wigan Station Pilot & Bank engine

Of the turns, two would head out Light Engine from the shed to Newton-le-Willows where they would pick up stock and work trains into Liverpool Lime Street. It seems the Liverpool service dominated the turns at this time because four more Springs Branch passenger turns involved this route with engines commencing on the 02:00, 06:15, 06:43 and 09:05 Lime Street trains. All steam working was severely curtailed in the late 1950's when DMU's took over, with just a couple of steam hauled 'rush hour' trains to Liverpool.

The remaining engines were employed on a couple of Preston locals, one each on Tyldesley & Blackburn locals, and a Chester train. The final loco in the passenger section worked the 20:35 Crewe which was actually the Wyre Dock (Fleetwood) to London (Broad Street) Fish and appeared to re-engine at Wigan. To paint the fuller picture, it should be remembered that these locos would go onto other trains in their respective diagrams and it can be seen, from the table above, that the 02:00 Lime St engine was diagrammed to go onto the 12:18 Manchester (Exchange) later in the day. Similarly, the engine on the 04:52 Newton would return to take out the 16:17 Leeds train as far as Huddersfield (as booked). It can also be seen that the 06:33 ROF train was, at this time, a Carlisle Upperby Black Five turn. The other passenger turns listed were 're-man' jobs that would probably be using a Springs Branch engine already out on its diagram.

WIGAN NW TO MANCHESTER EXCHANGE SERVICES

Ivatt 2-6-0 No 46447 heads away from Wigan NW station with the 16:17 Leeds via Manchester Exchange. The engine would work the train as far as Huddersfield before returning light engine to Rochdale for its next working.

23RD JUNE 1964 ● **JOHN BURGESS**

The Wigan to Manchester Exchange service was always sparse compared to that of the L&Y route to Manchester Victoria. In 1931 there were twelve weekday locals, plus one each from Wigan to Tyldesley and Leigh (via Pennington). On Saturday evenings the nightlife in Wigan must have been interesting because the railway provided two SO trains to Tyldesley, leaving at 22:40 and 23:00, suggesting quite a demand. At that time, the two weekday early morning Tyldesley workers' trains that became a regular sight after the war hadn't yet commenced, but both had appeared in the LMS timetable by 1945. There were also some through workings such as Windermere/Morecambe - Manchester Exchange and the Glasgow - Manchester expresses. The BR period brought about considerable changes and by 1951 there were only four local trains to Exchange plus the two Tyldesley workers' trains which were, until 1957, worked by railmotors on weekdays and engine with stock on Saturdays. In addition there were through services originating from Windermere (2), Preston, Blackpool Central and Glasgow Central (2) to Exchange, all calling at Wigan NW, plus more trains on summer Saturdays. The dated trains often started from Cross Lane - presumably because they could originate from the nearby carriage sidings at Ordsall Lane, but by the 1960's, these would be shown as starting from Eccles. On Sundays there were just four local trains and the Sunday local passenger service ceased completely in 1959.

Class 2P 2-4-2T No 6762 had a rather chequered career - indeed Eric Mason described the loco as a social outcast. Built in June 1890, it was sold by the Lancashire and Yorkshire Railway to the Wirral Railway in 1921 but survived into the BR period as No 46762 and became the last of its class in service. After electrification of the Wirral, it moved on, but for reasons unclear, never carried its intended LMS number - that of 10638. Instead it bore the Crewe-inspired No 6762. Its final work was as acting Station Pilot at Preston before withdrawal from the shed there in February 1952. It arrived at Springs Branch on New Years Day 1935 before leaving for Preston six months later. On 9th May 1936 the 'Radial Tank' returned for a further year before moving on to Sutton Oak. The engine awaits departure from Platform 2 at Manchester Exchange Station with a local train to Wigan North Western. On the left is an unidentified 'Claughton' working the Liverpool Lime Street service.   **MAY 1935 • W. POTTER**

Over the years the patterns changed slightly and some of the through services also didn't stop at Wigan at times. By 1959 the remaining weekday locals to Tyldesley ceased, although one still ran as a parcels train, but there were still Tyldesley to Wigan locals in the evening rush hour until 1965. By 1964 there were just five weekdays services to Manchester Exchange, excluding the Glasgow express. Summer 1965 saw the local service drop to just the one weekday train, the 08:22 (sx) DMU service which continued for a couple of years, but by May 1968 the local service had finished completely. Springs Branch shed was responsible for many of these services, but Patricroft shed also provided power for this route. In 1951, the 05:47 Tyldesley, 12:18 Manchester Exchange and 16:17 Leeds all commenced with engines and men from Springs Branch. Other workings would result from the return parts of these diagrams and there were other legs of diagrams that involved the Manchester route.

Approaching Bickershaw Junction is Black Five No **45425** on the 16:17 to Leeds. The Wigan engine would work this train as far as Huddersfield and then return light engine to Rochdale to bring a parcels train back. This spot is where the Bickershaw accident occurred in 1965 *(see page 161)*. The sidings in the foreground are those to Low Hall Colliery whilst the cooling towers of Westwood Power Station are seen in the background.   **SEPTEMBER 1964 • TOM SUTCH**

WIGAN NW TO WARRINGTON BANK QUAY SERVICES

Wigan and Warrington were well connected as the West Coast Main Line passed through both towns and many of the expresses called at both stations, thus offering an excellent service. There was also a local Wigan to Warrington stopping service that took the Earlestown route but this was relatively sparse and mainly catered for the local workforce. In 1951 there were two Wigan to Earlestown trains and two evening Warrington's, plus an extra late-night Earlestown train on Saturdays. There was also the 17:11 Chester and other through trains serving the route. The Earlestown locals finished in the mid 1950's and the Chester train terminated at Warrington. A Railmotor service operated on the weekday evening trains during the early 1950's. One interesting train was the 7:08am which, on summer Saturdays, was extended to Llandudno and was in the goods links. In the 1950's the loco and crew returned with a train for Sheffield and were relieved at Warrington Arpley. This extended working ceased after the 1961 summer season.

Ivatt 2-6-0 No 46506 approaches Springs Branch with the 17:22 Warrington to Wigan via Earlestown local train. This local service was shared between Springs Branch and Warrington (Dallam) MPDs with Dallam regularly supplying Ivatt 2-6-2 tanks.

20TH MAY 1964 • JOHN BURGESS

Standard Class 4 4-6-0 No 75039 heads south past Springs Branch No 1 signalbox with the 17:32 local train to Warrington.

16TH APRIL 1964 • JOHN BURGESS

By 1965 there were three trains to Warrington, with one extra train on Saturdays. All were loco hauled except the 17:35 (on summer Saturdays) and the 07:08 which soon changed to a DMU and by 1966, there was no weekday service, and just a handful of summer Saturday trains, the 08:25 (Loco) and 17:35 (DMU) to Warrington and the 12:20 (Loco) & 20:03 (DMU) return, although it must be remembered that other trains covered the Earlestown route, such as the Warrington to Carlisle and the Blackpool to Warrington. The situation in 1967 was unaltered, yet by 1968, the 17:35 was running six days a week throughout the year. Other services were now incorporated with these, such as the Warrington to Windermere, so effectively the Wigan to Warrington locals had all but petered out.

A couple of the trains that went beyond Warrington are described by local man Tommy Taylor. His father was a Springs Branch driver and Tommy shared the footplate with him, unofficially, on many occasions.

It was June 1946 and Tommy had, totally unofficially, become a reasonably competent fireman and accompanied his father on many journeys. One typical working was the 5:03pm stopper to Chester. Leaving from No 3 bay at Wigan NW station with a 2-6-4 tank and eight suburban coaches in tow, the train continued onto the Up slow at Wigan No 1 signalbox, whistled 2 long and 4 short to indicate that they were to stay on the Up slow to Golborne. Stops were made at Bamfurlong and Golborne before they turned off the main line at Golborne Junction and stopped at Lowton. Then it was further stops at Newton le Willows, Earlestown and then down the bank to rejoin the main line at Winwick Junction. At Warrington Bank Quay the opportunity was taken to fill the tanks whilst parcels duties were completed, then it was full first regulator and 45% cut off up the climb over the Ship Canal Bridge and into Daresbury station.

The ride on these tank engines was smooth except at very high speed when a knock was transmitted through the floorboards and seat and was so fierce that it was barely possible to sit down, and it was best to stand on one's toes. Fortunately this trip did not allow any high speed running so this was not a problem today. After a couple more stops the train arrived at Chester, stood for about 30 minutes waiting for its train to be drawn off, then it was light engine back to the North end of Warrington station to work a short passenger train all stations to Wigan. On arriving home the engine hooked off and went light to the Springs Branch shed where the crew was asked to take a container of water out to Rylands Siding signalbox, there being no water supply at that place. This was not unusual and often the loco would collect, on its return, the stores van that had come from Crewe Works with its load of urgently needed spare parts, and take this to the shed.

WIGAN NW TO LIVERPOOL LIME STREET SERVICES

Prior to the DMU's being introduced in 1959, Springs Branch supplied much of the motive power for the Wigan NW to Liverpool services and a few of these trains ran through to Preston, so the diagrams were a real mixed bag. Once the DMU's had taken hold, just two loco hauled services survived, namely, a 17:13 which lasted until 1962, and an 06:16 which finished in 1965. Throughout the BR period, a couple of interesting workings tied in with the Liverpool trains were the two light engines that left Springs Branch MPD between 6am and 7.15am to travel to Newton-le-Willows, pick up stock and work early morning commuter trains from there into Lime Street. After this, one of them would then work on to Manchester Exchange before taking a local back via Tyldesley to Wigan NW. The other engine is believed to have gone onto the Liverpool to Wigan service. Both these were steam hauled passenger workings from Springs Branch until they finally transferred over to DMU operation in 1966.

Other activity over the Lime St route were the parcels and fish trains. The 03:23 Lime St Fish, a portion off a train from Scotland which ran from LNWR days, disappeared during the war years, probably due to being combined with another train. The main Liverpool parcels had departed Wigan NW around 4am in LMS days but by Nationalisation it had become the 09:28 to Lime St which continued until 1963, albeit now diverted to Wavertree. During 1962 an additional Canada Dock/Tuebrook Parcels appeared and continued beyond 1968. Supporting these trains were a pair of Class 1 Mail or News trains leaving Wigan at 00:10 and 02:00, the latter can also be traced back to LNWR days. *A couple of these turns are described below by Driver Tommy Taylor.*

Stanier 2-6-4T No 42666 passes Gerards Bridge Junction on the 18:00 Wigan NW to Liverpool Lime Street service. The bridge below the coaches takes the line over the St Helens Sankey Canal whilst the huge mound on the right is sand that was used to polish glass at Rockware prior to float glass being invented. This mound, which still exists although now grassed over, stretches for over a mile alongside the canal and was originally reported to be up to 90 ft high in places.

c1957 • GERRY DROUGHT

Black Five 4-6-0 No 45431 brings an evening local out of St Helens Shaw Street towards Pocket Nook Bridge. The sidings on the right feed St Helens Goods Yard whilst in the right distance are the premises of the St Helens Gas Works. The fact that the loco is showing express passenger lamps remains a mystery - perhaps an oversight of the part of the footplate crew.

c1957 • GERRY DROUGHT

6.20 NEWTON - LIME SREET. We booked on at 04:45, prepared the engine taking 45 minutes for the 2-6-4 tank, then off light engine via Golborne Junction to Newton-le-Willows. Here we picked up our stock and drew into the station. We then proceeded all stations to Liverpool Lime St, arriving about 07:30. Shortly, the stock departed for Wigan behind another engine and we followed to the station throat before dropping back onto another rake of coaches to form the 08:15 semi fast to Manchester Exchange. So far as I can remember, this was all stations to Newton then express to Cross Lane. Although the engine would run at over 70 mph on the first regulator and 20% cut off, our ride was terrible with a knocking under the footplate that caused us to stand on our toes all the way across Chat Moss. We scooped water near Eccles and, after arrival at Manchester Exchange, we ran round and took the stock into a carriage siding for an hour or two. Then we backed into one of the bay platforms, leaving at 11:45 on the all stations to Wigan via Monton Green. Arrival at Wigan was about 12:45 and we hooked off and ran light to Springs Branch, left the engine for the fire droppers and went home.

LIME STREET FISH. This was a regular job, light engine from Springs Branch to the station, make a couple of shunts on the fish train from Scotland, almost certainly the Law Junction to Manchester Oldham Road fish train, then take the Liverpool section on to Lime St at 02:00. On one trip we had a Midland 2P which was a pleasant engine to drive, economical on coal, although not very powerful. We paused at St Helens Shaw Street and watered the coal in the tender by means of perforated pipes fitted down the sides and fed from an injector. This was my first and only encounter with this useful gadget.

WIGAN NW TO PRESTON SERVICES

Being on the main West Coast route, there were a considerable number of express trains stopping at both Wigan and Preston. In addition to these, there was a good local service stopping at all stations to Preston and these were generally shared by Preston (later Lostock Hall) and Springs Branch crews, although some trains originated from Warrington, Liverpool Lime St and Manchester Exchange, so Patricroft and Edge Hill engines and crews would also be involved. The occasional train would also go through to Blackpool or Morecambe, particularly on summer Saturdays.

A general overview of the trains shows that, in 1937, there were approximately a dozen (Down) trains, dropping to ten a decade later. Once BR took over the service, it settled at ten trains, including one for Leyland workers at the motor factory. A further Preston train was truncated to provide a second Leyland train in 1953 and this continued until the mid 1960's. The Wigan to Preston service gradually declined and by 1964 there were just six Preston locals plus the additional two Leyland workers' trains. For a couple of years the steam hauled service held the DMU's off until 1966 when all but the 06:48 Leyland and the 07:00 Preston became dieselised. The following year brought about both the end of the Leyland local service and steam operation.

The 19:10 Preston - Wigan NW transfers from the Up Slow to Up Main at Standish Junction behind Fairburn 2-6-4T No **42235**.

22ND JUNE 1965 • ALLAN HEYES

A regular on the Preston locals, Stanier 2-6-4T No **42456** leaves a pall of smoke at Farington Curve Junction whilst working the 12:20 Preston to Wigan local. Loads on these trains were normally three coaches but could sometimes be as many as six.

4TH APRIL 1964 • PETER FITTON

Six months earlier, the same long-time Springs Branch engine, No **42456** arrives at the south end of Preston Station with the 09:30 local from Wigan.

19TH OCTOBER 1963 • PETER FITTON

CHORLEY ROF AND BLACKBURN SERVICES

Prior to 1937, eight through services ran from Wigan to Blackburn during the day, but by 1945 it was just four with one from Liverpool. This continued until January 1960 when all passenger trains were withdrawn except for the Chorley ROF worker's trains. Thereafter, this direct route via Red Rock to Blackburn saw some holiday excursions and, while the West Coast Main Line was being upgraded in the late 1960s, some traffic was diverted this way, particularly at weekends. In BR days, the Chorley Royal Ordnance Factory (the ammunition factory) was served by workers' trains from places which included Blackpool, Bolton and Liverpool. The Wigan services traversed the Boar's Head Junction to Adlington Junction line which included the significant climb over Little Scotland. This factor, together with the load of usually 10 but sometimes 12 coaches, always ensured a large engine. Prior to the Royal Scots and rebuilt Patriots, two tanks (1940's) or a Black Five (1950's) would be used - two Black Fives were recorded on one occasion. In the early 1950's the Saturday train had more coaches and a 2P pilot would often be added. In 1937 there were no ROF services shown coming either through or from Wigan NW in the Working Timetable, but by 1945 there are three, all originating from the Liverpool area, namely the 04:53 and 19:53 from Edge Hill and the 13:00 from Prescot. The balancing trains show one to Broad Green and two to Edge Hill. The timings coincided with the workers' shifts.

By 1951, there only remained the familiar 06:33 Wigan to Chorley ROF and return. The diagram for this was originally linked to an Upperby Black Five and later a Camden Royal Scot but, with modernisation of the southern end of the West Coast route, the Royal Scots came onto Preston shed's books and later still to Springs Branch.

```
        Turn 2

        ONE CLASS 7P (EX LMS 4-6-0)

        Preston Shed    3. 5pm    LE      SX
23pm    Lostock Hall    4.10      ECS     SX (203)
25      R.O.F. Chorley  4.52      W'men   SX
17      Wigan           5.21      ECS     SX
24      Springs Branch

        Wigan           12.20pm   Pass    SO (8F/238)
17pm    Mancr. Ex.      2.22      ECS     SO
27      Ordsall Lane    3.40      ECS     SO
45      Mancr. Ex.      5. 5      Pass    SO
6       Wigan

        Springs Branch  6.12am    ECS     SX (8F/212)
15am    Wigan           6.33      W'men   SX
56      R.O.F. Chorley  7.18      LE      SX
32      Preston Shed
```

The empty stock forming the 16:29 ROF train rolls round the curve from Euxton Junction into Chorley ROF Halt Station with its regular engine at this time, No **46168 *The Girl Guide*.** Gunpowder wagons are evident in the ROF reception sidings. The stock for the 06:33 ROF was stored in a siding at Platt Bridge station until that station closed in May 1961. Thereafter it was stabled at Springs Branch North Sidings. On returning from Chorley, (this leg was usually worked by Preston men) the empty stock was run to Ince Moss Junction and reversed into North Sidings. The engine then went light, via Fir Tree House and Platt Bridge Junction, to the shed. The morning train would leave from platform 8 at Wigan NW station.   **11TH APRIL 1962 ● TONY GILLETT**

The late afternoon ROF ecs is seen once again approaching Euxton Junction with No **45531 *Sir Frederick Harrison*** in charge. (No 46168 *The Girl Guide* had recently been withdrawn and placed in store). In the latter years the load was much reduced and down to just six coaches. The works trains were discontinued on 31st August 1964 after which contracts were made with local bus operators which involved 18 vehicles, mainly from the Ribble fleet.   **26TH JUNE 1964 ● BILL ASHCROFT**

11.40(SO) WIGAN NW TO CARNFORTH

This was a winter Saturday only working, as the timings were covered by a Crewe train in the Summer Timetable. It ran as an 11:50 in the 1950's, changing to 11:40 with the start of the Winter 1960 timetable and this was possibly when Springs Branch engines took over the turn - although the working appears to have become a Carnforth job in 1965 and finished completely in April 1966. It was basically a stopping train, taking 95 minutes with calls at Leyland, Preston, Garstang, Hest Bank and Bolton-le-Sands. There was no return working and the stock may have got back on the 06:35 Carnforth to Preston on the Monday and hence back into the Wigan - Preston circuit. Although the train was booked for a Black Five during the Springs Branch period, other locos observed were Rebuilt Patriot No **45531** *Sir Frederick Harrison* (12th October 1963) and Stanier Moguls Nos 42977 (28th March 1964) and 42959 which appeared on 23rd May 1964 and again on 19th September 1964.

A diesel hauled excursion to Blackpool had trailed in off the Whelley line at Standish Junction and drawn alongside the 11:40 Wigan - Carnforth, hauled by Stanier Crab No **42959**. A race quickly ensued with the 2-6-0 topping 70mph before Leyland where it is making its booked call. The keen old driver looks back for the 'rightaway' with the brake already off, ready to pursue the Illuminations special which had not needed to stop.

19TH SEPTEMBER 1964 ● **STEVE LEYLAND**

The 11:40 is caught passing Hampson Green, north of Preston, with its three suburban coaches during the Christmas period of 1963. The motive power on this occasion is No **45070**.

28TH DECEMBER 1963 ● **PETER FITTON**

SPRINGS BRANCH ENGINES ON OTHER PASSENGER WORK

A Springs Branch Improved Precedent, No 253 *President Garfield*, is piloted by Whitworth No **2153 *Isis*.** at Wigan NW. According to his records, Driver Tommy Taylor had this Precedent back from Carnforth on 16/06/22.

20TH JULY 1914 ● **LNWR SOCIETY**

The 18:54 Wigan to Blackpool Central stopping train is in the hands of Stanier Mogul No **42961** at Ansdell & Fairhaven. This was normally a Blackpool turn but on 2nd July 1964, Carlisle Upperby's 0-6-0 No 44081 worked the train.

31ST AUGUST 1964 ● **PETER FITTON**

Webb 2-4-0 'Waterloo' Class No 1166 *Wyre* is caught heading north of Preston with an express passenger. They were also known as the 'Whitworth' Class in reference to the name of the first member but were more commonly referred to as 'Small Jumbos'. No 1166 entered service in January 1896, becoming LMS No 5108 in March 1924, but was withdrawn three years later.

c1911 ● **AUTHOR'S COLLECTION**

105

Long-time Springs Branch Black Five No 45408 drifts into Lancaster Castle Station with the 1L58 06:38 Workington to Preston train. At Preston the coaches would be added to the 10:00 Blackpool to Euston train. The 1964 Summer Timetable showed that the train ran independently to Euston on Saturdays, leaving Workington at 07:00. The shed provided the power for this as far as Crewe and Nos 45019/24/108/314/72/408/31 were all noted. At the start of 1965 the roles reversed with the 06:38 Workington to Euston (Saturdays and weekdays) being the principal train and the Blackpool train ran as a portion.
19TH MAY 1964 • PETER FITTON

Friday, 4th September 1964 was a momentous day in the Preston area. Not only did it herald the end of the celebrated 'club trains' between Blackpool and Manchester but the *Caledonian* also ceased running. The last Up train had D212 *(since preserved)* whilst the Down ran behind Coronation Pacific No 46238 *City of Carlisle*. Meanwhile Stanier 2-6-4T No **42647** goes about her daily business as she passes Skew Bridge signal box with the rear portion of a Glasgow train bound for Liverpool. The train engine, D374, went through to Manchester.

4TH SEPTEMBER 1964 • PETER FITTON

During the week ending 9th September 1961, Royal Scot 4-6-0 No **46161** *King's Own* became Springs Branch's own! The loco is caught passing Rylands Siding shortly after transfer with the morning Workington to Euston express.

16TH SEPTEMBER 1961 • ARNOLD BATTSON

106

The 10:05 from Blackpool South to Euston is pictured at St Annes with Springs Branch Standard Class 4 No **75059**. This is the train that is now added to the morning Workington - Euston at Preston.

4TH JANUARY 1965 ● PETER FITTON

The imposing Preston station plays host to Stanier Mogul No **42961**. Reporting number 1P73 indicates that this is the 18:41 Crewe to Blackpool Central train. Other Springs Branch engines appearing on this train during that summer were Black Fives Nos 45296 (12th July) and 45024 (9th August).

30TH AUGUST 1964 ● PETER FITTON

It was unusual to find a Springs Branch engine working the Manchester portion of a Glasgow train forward from Preston, which was normally a Newton Heath job. Crab 2-6-0 No **42777** is sitting in the south bay at Preston station waiting to perform such a duty once the 09:30 Glasgow to Liverpool portion has departed behind Type 4 No D326. The loco arrived from Stoke in July 1962, staying a mere 18 months before moving on to Birkenhead in December 1963.

12TH OCTOBER 1963 ● PETER FITTON

Weeton, near Kirkham, is the setting for this picture of Black Five No **45140** hauling the summer Saturday 14:10 Blackpool North to Nottingham train. Springs Branch engines Nos 45314 and 45024 worked the train on 25th July 1964 and 1st August 1964 respectively but 'Peak' diesels also appeared on occasions.
29TH AUGUST 1964 • PETER FITTON

Black Five No 45449 passes Farington Curve Junction and heads towards Preston Station for the second time with the summer Saturday 10:35 Glasgow Central to Blackpool Central. The train will have taken the East Lancs route from Preston station to circle round to Farington and hence through Preston station again to access the route to Blackpool. Interestingly, apart from one week, this train had an engine from a different shed every Saturday during July and August.
24TH AUGUST 1963 • PETER FITTON

Royal Scot No 46165 *The Ranger (12th London Regiment)* is unusually employed on the 15:55 Manchester Piccadilly to London Euston express. The train is passing over Newbold Troughs, near Rugby, from which the loco has replenished its tender.
1ST JULY 1962 • PETER FITTON

Passing through Bradkirk on the approach to Kirkham is No 45024 with the 12:15 Blackpool North to Birmingham. Although this appears to be a Crewe North turn, it would seem that their engines featured only occasionally. Another Springs Branch Black Five, No 45449 was also noted hauling this train on 14th July 1962.

8TH SEPTEMBER 1962 • PETER FITTON

Although only at Springs Branch for six months, it appears that No **45310** was a 'good un' as it was regularly noted on express passenger work. This dramatic view shows the engine leaving Preston and passing under the magnificent signal gantry whilst working 1L01 14:15 Wigan NW to Blackpool North relief. This was Wigan Wakes week and No 45310 was particularly busy this day as it had already powered a 1L00 10:40 Wigan to Blackpool North relief before returning for this train. Later that day the engine worked ECS to Heysham to take the 18:00 Heysham to Blackpool special back to Blackpool North and may even have worked an evening special back to Wigan.

8TH JULY 1967 • ALLAN HEYES

109

L&Y PASSENGER TURNS

Passenger work on the ex-Lancashire & Yorkshire lines around Wigan was transferred to Springs Branch when Wigan L&Y shed (27D/8P) closed in April 1964. By that time the majority of passenger work had gone over to DMU operation and what was left was chiefly the Liverpool Exchange to Rochdale turns plus a few parcels trains. Springs Branch worked these turns until full dieselisation in January 1966.

Stanier 2-6-4T No 42456 eases itself into the former East Lancashire platforms at Preston with a local train. This loco would have found itself on a Wigan Wallgate to Southport diagram which would also include a run from Southport to Preston and back as a fill-in.
10TH JANUARY 1963 ● **D. HAMPSON**

An arrival in Platform 13 at Manchester Victoria Station is Fairburn 2-6-4T No **42174** with the 08:00 from Orrell. This commuter train was the only one to originate from Orrell although a similar morning service ran from Rainford Junction to Manchester Victoria.
21ST APRIL 1965 ● **PETER FITTON**

Although Wigan L&Y shed had not yet closed, Springs Branch Black Five No **45024** has charge of the 12:03 Liverpool Exchange to Wigan Wallgate service at Pemberton Junction. Perhaps it was a case of locomen familiarising themselves in readiness for the forthcoming work.
21ST MARCH 1964 ● **BRIAN BARLOW**

The 17:15 Rochdale to Southport became a regular Springs Branch working. The four-coach stopping train is pictured at Westhoughton with Stanier 2-6-4T No **42577** arriving in the platform.

31ST AUGUST 1965 ● **PETER FITTON**

Ivatt 2-6-0 No 46486 had been a Springs Branch engine for only one month when it was noted here approaching Hindley North with what is almost certainly a Liverpool Exchange to Rochdale service.

13TH MAY 1964 ● **JOHN BURGESS**

Royal Scot 4-6-0 No 46115 *Scots Guardsman* stands ready to depart from Southport Chapel Street with an express to Manchester Victoria. There were a few rush hour expresses that ran from Manchester to Southport with few or no stops and Class 6P and 7P engines were often found on these trains. No 46115 was one of seven Royal Scots that became allocated to the shed although this particular engine only spent seven weeks there in June/July 1964.

JULY 1964 ● **PHOTOMATIC**

Stanier 2-6-4T No 42456 is seen yet again - this time at Craddock Street on the approaches to the Croal viaduct and Bolton Trinity Street Station. The train is the Saturdays Only 8:09 stopper from Clitheroe to Manchester Victoria - a most unusual working for a Springs Branch engine. Had it been 'nicked' off one of the Blackburn or Colne parcels trains as a substitute for a failed locomotive?

25TH AUGUST 1962 • D. HAMPSON

Rebuilt Patriot No 45521 Rhyl has just dropped off the last of its passengers at Hindley North and the lamps have been reset for ecs running. Loco and stock are seen leaving Hindley and will take the slow line to Wigan Wallgate for its next turn. No 45521 had previously brought the 17:05 from Manchester Victoria via Atherton - a case of another 'one off' rush hour train to an unlikely destination.

16TH SEPTEMBER 1963 • JOHN BURGESS

Another Springs Branch tank finds itself on an East Lancs service, with Fowler 2-6-4 No **42327** approaching Bolton on the 15:55 Manchester Victoria to Blackburn train. Note the fine signal gantry guarding the southern approach to Bolton Trinity Street Station.

2ND APRIL 1963 • D. HAMPSON

WIGAN CENTRAL TO MANCHESTER CENTRAL

On the closure of the former Great Central engine shed at Lower Ince in 1952, all its J10 0-6-0 locomotives were transferred to Springs Branch, which took over the workings on the Wigan Central to Manchester Central route. This coincided with the withdrawal of services over the St Helens Branch from Lowton St Mary's but the line continued to be used for trip freights. The ageing J10's gave way to more modern locos and the ex-LMS 2-6-4 tanks, supported by Ivatt 2-6-0's, became the staple motive power.

The fireman of J10 No 65170 replenishes the tender whilst running round its train prior to departure from Wigan Central to Manchester Central. **23RD AUGUST 1952** • H. C. CASSERLEY

The ex-GC passenger turns in 1952 under Springs Branch

Turn	Book on	Off shed	Train Working
54 SX	03:30	04:15	LE to Wigan C
		05:04	Wigan C - Irlam
		06:13	Irlam to Wigan C
28 6d	05:05	05:20	LE to Wigan C
		06:10	Wigan C - Man C
		07:38	Man C - Wigan C
59 6d	03:50	05:20	LE to Wigan C Gds, ecs to Wigan C
		06:21	Wigan C - Partington ecs to Glazebrook
		07:24	Glazebrook - Wigan C Loco does turn 30 later
46 SX	03:55	05:25	LE to Wigan C Gds, ecs to Wigan C
		06:34	Wigan C - Man C
		08:00	Man C - Lowton St Mary's
35 SX	05:05	06:35	LE to Lowton St Mary's
		07:25	Lowton SM - Irlam ecs to Lowton St Mary's
60 SX	14:20	14:35	LE to Lowton St Mary's
		15:26	Lowton SM - Wigan C ecs to Partington
		17:09	Partington - Wigan C
51 SX	15:40	16:25	LE to Risley
		17:50	Risley - Wigan C ecs to Lowton St Mary's

Shows first few workings only

A fine view of Wigan Central station with No **42554** ready to leave with the 1pm to Irlam. This was essentially a workmens' train, timed to coincide with the shift changes. The tank moved on to Bolton shed one month later. **2ND OCTOBER 1964** • PETER FITTON

The pattern of workings from 1952 was eight weekday through Wigan to Manchester Central trains. In addition there were others specifically for workmen, with two to Partington, three to Irlam (for Lancashire Steel) and one to Risley. In 1959 one of the Partington trains ceased and a year later, one of the Irlam's became a through train to Manchester Central. By 1961 the Risley train had been withdrawn, leaving a rather spartan service that continued until the line closed to passengers in November 1964.

Lowton St Mary's station provides the setting for No **42456** as it heads south on a Wigan Central to Manchester Central local train. During 1964, the shed's Black Fives and Standard Class 4's made occasional appearances as did Class 25 diesels from Trafford Park and the odd DMU. Springs Branch provided virtually all the motive power for this line and there were a considerable number of light engine movements between Wigan Central and the shed, particularly early morning and late evening.

2ND OCTOBER 1964 • I. G. HOLT

The cameraman captures 2-6-4T No 42572, deep in the cutting to the south of Lower Ince station. The Stanier locomotive is hauling a six coach train, probably from Irlam conveying the workmen from the steelworks and bound for Wigan Central. The bridge above carries the ex-L&Y Westwood Loop from Hindley to Pemberton, a route much used by the large number of coal trains to Liverpool via the L&Y.

8TH JUNE 1963 • JOHN BURGESS

Standard 4 4-6-0 No 75057 arrives at Bickershaw & Abram station, heading south on the last day of passenger services on this line. This loco was one of a batch of eight, all arriving from Derby shed during November 1963. They similarly left en-bloc for Skipton MPD in March 1965

1ST NOVEMBER 1964 • ALLAN HEYES

Taking the Wigan route from Glazebrook is Ivatt Mogul No **46448** on the 14:15 Irlam - Wigan Central train. This loco had three spells at the shed, finally moving on to Bescot in February 1962.

14TH SEPTEMBER 1959 • P. HUTCHINSON

Another of the Springs Branch stud of Stanier tank engines, No **42426,** waits to depart from Platform No 3 at Manchester Central with a Wigan train. This loco arrived from Upperby in February 1962 and stayed until November 1964 before going up the road to Bolton.

2ND APRIL 1964 • G. WHITEHEAD

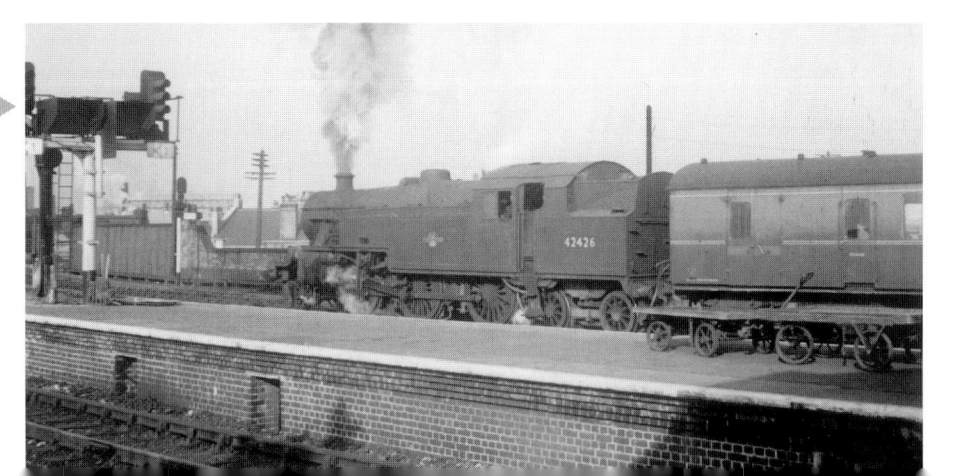

A superb view of the Wigan Central goods area as No 42494 arrives with the 14:15 from Irlam. To the left of the loco is the original terminus of the line at Darlington Street. The goods yard is to the right. Although double track existed from Glazebrook to here, the line was single into Central Station.

6TH SEPTEMBER 1964 • ALLAN HEYES

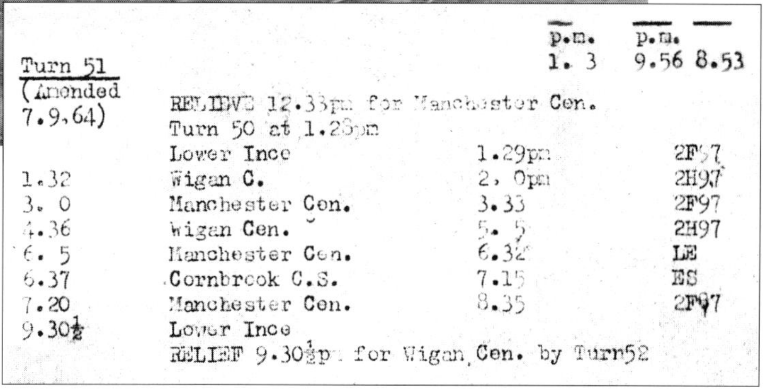

		p.m.	p.m.
Turn 51		1. 3	9.56 8.53
(Amended 7.9.64)	RELIEVES 12.33pm for Manchester Cen. Turn 50 at 1.28pm		
	Lower Ince	1.29pm	2F57
1.32	Wigan C.	2, 0pm	2H97
3. 0	Manchester Cen.	3.33	2F97
4.36	Wigan Cen.	5. 5	2H97
6. 5	Manchester Cen.	6.32	LE
6.37	Cornbrook C.S.	7.15	ES
7.20	Manchester Cen.	8.35	2F97
9.30½	Lower Ince		
	RELIEF 9.30½pm for Wigan Cen. by Turn52		

The line has a month to go and Wigan Central station is host to Standard Class 4 No **75015** in charge of the 2pm to Manchester Central. During the last year of the line, the Standards put in regular appearances, sharing duties with the 2-6-4 tanks.

2ND OCTOBER 1964 • PETER FITTON

Long term resident tank No 42456 is seen hauling the 15:33 from Manchester Central to Wigan Central and passes under the Wigan NW to Manchester Exchange line. The photographer is looking east, and the line crossing over the bridge (far left) is the access to Low Hall Colliery. The bridge slightly to the right allows one of the chords from Bickershaw Junction to dive under the ex-LNWR line and join the GC. The other chord can be seen above this bridge, running left to right to join the Manchester Exchange route at Bickershaw Junction. The view in the opposite direction is seen on page 99.

SEPTEMBER 1964 • TOM SUTCH

EXCURSIONS

Flagship engine No 45425 reverses past Llandudno No 1 signal box prior to departing for home. The loco's condition suggests that it has recently been used on Royal Train duty. On summer Saturdays, the morning local train from Wigan to Warrington was extended to Llandudno. In the 1940's the LMS also regularly ran an excursion to Llandudno during the Wigan Wakes week leaving at 7.30am and calling at Warrington, Rhyl and Colwyn Bay. Tommy Taylor joined his dad on one of these turns and describes the trip below.

AUGUST 1959 ● G. HARROP

"My father booked on at 6.45am to find the engine, a smart looking Black Five, already prepared and ready to go. From the shed exit we proceeded to Springs Branch North Sidings to collect the empty stock, then on to platform 4 at North Western station. After running round the train using platform 5, we coupled up and watched the passengers arrive, some armed with buckets and spades. It was time to fill the firebox with the larger lumps of coal, making sure the back corners were well filled. We departed bang on 7.30 onto the Up slow, whistling 'two and one' telling the bobby we were on the slow line and wanted the fast line which we duly got at Springs Branch. Then we could open her up for the run to Warrington. On this occasion the engine was fresh from overhaul at Crewe Works and the expectation was for a good trip, however, the engine seemed a bit sluggish and was reluctant to pick up speed on the easy run to Chester. On departure from Chester progress was reasonable but steam was leaking from several places with a bad blow from the left hand piston rod gland. Fortunately we were one of the early excursions down the coast so had a clear run as far as Rhyl, then it was on to Colwyn Bay and the customary stop outside of Llandudno Junction. From here it was a short run into Llandudno station and a well deserved rest.

The return trip was the 11:40 to Nelson and Colne and, although the fire had been cleaned, most of the firebox tubes were leaking and a river ran down the tubeplate. We never raised steam to full pressure, both injectors having to be left on all the way back to Wigan. Due to the volume of holiday traffic we had to stop at virtually every signal to Chester so had time to recover steam pressure. After 15 minutes stopped in the middle road at Chester station we were given a clear run to Wigan. On full regulator and 25% cut off she could not make more than 50 mph on the easiest of roads, however, a little leeway with the speed restrictions near Bamfurlong saw us finally arrived back in platform 4 at Wigan only 15 minutes late. From here an assisting engine was waiting to help over the 'alps' to Blackburn and we briefed the relieving crew on the condition of the loco before walking to the shed to book off".

The folk of Wigan were, and still are, staunch supporters of their Rugby League team, especially when they reach Wembley in the Challenge Cup final. A number of them gather on Wigan (NW) platform before the exodus to London hoping that they might appear in next week's local press. Jubilee 4-6-0 No **5668 Madden,** borrowed from Patricroft, is adorned with headboard and Reporting Number, although it's doubtful if the ribbon and replica cup would survive the journey. Play up they did. Wigan won 8 - 3 against Bradford Northern and a good day out was had by all. **8TH MAY 1948 ● AUTHOR'S COLLECTION**

Two specials were provided for the workforce of Coop & Co, Wigan for their annual outing to Blackpool. The first, leaving at 09:15, went behind Black Five No 45431 whilst the second, pictured here passing Skew Bridge, left 23 minutes later and is in the hands of sister engine No **45449**.

25TH AUGUST 1962 ● PETER FITTON

Super D's rarely saw passenger work but in earlier years, anything with wheels would be commandeered for use at the height of the summer. No **49119** became a Springs Branch engine after this date but it had been borrowed to haul a Blackpool North to Wigan return excursion on this occasion.

AUGUST 1938 ● FRANK DEAN

Another Blackpool excursion sees No 45521 Rhyl passing through the South Station, nearing the end of its journey on 1Z41 Wigan NW to Blackpool Central.

15TH SEPTEMBER 1962 ● PETER FITTON

A pair of Black Fives, Nos 44678 and 44962 haul the 09:53 excursion (1T81) out of St Helens Shaw Street en route to Wembley Central. The pair worked tender first from St Helens via Widnes before reversing at Ditton Junction. **21ST MAY 1966** ● **BEV PRICE**

Another Rugby League special, this one returning from Wigan after the derby game with St Helens. Black Five No **45026** has charge of one of four Rugex trains that day and is seen on 1Z18, the 17.09 Wigan NW to St Helens. The train is passing Pocket Nook Junction as it arrives at Shaw Street. The loading platform of a local glass bottle company is seen beyond the engine, with Pocket Nook signalbox above the rear coaches. Wigan lost 4-24 on this occasion. **12TH APRIL 1963** ● **BEV PRICE**

THE ROYAL TRAIN

Springs Branch engines and men were frequently involved with diagrams involving the Royal Train. Relatively near to the shed lay the quiet and secluded cutting at Lowton Manchester Curve which was considered to be a suitable and secure place to stable the Royal Train overnight when Royalty was aboard. It was utilised on a regular basis and even if the shed didn't provide the motive power for the train - which it frequently did - it would certainly provide the locomotive that steam heated it - usually a Super D. The favoured engines for the train itself during the BR period were the Black Fives of which Nos 45425, 45431 and 45449 were regular performers. Two engines were nearly always provided for cover in the event of failure. The tradition was maintained well into the diesel era when the shed usually provided English Electric Type 4's (Class 40's), again working in tandem. Such an occasion fell on 7th September 1973 when Springs Branch men were observed busily preparing Class 40's 308/9 for a forthcoming Royal working.

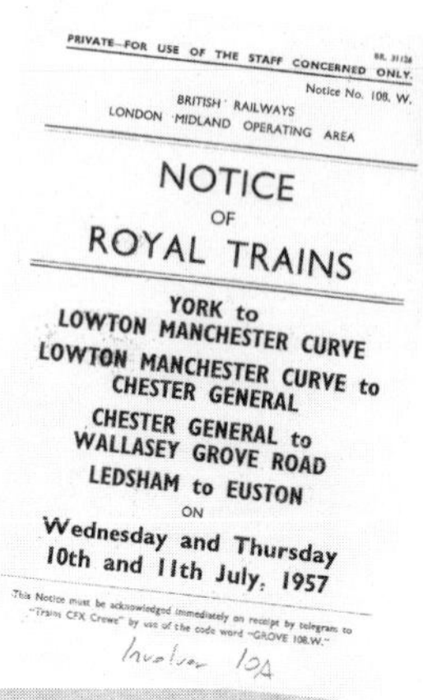

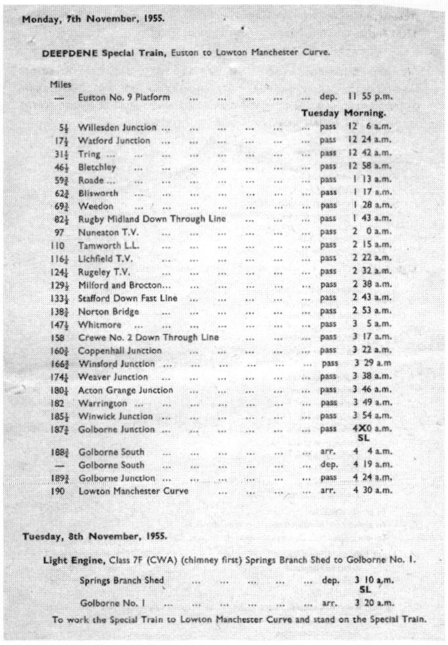

Polished up and ready to go, the shed has provided No **45425** on this occasion. Springs Branch men (L-R) Ben Bainbridge, Harry Ackers, Tommy Taylor and Frank Jennings pose for the record. Note all four have clean overalls and are wearing ties. The crews for the Royal train tended to be selected from those men considered most experienced and courteous.
1957 ● **COURTESY MARGARET TAYLOR**

Driver Tommy Taylor and Fireman Frank Jennings.
1957 ● **COURTESY MARGARET TAYLOR**

Black Fives Nos 45449 & 45431 stand at the rear of the shed buffed up and ready for duty. **20TH MAY 1961** ● **RICHARD STRANGE**

FREIGHT WORKINGS

Rebuilt Patriot No 45530 *Sir Frank Ree* forges past Springs Branch with a northbound mixed freight and overtakes engine and brake van on the Down Slow. The Black Five is a local engine - No **45108**. **6TH SEPTEMBER 1965 ● TOM HEAVYSIDE**

WIGAN AREA FREIGHT OPERATIONS

The majority of freight movements in the Wigan area involved the yards near the shed, namely Bamfurlong Yard, Ince Moss Sidings and Springs Branch North Sidings, and freight trains started from all these yards, depending on the destination. Engine Shed Sidings, the yard alongside the shed, was mainly used in connection with local trip workings. The freight turns from Springs Branch shed were divided into five groups, depending on whether the work was yard work, local, banking or further afield.

1 - BOOKED FREIGHT Regular timetabled freight trains worked by engines off the shed to the likes of Carlisle, Carnforth, Preston, Birkenhead, Warrington, Edge Hill and Northwich.

2 - TRIPS Involved workings to/from local Colliery sidings and small yards, generally to/from yards in the Bamfurlong area.

3 - SHUNTS Engines employed shunting local yards.

4 - BANKERS Banking engines employed for assisting trains over graded sections, generally from Bamfurlong over the Whelley line.

5 - SPECIAL FREIGHT Non Timetabled freight trains arranged and run as required.

Whilst Bamfurlong Yard was the hub of freight operations in the Wigan Area, it might be conceivable to believe that it would be dealing mainly with coal traffic. The actual situation was much the opposite, as during the late 1950's and early 60's, about 75% of traffic through the yard was general merchandise. In the mid-1960's plans were well advanced for a new marshalling yard at Golborne, just south of Bamfurlong, to replace the Wigan yards, however it never materialised.

Much of the coal went directly from the collieries to the power stations and rail heads/docks.

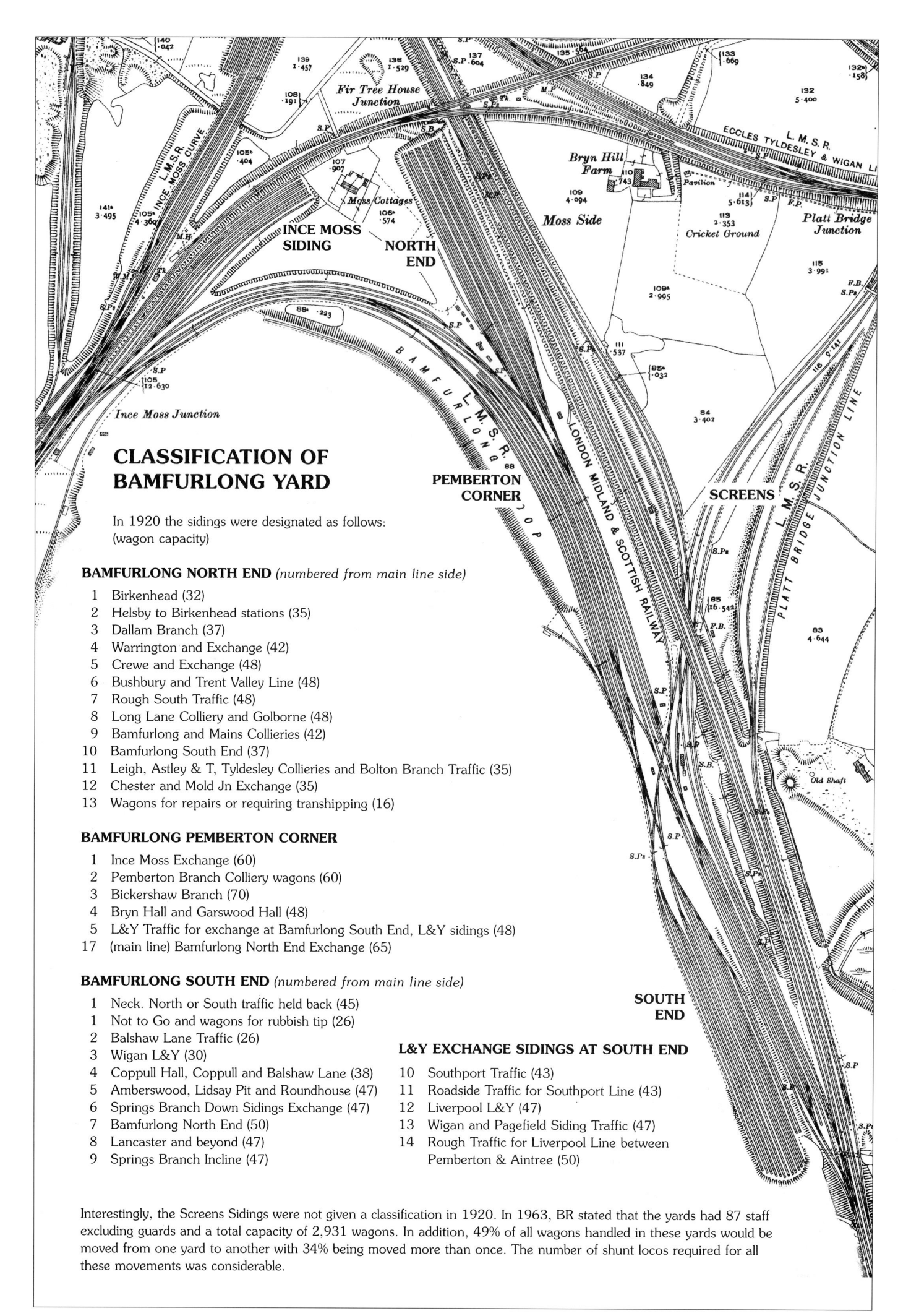

CLASSIFICATION OF BAMFURLONG YARD

In 1920 the sidings were designated as follows:
(wagon capacity)

BAMFURLONG NORTH END *(numbered from main line side)*

1. Birkenhead (32)
2. Helsby to Birkenhead stations (35)
3. Dallam Branch (37)
4. Warrington and Exchange (42)
5. Crewe and Exchange (48)
6. Bushbury and Trent Valley Line (48)
7. Rough South Traffic (48)
8. Long Lane Colliery and Golborne (48)
9. Bamfurlong and Mains Collieries (42)
10. Bamfurlong South End (37)
11. Leigh, Astley & T, Tyldesley Collieries and Bolton Branch Traffic (35)
12. Chester and Mold Jn Exchange (35)
13. Wagons for repairs or requiring transhipping (16)

BAMFURLONG PEMBERTON CORNER

1. Ince Moss Exchange (60)
2. Pemberton Branch Colliery wagons (60)
3. Bickershaw Branch (70)
4. Bryn Hall and Garswood Hall (48)
5. L&Y Traffic for exchange at Bamfurlong South End, L&Y sidings (48)
17. (main line) Bamfurlong North End Exchange (65)

BAMFURLONG SOUTH END *(numbered from main line side)*

1. Neck. North or South traffic held back (45)
1. Not to Go and wagons for rubbish tip (26)
2. Balshaw Lane Traffic (26)
3. Wigan L&Y (30)
4. Coppull Hall, Coppull and Balshaw Lane (38)
5. Amberswood, Lidsay Pit and Roundhouse (47)
6. Springs Branch Down Sidings Exchange (47)
7. Bamfurlong North End (50)
8. Lancaster and beyond (47)
9. Springs Branch Incline (47)

L&Y EXCHANGE SIDINGS AT SOUTH END

10. Southport Traffic (43)
11. Roadside Traffic for Southport Line (43)
12. Liverpool L&Y (47)
13. Wigan and Pagefield Siding Traffic (47)
14. Rough Traffic for Liverpool Line between Pemberton & Aintree (50)

Interestingly, the Screens Sidings were not given a classification in 1920. In 1963, BR stated that the yards had 87 staff excluding guards and a total capacity of 2,931 wagons. In addition, 49% of all wagons handled in these yards would be moved from one yard to another with 34% being moved more than once. The number of shunt locos required for all these movements was considerable.

BAMFURLONG YARD

Situated just a few hundred yards from Springs Branch Shed, Bamfurlong played a massive part in the whole freight operation handling. The scale of the operation can be revealed by figures extracted from February 1963 traffic analysis documents. In 1961, for example, 70,000 wagons were handled per month in the Wigan area. Although given the collective title of Bamfurlong Sorting Sidings, there were really four distinct parts to the yard.

NORTH END SIDINGS. A fan of thirteen dead end roads. Trains for Warrington, Crewe, Birkenhead and the Patricroft area departed from this yard.

SOUTH END SIDINGS. Two fans of sidings - the 'Wessie' side (ex-LNWR) consisting of nine dead end roads and the 'Lanky' side (ex-L&Y) which had five. All roads had buffer stops at the South end. Used for departures to Carlisle, Hellifield, Aintree, Southport, Bolton and Blackburn.

PEMBERTON CORNER. A group of sidings lying virtually between the two gridirons which curved from the South round towards the West (Ince Moss) end of the complex. Many of these were through roads and this allowed much flexibility with the marshalling of trains. Only the odd train departed from this yard, such as the 13:30 Trip 138 to Atherton Bag Lane.

BAMFURLONG SCREENS. About six sidings (varied over the years) on the East side of the Main Line which could only be accessed from the Whelley Line or by reversing from the Main Line. Some through trains were shunted here and freight to the Western Region used this yard.

The L&Y had running rights into Bamfurlong Yard and also their own sidings at the South Gridiron (South end). Their trains mainly served the likes of Aintree, Fazakerley and Southport. Prior to the former GC coming under Springs Branch, their trip freights could exchange traffic via Amberswood Sidings. Direct freights also ran to destinations such as Glazebrook, Lowton and Dewsnap from Bamfurlong Yard.

There were also two other significant yards close by that were used in a similar manner:

INCE MOSS SIDINGS. Trains to Clock Face, Liverpool, Widnes and Ordsall Lane departed from this yard. Lying North and West of Bamfurlong, there were sidings on both the North and South sides of the line. Those to the North were originally used during shunting operations at the West end of Springs Branch North Sidings and also traffic leaving the adjacent Ince Moss Colliery, which closed in 1962. In later years they were used for the Ince Moss tip (an area used heavily from the late 1950's for dumping of virtually any railway rubbish) and from the 1980's mainly for permanent way spoil (used ballast). There were eight dead end sidings on the south side, facing west.

SPRINGS BRANCH NORTH SIDINGS. Trains to Preston, Carnforth, Wyre Dock and Blackburn departed from this yard. Situated directly across the main line from the engine shed, this set of twelve roads curved round towards Ince Moss Junction. This yard was generally used by Down trains. In the mid 1960's, some Bamfurlong departures were re-directed to depart from North Sidings.

SPRINGS BRANCH UP SIDINGS. Situated just west of the shed and also known as Engine Shed Sidings. Used chiefly for trip workings, especially those involved with the incline.

A panoramic view of the Bamfurlong complex looking south from Fir Tree House Junction.   SUMMER 1965   IRWELL PRESS

SCREENS   NORTH END   PEMBERTON CORNER

BOOKED FREIGHT

The regular booked freight trains from the Wigan area didn't vary much during the LMS and BR periods, and a few can be traced back to Pre-Grouping days. It was the mid 1960's when major changes occurred. Of significance over the years was the gradual decline of traffic, in particular coal. During the LMS period there had been daily freights to Birmingham, Bushbury, Dewsnap, Oxenholme, Rugby and Shrewsbury, but these barely continued into BR days. Freights were not necessarily all 'Out and Back' as there were several inbound workings with no apparent balancing outbound train. For example, the 21:08 Buxton to Bamfurlong which appears to have arrived at Buxton from the Chester area with a Springs Branch engine. There had been freights running directly from collieries to power stations from at least 1937 with a 12:20 Bickershaw Colliery to Bullfield and a 17:05 Garswood to Halliwell appearing in the working timetable. By the mid 1960's this type of operation had increased considerably. leaving far less traffic for the local yards to handle.

The GC tended to run 'Trip Freights' and these are dealt with in the 'Trip' section. Before Wigan L&Y shed closed, the only turns worked by Springs Branch crews over L&Y metals were the morning Bamfurlong - Halliwell and the afternoon Chanters - Kearsley. When the ex-L&Y duties were taken over, they consisted of a few local workings which, in many cases, became 'Trips' from Springs Branch. Looking at the principal freight workings in the table below, those shown represent the regular ongoing daily trains that ran for a significant period. Short lived freights or those operating on a 'one day only' basis are not included. It also reveals the same trains operated, albeit at slightly different times over many decades.

PRINCIPAL FREIGHT ORIGINATING FROM WIGAN YARDS

Lower Darwen loco	H	00:55	MX	S Branch N Sidings	Farington Junction	Direct	Ran to Lostock Hall in 1960's
	H	02:25	MX	S Branch N Sidings	Blackburn	Mixed, Direct	Ran from LMS days through
	J	04:15	MX	S Branch N Sidings	Carnforth	Mixed, Shunts at Lancaster	
	J	07:26	SX	S Branch N Sidings	Wyre Dock	Mixed, Shunts at Kirkham	Ran from LMS days through
	H	09:30	SX	S Branch N Sidings	Ribble Sidings	Direct	
L&Y JOB	K	10:25	6d	S Branch N Sidings	Blackburn	Shunts at Chorley & Heapey	Ran from LMS days through
	J	14:10	SX	S Branch N Sidings	Farington Junction	Mixed	Ran to Lostock Hall in 1960's
	J	14:15	SX	S Branch N Sidings	Carnforth	Mixed	Ran from 1957 through
	J	19:00	SX	S Branch N Sidings	Farington Junction	Mixed, Direct	To Bamber Bridge in 1960's
	J	21:00	SX	S Branch N Sidings	Wyre Dock	Mainly coal, Shunts Blainscough & Kirkham	
	H	02:10	MX	Bamfurlong SE	Carlisle	Direct	
L&Y JOB	H	02:40	MX	Bamfurlong SE	Aintree		
Lower Darwen loco	E	02:45	MX	Bamfurlong SE	Colne	Mixed	Ran from LMS days to 1957
L&Y JOB	H	04:50	MX	Bamfurlong SE	Aintree		Ran until 1961
L&Y JOB	H	07:00	6d	Bamfurlong SE	Blackburn	Mixed, Shunts White Bear or Chorley	Ran from LMS days through
L&Y JOB	J	07:24	SX	Bamfurlong SE	Ormskirk, later Rainford		
L&Y JOB	K	08:15	SX	Bamfurlong SE	Southport		
	E	09:40	MSX	Bamfurlong SE	Carlisle Canal via S&C	Direct, Later only to Hellifield	Finished 1961
L&Y JOB	J	14:50	6d	Bamfurlong SE	Aintree		Ran until 1961
Not SB JOB	H	21:50	SX	Bamfurlong SE	Blackburn	Direct	
L&Y JOB	H	22:30	6d	Bamfurlong SE	Southport		
	H	03:25	MX	Bamfurlong NE	Arpley	Shunts Winwick Quay, Warrington S End Yard	
	H	05:05	MX	Bamfurlong NE	Crewe Gresty Ln		
Birkenhead loco	J	06:00	6d	Bamfurlong NE	Birkenhead	Shunts Winwick Quay, Ellesmere Port & Hooton	
	K	08:25	6d	Bamfurlong NE	Astley Gn/Patricroft	Shunts Kenyon Jn & Pumping Station	Ran until 1961
	J	10:30	6d	Bamfurlong NE	Dallam Sdgs	Shunts Cross Tetley, later Golborne & Winwick Quay	
	J	10:40	6d	Bamfurlong NE	Northwich	Mixed, Calls Walton Old Junction	Ran from 1957
	E	11:55	SX	Bamfurlong NE	Crewe Basford Hall	Mixed	Ran until 1957
	J	17:55	6d	Bamfurlong NE	Dallam Sidings	Mixed, Later SX, Shunts Golborne Line Collieries	
Not L&Y JOB	J	08:55	6d	Bamfurlong Sidings	Halliwell	Coal, Shunts Westhoughton & Bullfield	
L&Y JOB	J	17:50	6d	Bamfurlong Sidings	Bullfield	Coal, Later SX	
L&Y JOB	J	20:20	SX	Bamfurlong Sidings	Burnden (Bury in LMS)	Coal, Shunts Westhoughton & Bullfield	
Sutton Oak men	K	00:45	MX	Ince Moss Junction	Clock Face	Coal	
	J	10:00	6d	Ince Moss Junction	Garston	Mainly Coal	
	K	11:00	6d	Ince Moss Junction	Widnes	Incl Chemicals, Shunts Clock Face	
	J	18:30	6d	Ince Moss Junction	Clock Face	Coal, Shunts Garswood & Ravenhead Junction	
	J	19:20	6d	Ince Moss Junction	Edge Hill	Mixed, Shunts Garswood Hall & St Helens	
	J	20:10	6d	Ince Moss Junction	Garston	Coal	Ran until 1961
	K	23:45	6d	Ince Moss Junction	Weaste	Mixed, Direct	
GC Line	K	10:30	6d	Bamfurlong	West Leigh & Bedford	Mainly Coal, Later SX and to Lowton St Marys	
	C	20:25	SX	Wigan North Western	Chester	Fish, runs FO as required. Portion off Wyre Dock to Broad Street	

The following pages feature a selection of the daytime freights with their Springs Branch engines.

THE 08:54 BAMFURLONG - HALLIWELL
(later 09:20 Abram North-Halliwell)

Starting from the sorting sidings at Bamfurlong, this train would have the banker on the front as it climbed past Amberswood Junctions and along the Whelley line to De Trafford Junction. At this point it was allowed 26 minutes to complete the reversal, and the train engine (which had banked the train up from Bamfurlong) was now at the head and the banker would assist round the curve to Hindley - quite a steep gradient itself. The consist of this train was mainly coal for the Back O'Th' Barn Power Station at Bolton. When it originated from Bamfurlong, other traffic could be conveyed and deposited where required, for the train was originally booked to shunt at Westhoughton and Bullfield. The vans may have possibly been left at Bolton goods yard. In 1966 it was retimed to depart from Bamfurlong at 05:32, but no longer called anywhere en route.

During the following year it was again retimed and started from Abram North, the exchange sidings for Bickershaw Colliery, at 09:20. From here the train ran through Platt Bridge and Springs Branch to Wigan No 1 where it reversed and took the ex-L&Y line directly to Bolton.

Super D No 49438 passes the sidings at Lostock Junction with the 08:54 Bamfurlong to Halliwell. The 32 lever Lostock Sidings South signal box closed on 4th April 1967.
25TH APRIL 1962 • PETER FITTON

The 09:20 Abram North to Halliwell coal, now running via Wigan NW, passes by the shed hauled by No **45350**.
31ST MARCH 1967 • ALLAN HEYES

10:40 BAMFURLONG NORTH END - NORTHWICH

This train first appeared in the 1956 Working Timetable, calling at Walton Old Junction yard and Wallerscote Sidings. The front (Northwich) section was hopper wagons for the ICI plant. The turn started with a light engine from the shed. On this occasion the loco concerned had been prepared by another crew who would then proceed on to other work. The loco was allowed 30 minutes to travel from Springs Branch shed to Bamfurlong North End yard, couple up and prepare to leave. From the Grid Iron Sidings at North End Yard, this train would then proceed south through the reception sidings, Bamfurlong Sorting Sidings and Bamfurlong Junction. So as to avoid stopping on the incline up to Bamfurlong Junction, a clear road would usually be made available to allow the train enough momentum to tackle the incline unassisted. This working had a balancing return trip leaving Northwich at 14:45. Historically, this had been a Super D or WD turn, but by 1965 it was booked for a Black Five with the following schedule.

Stanier Class Five No 45372 is caught working the 10:40 Bamfurlong - Northwich near Golborne. The loco is in ex-works condition

30TH OCTOBER 1963 • JOHN BURGESS

```
Turn 484                                              09 53  18 40  8 47
         ONE CLASS 5 (EX. L.M.S. 4-6-0)
         ENGINE PREPARED By Turns 358 (MO) 440 (MSX)
         Springs Branch M.P.D.  10 03   LE     SX
         Bamfurlong             10 33   8F24   SX
13 50    Northwich              14 45   7K67   SX
18 05    Bamfurlong                     LE     SX
18 20    Springs Branch M.P.D.
         Engine Prepared by Turn 421 (SO)           )
         Springs Nranch M.P.D.  10 03   LE     SO   )
         Bamfurlong N.E.        10 33   8F24   SO   )  COMM 11 SEPT
13 50    Northwich              15 00   6P54   SO   )
18 02    Bamfurlong                     LE     SO   )
18 17    Springs Branch
```

WD 2-8-0 No 90173 approaches Winwick Junction with the train. Note the wooden bodied buffer wagon behind the tender.

3RD SEPTEMBER 1962 • JOHN BURGESS

Another WD - No 90268, this time at Cross Tetley Sidings. The train was often lengthy and, once more, a pair of wooden bodied buffer wagons are in evidence

13TH OCTOBER 1962 • JOHN BURGESS

14:40 SPRINGS BRANCH NORTH SIDINGS - RIBBLE SIDINGS

This Class K freight turn would start out from Springs Branch North Sidings and the fireman would have put plenty of coal in the box so as to have a good supply of steam to tackle Boar's Head Bank, a formidable climb of two miles starting at Wigan North Western Station. The gradient varied from 1 in 116 to its steepest of 1 in 80 and quite a few trains came to grief here over the years. On such occasions the Wigan Bank Engine (NW pilot) would be summoned to come up behind the train to offer the necessary assistance. The incline continued for another four miles beyond Boar's Head but the gradient became much easier after this point.

Stanier Mogul No 42960 departs from North Sidings with the 14:40 to Ribble Sidings, calling at Coppull and Blainscough yards.
10TH APRIL 1964 • JOHN BURGESS

18:50 SPRINGS BRANCH NORTH SIDINGS - WYRE DOCK

Rebuilt Patriot No 45521 *Rhyl* heads the 07:10 Springs Branch to Fleetwood Wyre Dock past Skew Bridge. The formation of this train was mainly coal for the docks at Fleetwood.
19TH JUNE 1963 • PETER FITTON

18:08 SPRINGS BRANCH - BAMBER BRIDGE

This train can be traced back to 1948, when it called at various collieries en route to Farington Yard. The turn started with the engine leaving the shed at 17:48 before making its way to Springs Branch North Sidings, on the opposite side of the main line from the shed. To prevent congestion across all the main lines, it would almost certainly go via Crompton's Sidings Signal Box to Platt Bridge Junction, (reverse) then over Fir Tree to Ince Moss Junction (reverse) and onto its train in the North Sidings. The train consist was a mixed lot with all types of wagons conveyed. From North Sidings, the Whelley Line couldn't be used unless a reverse to Ince Moss Junction was undertaken, so the main line via Wigan North Western Station would be the route to Bamber Bridge. From 1967 this train became the 18:50 Abram North to Ribble Sidings Class 9 coal train.

Passing the shed is Standard Class 4 No 75041 hauling the 18:08 Springs Branch - Bamber Bridge. On this occasion the train appears to have started out from Bamfurlong.

22ND JUNE 1964 • **ALLAN HEYES**

WD 2-8-0 No 90686 passes Standish Junction on 18:08 Springs Branch North Sidings to Bamber Bridge freight.

15TH MAY 1964 • **ALLAN HEYES**

```
                                                    p.m.   a.m.
                                                    4/48
turn 553. Amended    Turn 553                       5.3   12.47  7.44
     3/2/64         (Amended
                     3.2.64)   Springs Bchm MPD    5.48pm  LE    SX
                               Springs Bch          6. 8   9L06  SX
                    7.35pm     Bamber Bridge        8.55   LE    SX
                    9.10       Preston N.U.        11.14   7K28  SX
                    12.12am    Bamfurlong Jn.              LE    MX
                    12.27      Springs Bch. MPD
```

11:30 PARKSIDE COLLIERY - WHITEBIRK

This is one of the new services that commenced in 1966, although a mineral train had run in similar timings from Springs Branch Engine Shed Sidings to Preston North Union yard since the late 1950's. The late 1960's was a period when substantially more coal was moved directly from source to end user. On this turn the engine went light to Parkside Colliery, accessing at Newton-le-Willows and hence via Wigan, Euxton Junction and Blackburn to near Accrington. The return working, the 12:20 SX Whitebirk to Parkside Colliery, brought the empties back to Parkside ready for another trip. The engine then retired to Springs Branch shed.

Blackburn station is awakened by Stanier 8F 2-8-0 No 48187 thundering through with the 11:30 Parkside Colliery to Whitebirk. No fewer than three clocks are visible - all set at differing times!   **SEPTEMBER 1966 • ALLAN HEYES**

Turn 380	ONE CLASS 8F (STD 2.8.0)					
	19 June to 4 Sept				06 30	- -
	Springs Bch. M.P.D.	07 30	LE	SO		
07 55	Parkside Colly	08 15	8P11	SO		
11 00	Whitebirk	12 34	8F44	SO		
14 30	Parkside Colly	-	LE	SO		
	Springs Bch. M.P.D.					
	Except Sats 19 June to 4 Sept					
	Springs Bch M.P.D.	08 15	LE	D	07 15	- --
8 35	Parkside Colly	09 00	8P11	D		
11 58	Whitebirk	12 20	8F44	SX		
15 35	Parkside Colly					
11 58	Whitebirk	13 10	8F44	SO		
15 10	Parkside Colly		LE	D		
	Springs Branch M.P.D.					

18:50 ABRAM NORTH - RIBBLE SIDINGS

Leaving Wigan behind, 8F No 48261 works the 18:08 Abram North to Ribble Sidings coal train up the 1 in 104 Boar's Head Bank.
19TH JUNE 1967 ● **ALLAN HEYES**

Abram North was the point where exchange sidings were situated to serve the Bickershaw Colliery complex. Coal wagons were marshalled into trains and this particular working would travel via Bickershaw Junction to Springs Branch, where it would join the West Coast Main Line. The train would then climb up Boar's Head bank and continue to Ribble sidings. Again, these were exchange sidings on the Down (West) side of the main line, about half a mile South of Preston Station. From Ribble Sidings, some of the coal wagons would probably go down the steep branch to Preston Docks and some would go to local coal yards and be available as domestic fuel.

BUXTON

Somewhat off its beaten track is LMS 0-8-0 No **9564** emerging from the south end of Dove Holes Tunnel en-route to Buxton. According to records, there wasn't a direct working from any of the Wigan yards to Buxton and this engine's presence on the former Midland main line is probably the result of a more complex diagram. There was a regular evening freight from Buxton to Bamfurlong but the outward working appears to have been via Hooton or Birkenhead. The 'Austin Sevens', as they were referred to, were more associated with the ex-L&Y routes and several worked out of the town's L&Y shed. No 9564 became a Springs Branch engine for a mere nine months in 1937, but none were allocated during the BR period.

1937 ● **STEAM IMAGE**

OVER SHAP

Although Springs Branch crews worked freights from the Wigan yards through to Carlisle, these turns were chiefly overnight. In addition to these jobs, the depot's engines could be found continuing other diagrams which would take them over Shap with crews from other depots.

◂ **Having been offered the road, No 44962** comes out of the Down loop at Shap Summit with a northbound freight. The closure of Springs Branch MPD to steam eight weeks later brought about this loco's demise.

11TH OCTOBER 1967 ● **TOM HEAVYSIDE**

No 44873 makes a stirring sight whilst tackling the 1 in 75 Shap incline with the aid of a banker. The passing time is recorded as 09:50 and this train may well be the Camden - Carlisle fast fitted freight running late.
30TH JULY 1965 ● **M. WELCH**

Similarly Springs Branch crews would work engines from other depots such as Carlisle, Carnforth or Crewe. They would return with Warrington or Crewe bound freights, most likely being relieved at Bamfurlong Sorting Sidings by Dallam or Crewe men. There would also be some additional 'Control' freight workings which could again take the engines and crew over Shap.

A northbound Class F freight breasts the summit at ▸ Shap with yet another of the depot's complement of Black Fives. The loco on this occasion was No **45281**.

11TH OCTOBER 1967 ● **TOM HEAVYSIDE**

THE CARLISLE LODGING TURNS

Super D No 9140 passes over Dillicar troughs on the approach to Tebay with a northbound freight. c1935 • STEAM IMAGE

LNWR records dated 14th January 1910 show that the shed had lodging turns to Carlisle, Shrewsbury and even as close as Birkenhead, Sutton Oak and Wyre Dock at Fleetwood. By the mid 1930's the shed had a through Carlisle freight with two returning Up trains. Additional traffic for Carlisle from Bamfurlong was forwarded on from Preston and Carnforth within other trains. By 1951 the through trains had increased to two out and two back with a couple of single day trips (Saturday or Monday only), but by the mid 1950's the through freights had increased considerably with two out via Shap and one via the Settle & Carlisle route with four returning (all via Shap) plus five single day and five Sunday trains. This represented the peak of the service as it then tailed off and, by 1964, there was but one outward and two return trains to Carlisle, plus two Saturday Only runs and no Sunday trains.

Stanier Mogul 2-6-0 No 42954 toils up the bank at Shap Wells just after 08:00 with the overnight 01:43 Bamfurlong to Carlisle freight. The loco is hardly in the best of condition and of further interest are the engineers' vehicles at the front of the train. Fairburn tank No **42095** brings up the rear. 4TH JUNE 1965 • M. WELCH

By the end of steam there only remained the 14:40 Bamfurlong to Carlisle with no balancing return, although the loco would have worked to another yard such as Warrington. It is of interest that many Up freights from Carlisle arrived at Ince Moss Junction with a few coming into the Screens Sidings, however all freights in the Down direction left from Bamfurlong Sorting Sidings. During the LNWR and LMS periods, the Super D's would often tackle these Carlisle freights and, despite complaints from enginemen attempting to obtain a fresh engine, the same loco would always be waiting for them on their return. In later years, Stanier 2-6-0's and WD's were occasionally utilised but the Black Fives became the main locomotives, being ideally suited for these duties. In the 1950's and 60's, Upperby shed had numerous Patriots, Jubilees and Scots as well as Black Fives to call on and all were common visitors on these workings. From 1965, Kingmoor Britannia Pacifics were regularly observed, again residing on the shed between turns.

During the British Railways era, only one regular lodging turn remained - the early morning Carlisle freight. Booked for a Black 5 and often an Upperby engine, the train left from the neck at Bamfurlong Sorting Sidings, having been marshalled during the previous day. It comprised a mixed freight and would take the Whelley line from Bamfurlong through to Standish Junction. The train was booked to arrive at Carlisle around 10.00am whereupon the men would lodge before bringing the 9.50pm freight back the following day.

Springs Branch Driver *Tommy Taylor* also recalls another regular Carlisle job where Springs Branch supplied 'men only' forward from Wigan. They relieved Edge Hill men who brought in the train which had originated at Garston. A typical trip was a train consisting of up to 40 vans, all fitted with vacuum brakes.

'Crab' 2-6-0 No 42894 crosses the River Ribble on the southern approaches to the Sidings at Preston with a northbound freight, described as above and possibly bound for Carlisle.

21ST DECEMBER 1963 ● PETER FITTON

Super D 0-8-0 No 9055 approaches ▷ the camera at no more than walking pace on the familiar northbound ascent of Shap. It was rather unusual to find a member of the class carrying a makeshift front number.

1935 ● P. WILSON

OTHER FREIGHT

The following three pages offer a selection of Springs Branch engines engaged in other freight work. Identification of trains is always difficult due to the lack of visible information, although the load can sometimes give clues to the possible originating point or destination.

A loco that spent over 15 years at the shed, Black Five No **45408** heads past Springs Branch with a northbound freight.

28TH AUGUST 1965 ● JOHN BURGESS

Heading south towards Golborne with either a Warrington or Crewe bound freight is No **49447**.

1ST JUNE 1962 ● JOHN BURGESS

It was unusual to find a pair of Standard Class 4 4-6-0s working in tandem. On this occasion Nos **75057** and **75011** (both Springs Branch engines) are caught hauling a northbound mixed freight at Springs Branch. Both these locos came from Derby in November 1963 and both left for Skipton in March 1965.

10TH APRIL 1964 ● JOHN BURGESS

Heading north past the famous Carnforth clock immortalised in the epic film *Brief Encounter* is Wigan Super D 0-8-0 No **49154**. The mixed freight is bound for Kendal and was probably a special working for although Springs Branch had booked freights to Carnforth, there were none to Kendal in the Working Timetable for the period. Perhaps some of the vans were in association with the K shoe factory, a major employer in the town.

29TH AUGUST 1960 ● PETER FITTON

▲ **The open expanse of Winwick Junction** remains an attraction for a succession of railway photographers. Class Five No **45395** passes on the Down Fast at 2.50pm with a fitted freight. **23RD MARCH 1967** ● M. WELCH

Running down the bank from Standish Junction is Royal Scot No ▶ **46115** *Scots Guardsman.* The engine is entrusted with the 14:53 Wyre Dock to London Broad Street fish, which will split at Wigan NW, with a portion going forward to Chester. **17TH JUNE 1964** ● ALLAN HEYES

◀ **A Down freight passes Farington Curve Junction** behind Standard Class 4 No **75042** with what is possibly china clay or sand in the formation.

24TH JULY 1964 ● PETER FITTON

9F 2-10-0 No 92109 and an unidentified Black Five in early mist at Springs Branch with breakdown cranes.

4TH NOVEMBER 1967 • ALLAN HEYES

Class 4F 0-6-0 No 44121, standing on the Up Slow line, assists with ballast operation at Leyland Coal Sidings at 16:25.

25TH APRIL 1962 • PETER FITTON

Super D No 49447 brings a northbound mixed freight past Springs Branch.

24TH AUGUST 1961 • JOHN BURGESS

Trip, Shunt and Banking Workings

TRIP WORKINGS

Virtually all Motive Power Depots had local trip workings and Springs Branch had, perhaps, more than most. By the end of the 19th Century there were dozens of collieries which fanned out in all directions and within close proximity of the shed. All were catered for and records reveal that in 1920, a period late in the LNWR era, the local coalfields were sufficiently productive to require a total of 29 Springs Branch Trip Workings. From then on, however, it was a case of gradual decline. By 1937 this number had reduced to 20 and by 1951 there remained but 15. The situation further deteriorated and by 1965 there were a mere 8 Trip Workings. A handful survived into the 1970's.

In 1963, BR stated that practically the whole of the local trip service was engaged in clearing local collieries. Another factor in the 'Trip Work' decline was that from the mid 1960's, more coal was going directly from the main collieries such as Bickershaw to the end users, for example the power stations at Halliwell (Bolton), Whitebirk or Kearsley. From 1976, an underground tunnel connected Bickershaw Colliery with Parkside and Golborne pits, after which all coal dispatch was concentrated on Bickershaw, where an MGR system operated until 1992, at which time the last of the coalfields closed. Other trip workings that did not involve coal continued for a while and there were local jobs to Horwich Works and Chorley ROF until their respective closures.

TRIP WORKINGS TO THE NORTH

Trippers worked through Wigan NW station to Rylands Siding, Victoria Colliery and along the Preston line, generally as far as Farington Sidings. Alternatively they would run via the Whelley line, calling at its sidings, then on to join the Preston route at Standish Junction, also serving the sidings (mainly collieries) to Farington. Both these routes could also trip through to Brinscall and Chorley via Adlington Junction. Springs Branch enginemen report that ex-L&Y 0-6-0s locos were the only BR engines allowed into Victoria colliery yard.

TRIP WORKINGS TO THE EAST (ex-L&Y lines)

These went via the Whelley line to De Trafford Junction (reverse), then to several destinations in the Bolton area. Whilst most of the services on this route were undertaken by the Lanky there were a couple of turns operated by Springs Branch to Bullfield and Kearsley (for Power Station) so the majority of traffic was coal.

TRIP WORKINGS TO THE EAST (ex-LNWR lines)

Via Bickershaw Junction on the Manchester line to sidings on the Tyldesley route to Howe Bridge West but some continuing through Atherton Bag Lane to Bolton Fletcher St. Also to sidings along the Bickershaw Branch to Kenyon Junction (closed 1965 but had little traffic in the latter years), some returning direct from Kenyon Junction to Bamfurlong via Lowton and Golborne. Although originating from 1877, Bickershaw Colliery was the principal pit in this area, having been modernised in 1933 and again in 1951. In the diesel era, it was connected by underground tunnels to two other collieries and all output was dispatched from Bickershaw.

TRIP WORKINGS TO THE SOUTH

Along the Warrington route calling at yards, (virtually all colliery sidings) usually as far as Haydock and Earlestown Wagon Works and some trips would go to Bickershaw via Kenyon Junction and vice versa.

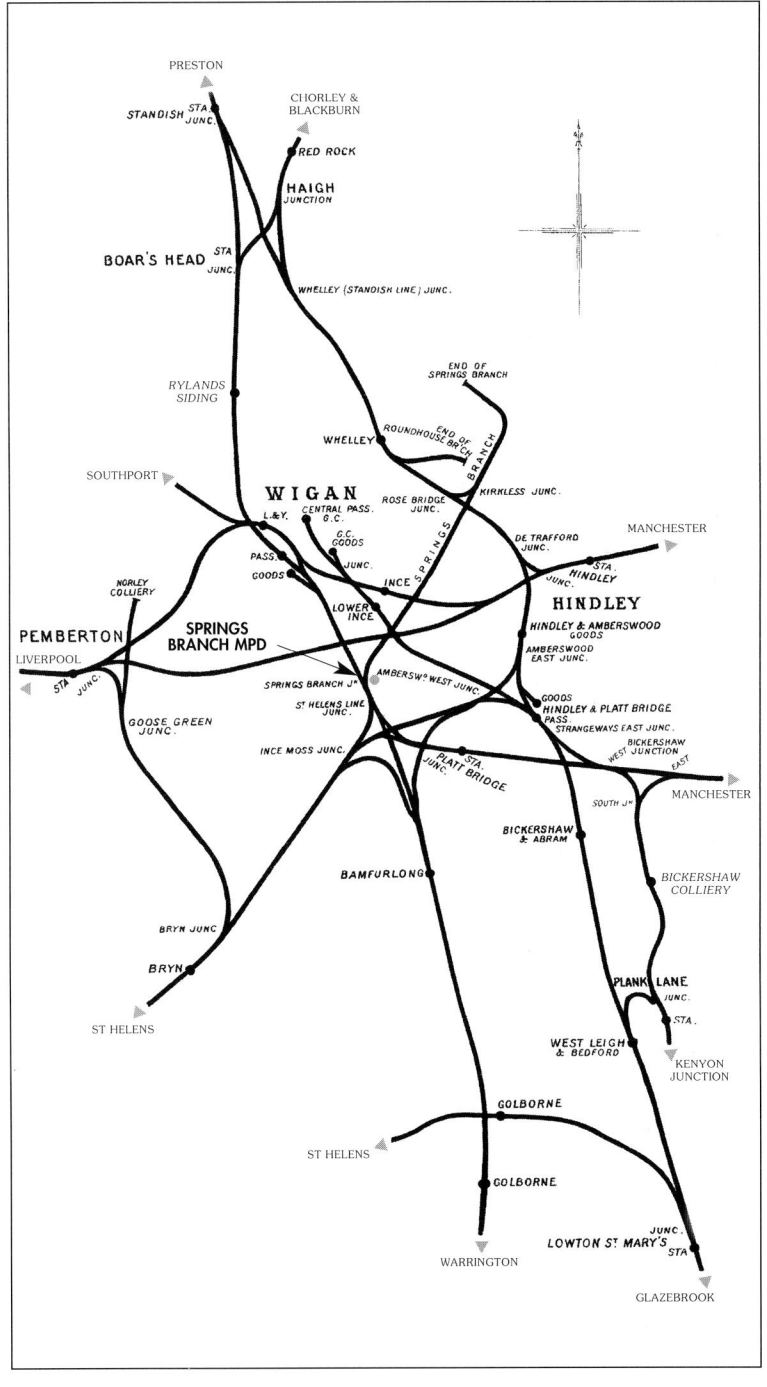

TRIP WORKINGS TO THE WEST (ex-LNWR lines)

Along the St Helens line calling at sidings en route, usually as far as Garswood but a few turns went to Ravenhead and Clock Face (Clock Face also had a daily full freight). There was also a branch off this route at Bryn Junction (approx one mile from Ince Moss Junction) for the collieries towards Pemberton.

TRIP WORKINGS TO THE WEST (ex-L&Y lines)

Springs Branch didn't generally work any trips along the Aintree or Southport ex-L&Y lines until the L&Y shed closed. The L&Y shed tended to work freights and not trips to these places.

LOCAL TRIPS

There were also two local workings that spent all day tripping between the Bamfurlong yards, Wigan NW and Wallgate Stations and Wigan Canal Goods Yard. There was a separate local trip conveying water cans etc to some of the signal boxes without mains supply, but this doesn't seem to have been given a trip number and would often be arranged as required.

Typical Trip workings would commence with either a light engine (LE) or Engine + brake van (EBV) from the Shed to one of the Bamfurlong or Springs Branch yards. They would then pick up any relevant wagons, often empty coal, before calling at most sidings on a particular route and exchange wagons as required. In the case of collieries, that would generally involve depositing empty mineral wagons and collecting loaded ones. Often the locos would shunt the yards as required, particularly if the site did not have a shunt loco, although most of the pits would have an NCB loco for internal shunting. At the end of the trip the loco brought the exchanged wagons back to one of the yards in the Bamfurlong area and then returned LE (or EBV) to shed.

Over the years the collieries gradually closed and the trip workings would serve fewer sidings so that occasionally certain jobs would be completely discontinued. Others would be modified to suit what traffic and sidings remained. In 1961 the North West division of the NCB contributed 11.5 million tons of deep mined coal in the Wigan area, so there was still a considerable quantity to be transported by rail.

TRIP WORKINGS - OCTOBER 1920

Turn	Loco	No/Shift			Covers
20	CTE	V	varies	22:30 off shed, then ebv	Scowcrofts, Hindley Green, Atherton, Hulton S, Atherton, Kenyon, Blong, L&Y, local
21	CTE	3	5.45am - 2.05am	05:45 off shed	Platt Bridge, Scowcrofts, Hindley Green, Scowcrofts, Moss Hall, Abram, Bickershaw Col
22	CTE	2	6am - 7.30pm	06:00 off shed	Golborne, Long Lane and Bamfurlong Yards
23	CTE	2	6.30am - 8.30pm	06:30 off shed	Hindley Field, Abram, Bickershaw (GC), Shed to reman, Wigan Goods, Rylands Mill, L&Y
24	CTE	2	7am - 9.10pm	07:00 off shed	Wigan Goods, Rylands, Victoria, Broomfield, via Kirkless to shed (reman), repeat trip
25	CTE	2	6.45am - 7.15pm	06:45 off shed	Blainscough, Balshaw Lane, Darlington S, Coppull Hall, Wigan (reman), repeat trip
26	STCE	2	7.15(6.30MO)am - 9.15pm	07:15MX 06:30MO	L&Y & Bamfurlong Yards, Reman at shed, Bamfurlong Colliery, Long Lane, Mains Colliery, SB
27	D	2	9.00am - 9.00pm	09:00 off shed, then ebv	Coppull Hall, Lindsay, WSTH, ebv - Lostock sdgs, Blainscough, Reman, Hindley, Coppull Hall, Bamfurlong Yards
28	CTE	3	6.50am - 4.00pm	06:50 off shed	Park Lane, Blundells, Norley, SB reman, Norley, Blundells, Park Lane, SB reman, L&Y, Bamfurlong Yards
29	CTE	2	7.15am - 9.00pm	07:15 off shed	Fir Tree, Ince Moss, Long Lane, Mains Colliery, SB reman, ebv - Howe Bridge, Kirkless, Scowcrofts, Kirkless, SB
30	CTE	3	8.30am - 6.55pm	08:30 off shed	Mains Colliery, AW, Bamfurlong Yards, SB reman, ebv - Bamfurlong Yards, AW, Garswood Hall, Bryn Hall, SB
31	CTE	2	9.10am - 11.30pm	09:10 off shed	Ince Moss, Kirkless, Lindsay, Victoria, Rylands, Kirkless, SB reman, ebv - Bickershaw Col, Diggles, Kenyon, HF, SB
32	CTE	1	9.15am - 3.30pm	08:15 off shed, then ebv	De Trafford, AW, Blong, Bryn Hall, Garswood Hall, Ince Moss, SB
33	CTE	1	10.05am - 5.30pm	10:05 off shed	SB, Wigan Goods, Red Rock, White Bear, Adlington Jn, Brinks, return - Rose Bridge, Bamfurlong Yards
34	CTE	2	10.30am - 10.00pm	10:30 off shed, then ebv	SB, Bickershaw, Abram Colliery, Rylands, Chorley reman, Heapey, Brinscall, Chorley, Roundhouse
35	CTE	2	8.00pm - 9.00am	20:00 off shed	SB, Coppull Hall, Amberswood E, reman at 02:00 then control orders
36	CTE	2	7.00pm - 7.30am	19:00 off shed	Blong, Blundells, Garswood Hall, IM, SB reman, Garswood Hall, Ince Moss
37	CTE	2	11.50am - 1.30am	23:50 off shed	Ince Moss, Scowcrofts, Howe Bridge, Hindley (repeat), SB reman, Wigan Goods, Park Lane, Garswood Hall, SB
38	CTE	2	12.00pm - 1.10am	12:00 off shed	Blong, Garswood Hall, Carr Mill, Billinge C, Garswood, Ince Moss, P Br Jn reman, Bickershaw C, Abram, Scowcrofts, SB
39	CTE	1	2.15pm - 8.15pm	14:15 off shed	SB, Edge Lane, Golborne, Long Lane, Mains Colliery, SB
40	CTE	2	12noon - 4.30pm	12:00 off shed	Lindsay, Coppull Hall, Brinks, Chorley, ebv - Roundhouse reman, Hindley Sidings, SB then control orders
41	CTE	2	1.15pm - 3.30am	13:15 off shed	SB, Fir Tree Colliery, SB, ESX, Ince Moss reman, Fir Tree, Scowcrofts, Hindley Green, Howe Bridge, (repeat), SB
42	SPARE				
43	CTE	2	5.30pm - 7.20pm	05:30 off shed	SB, Rylands, Kirkless, Rose Bridge, AW, Blong reman, HF, Abram, Bickershaw Col and via Kenyon to Bamfurlong Yards
44	CTE	2	5.10pm - 7.15am	17:10 off shed, then ebv	SB, Moss Hall, Hindley Fields, Bickershaw, Moss Hall, SB, ESX reman, Kenyon, Bickershaw Col, Abram, SB
45	CTE	1	5.45pm - 12.30am	17:45 off shed	SB, Blong, Hindley Fields, Bickershaw, Abram, Hindley Fields, Engine Shed Exchange Sidings
46	CTE	2	5.00am - 8.10pm	05:00 off shed	SB, Wigan Goods, Ince Moss, SB Down Sidings reman then control orders
47	Off Frt	1	3.00am - 10.00pm	eng off 00:30 Rav - IM	Ince Moss, Hindley Fields, Abram, Bickershaw Col, Ince Moss, Amberswood, Kirkless, Rylands, ebv Eng shed exchange
48	CTE	2	6.15pm - 6.30am	18:15 off shed	SB, Rylands, Kirkless, Rylands, L&Y, Bamfurlong Yards control orders & reman, L&Y, Bamfurlong Yards
49	CTE	2	9.30am - 11.00pm	09:30 off shed	Moss Colliery, Amberswood, Roundhouse, Ince Moss, Moss C, AW, Bamfurlong Yards, SB then control orders & reman

CTE: Coal Tender engine   D: Super D
STCE: Small Tender Coal engine
Blong: Bamfurlong
SB: Springs Branch Yards
AW: Amberswood West
WSTH: Westhoughton
HF: Hindley Fields
ESX: Engine Shed Exchange Sidings

◀ **Ex-L&Y 2F No 12045** stands in the shed yard with its Trip 23 plate leaning against the sand box. It was mainly the trip and shunt engines that carried these plates to assist identification of their working. At busy times there would be numerous light engines (or engines & brake vans) in the vicinity of Springs Branch.

14TH MAY 1938 ● **R. J. BUCKLEY**

TRIP WORKINGS 1951

Turn	Loco	Shift & Time	Covers
101	BL5	Mon - Fri 7.00am, 3:30pm, Sat 7.00am	Cross Tetley, Golborne, Earlestown, Haydock
102	SD	Sun Only 7:00am	Clock Face (others as required)
109	SD	Mon - Sat 2:00pm	Moss Hall, Scowcrofts, Kenyon Junction, Bickershaw
112	SD	Mon - Fri 5:00pm, Midnight Sat 3:00pm	Bickershaw, Springs Branch, Kenyon Junction
116	SD	Mon - Sat 1:00pm	Garswood Hall, Springs Branch, Ince Moss, Garswood
122	BL5	Mon - Sat 7:40am	runs (but not shown in WTT)
123	L&Y	Mon - Fri 9:00am, Sat 6:50am	Victoria Colliery, Ince Moss
124	SD	Mon - Fri 2:00pm	Coppull Hall, Rylands Siding, Bamfurlong Yards
126	BL5	Mon - Fri 2:00pm, Sat 11:00am	Darlington Sidings, Ince Moss
132	BL5	Mon - Fri 7:00am, 1:20pm, Sat 8:15am, 2:50pm	Rylands Siding, Ince Moss, Howe Bridge (SO Darlington Sidings)
133	L&Y	Mon - Sat 5:00am, 11:30am & 6:30pm	Wigan Wallgate, Bamfurlong Yards
134	Varies	Mon - Sat 1:00am, 6:00pm Sat+11:00pm	Ince Moss, Bamfurlong Yards, Wigan Wallgate, Springs Branch
136	SD	Mon - Sat 11:00am	Moss Hall, Abram N, Bickershaw
137	SD	Mon - Fri 2:00pm	Amberswood, Moss Hall, Bag Lane, Chanters
138	SD	Mon - Sat 8:00am	Bamfurlong Yards, Halliwell
140	BL5	Mon - Fri 6:30pm	Bag Lane, Howe Bridge, Scowcrofts, Moss Hall

TRIP WORKINGS 1963

Turn	Loco	Shift & Time	Covers
T2	Ivatt	double shift	Bickershaw
T4	WD	double shift	Abram North
T5	BL5	single shift	Ravenhead/Bickershaw
T6	CL7	single shift	Rylands Siding
T8	4F	double shift	Roundhouse, Kirkless
T9	4F	treble shift	Local yards
T10	BL5	double shift	Canal Sidings, Local yards
T11	BL5	single shift	Bamfurlong, Bickershaw
T12	BL5	double shift	Golborne, Parkside (Earlestown)
T13	BL5	double shift	Bolton C St
T14	4F	single shift	Ince Moss, Jacksons Sidings
T15	Jinty	double shift	Incline

TRIP WORKINGS 1966

Turn	Loco	Shift & Time	Covers
102	BL5	10:00am	Bickershaw, Abram North
105	S Mogul	7:00am	Ravenhead, Bickershaw
108	204DS	4:40am - 10:55pm mo, 6:55am - 9:05pm mx	CWS sidings Roundhouse
110	204DS	9:50am sx - 6:25am mx	Canal Sidings, Local yards
111	BL8	11:50am - 7:20pm sx	Bamfurlong, Bickershaw
112	BL8	9:30am - 4:15pm sx	Golborne, Parkside
113	BL8	9:45am - 3:40pm sx	Howe Bridge, Patricroft
115	204DS	6:10am - 12:30pm sx, 2:40pm - 8:00pm sx	Incline
125	BL5	6:20am - 8:33pm sx, 7:58am - 11:15am so	Douglas Bank, Gathurst

The view looking north on the main West Coast line. Super D 0-8-0 No **49267** crosses on the way from Platt Bridge Junction to Ince Moss and is about to pass Fir Tree House Junction signalbox which appears to be somewhat precariously supported by struts. Looking ahead beyond the nearest overbridge, the main line passes under Taylor's Lane, after which lie Springs Branch Nos 1 and 2 signal boxes, both of which are just visible. Needless to say, photographer Ray Farrell had a lineside permit for this stretch of track.

24TH JUNE 1961 • RAY FARRELL

The view from Taylor's Lane as mentioned above. Ivatt Class 2MT No **46419** is nicely portrayed propelling a brake van coming up the incline from Bamfurlong Sidings, having completed a trip working. The throat of the shed yard is prominent and a Stanier loco awaits the signal to move off, whilst beyond a Jinty 0-6-0 tank may well be on shed pilot duties. Of further interest is the line of stabled locos. A trio of withdrawn Stanier 2-6-4 tanks, Nos **42456, 42565** and **42670** are brought up in the rear by ex-GWR Pannier Tank No **9753**.

3RD SEPTEMBER 1965 • EDDIE BELLASS

TRIPS 133 & 134 (LOCAL)

There were two trips that were regarded as local workings and would usually be the preserve of the older men and often the older engines too. Trip 133 earned the nickname of 'City Goods'. The purpose of these trips was to collect and distribute wagons between the local marshalling yards and Wigan NW and Wallgate stations. They would quite literally travel constantly between all the Bamfurlong Yards, Ince Moss and Springs Branch, then trip over to the stations and back to the yards again throughout their shifts. This created a fast and efficient service between these points and meant that any wagonloads would be dealt with quickly. It also reduced congestion in the yards by constantly transferring some wagons away that were destined for another Wigan yard.

Black Five No 45024 shunts the yard at Wigan Wallgate station. It would then take any relevant wagons either to the exchange yard at the south of the station, Canal Sidings or Bamfurlong Yards.

18TH APRIL 1967 • ALLAN HEYES

Stanier 8F No 48275 trundles through Springs Branch North Sidings as Hunslet 0-6-0 Diesel Shunter **D2560** passes, almost certainly working either Trip No 133 or 134 heading for Wigan North Western.

7TH SEPTEMBER 1966 • RAY FARRELL

Shunting Wigan Exchange Sidings, situated at the side of the North Western Station, is Ivatt 2-6-0 No **46486**. Just visible in the background is Standard Class 4 No **75057**. Several trip workings would bring different engines into the yard during the course of a day.

2ND OCTOBER 1964 • PETER FITTON

TRIPS 122 - 126 (TO THE NORTH)

A busy period at Rylands Siding with Black Five No **44675** passing the signal box with a northbound freight. The yard shunter, complete with pole, converses with a colleague whilst WD 2-8-0 No **90667** rests in the sidings. All the traffic dealt with here was coal from the Standish and Shevington area, which ceased in 1964. The collieries feeding Rylands Siding had their own locos, initially around four were involved but they were later replaced by two Yorkshire diesel shunters.   **AUGUST 1963 ● D. COUSINS**

There were a series of collieries to the north of Wigan alongside the main line to Preston and several trip workings served these. They would travel either via North Western Station or via the Whelley line. Both routes served the various colliery sidings and would shunt as follows.

Via North Western station to Rylands Siding (busy exchange for coal traffic), Victoria Colliery (closed 1958), Coppull Hall Sidings (for Chisnall Hall colliery), Blainscough Siding (for Coppull Goods Yard) and Darlingtons Siding (for Coppull Ring Mill) and sometimes Balshaw Lane Yard. The route via the Whelley line served Roundhouse Sidings and Alexander Pit, both situated at Whelley itself.

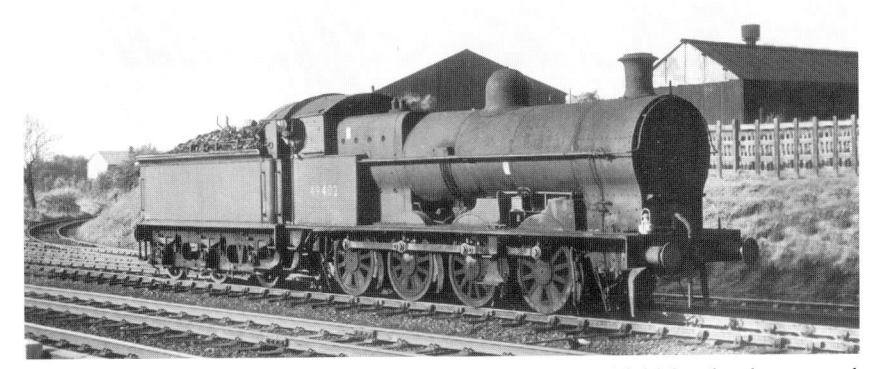

An example of the shed's tender cab Super D, No 49402 is busily engaged re-arranging wagons at Rylands siding.   **16TH SEPTEMBER 1961 ● ARNOLD BATTSON**

By 1967, former Royal Train Engine No **45425** had been reduced to similar menial duties in Rylands Siding. They were used for storing PW wagons after the pits closed in 1964.   **1967 ● CHRIS COATES**

RYLANDS COAL TRAIN

In the middle of the afternoon a Super D would arrive at Rylands Siding from the Wigan direction. The engine usually had two brake vans in front which it propelled up the headshunt, then dropped back to allow one van to roll down under the influence of gravity, eventually to be stopped at the bottom end of the departure road. The engine would then spend several hours shunting the wagons in the Wigan Coal Corporation Sidings here, a difficult job due to the short handled regulator and a large superheater which took a long time to fill with steam. After the shunting was done and a brake van picked up at the rear, the other brake van was dropped down so that there was a brake van at either end. The engine then attached to the south end of the train.

Shortly after 6pm, another Super D would arrive and couple up to the north end of the train and when the dummy (ground) signal cleared, both engines crowed up and opened their regulators to drag and push this heavy coal train up the bank past Boar's Head Junction, over the lofty viaduct and into Red Rock station. Here the guard climbed down from the south end brake van and walked to the other end to ensure the front engine at that end had hooked off. The original engine now became the train engine and, when the signal was given, the train set off for Whelley Junction and over the Whelley line to Platt Bridge and Bamfurlong Screens Sidings where the train was left and the engine went to the shed. The reason the train didn't go directly via Wigan station was because it would have had to reverse into the Screens siding from the Up Main, there being only a trailing junction there. This would be a time consuming exercise at a very busy time of the day. If the load didn't warrant a banker, the train would proceed to Red Rock station and the engine would travel light to White Bear to cross over, run back to Red Rock, across again and couple at the (now) front of the train, and proceed to the Screens as above.

UN-SUPER D

Although Super D's were generally very reliable and could manage virtually anything thrown at them, sometimes a crew would get a 'duff' one and Driver Tom Taylor describes one such occasion.

We booked on at about 2am and joined our engine, a Super D, standing just outside the shed in light steam, about 40lbs showing on the gauge. The fire consisted mainly of a pile of half-burned coal lurking under the firehole door so I pushed it with the pricker to spread it all over the grate then turned the blower on. Nothing happened despite fiddling with the blower control, the fire remained dull and smoky. After some time we gave in and called a fitter, who made some adjustment which improved the situation slightly, the fire beginning to look as if it meant business. Eventually we raised enough steam to move the engine, so we proceeded to the shed exit ground signal, now being at least one hour late off shed. The signal came off allowing us out to Cromptons signalbox where the pointsman enquired after our health and offered to subscribe towards an alarm clock to help us to get to work on time. In fact he would be well aware of the cause of the delay since the Running Shift Foreman would have informed the bobby as well as Control that the engine was not inclined to work. We now ran slowly to Ince Moss, backed onto our train and learned our load from the guard and then started off up the bank to Fir Tree Junction and Platt Bridge, looking back for the guard to inform us that he was aboard his van. His signal consisted of a white light waved to and fro which we answered by waving a gauge glass back at him. With the aid of the Ince Moss bank engine at the rear, which was doing most of the work, we staggered over the top and set off along the reasonably level track through Bickershaw Junction, Scowcrofts Sidings, Hindley Green, Howe Bridge and down the dip beyond Howe Bridge West Junction. Our geriatric 'D' had been holding a race between the water gauge and the pressure gauge as to which could reach the bottom first so we were not making much speed. I gave it full regulator in an attempt to pick up enough speed to climb the bank beyond the dip but we gradually came to a stand halfway up the hill. After a few minutes our reluctant dragon had regained some breath so we proceeded to lift the train up the bank to Tyldesley yard, where we were due to shunt.

To help start the train, instead of repeatedly winding the reverser into back gear, I released the brake and opened the cylinder drain cocks. This action released compression in the cylinders and allowed the loco to slowly drift backwards down the bank, buffering up the wagons against the brake van, on which the guard had wound the handbrake, holding the train on the bank. When the engine stopped, leaning back against the train, the taps were closed and the engine given as much steam as the boiler could supply. She started briskly, pulling out the couplings one by one and slowing gradually as she picked up more wagons plus the brake van. We gained about one hundred yards before grinding to a halt, applying the brake to allow the guard to apply his, then repeating the procedure time after time, gaining ground each time. After twenty minutes of the quadrille we surmounted the bank into Tyldesley station where we could see help on the horizon in the form of another 'D' which had been summoned from Patricroft shed. The signalman had sent for help when he heard us performing the military two-step in the dip. The other engine crossed on to our road then backed up and coupled to our engine, chimney to chimney. The two engines then set about shunting some wagons into the yard and picking up the other traffic. When our train was pieced up we departed down the bank to Monton Green reception siding where we left the train and took the engine on Patricroft shed. Here I went to the office and put in a repair card stating the engine was a bad steamer and unfit to be sent off shed only to be informed that they would get another turn out of it. I suspect that it was a well known cripple which was used on very light duties or foisted off on unsuspecting crews from other sheds. Luckily we escaped another trip with this old rip and were given another 'D' to take home to Springs Branch. As there was no returning train I had to bring it home light engine.

TRIPS 102 (SUN ONLY) AND 116 (TO THE WEST)

Taking the Liverpool route from Ince Moss Junction, there were collieries all the way up the bank to Garswood and these trippers covered both the collieries and the yards towards St Helens. They also traversed the Norley Branch from Bryn Junction which included the huge Blundells Colliery at Pemberton. In 1951 there was a Sunday trip working to Clock Face whereas in the week, two regular freights ran to this colliery. The Norley Branch appears to have closed in the late 1940's.

◀ **This is the view the fireman** would have as he pushed coal forward in the tender. Enginemen working on Super D's without tender cabs were somewhat exposed to the elements. No **49025** is shunting Garswood yard as part of its trip working.
c1960 ● LEN BALL

A Super D 0-8-0 with tender cab, No 49422 heads down the bank from Bryn towards Bamfurlong with a short trip freight.
12TH AUGUST 1960 ● N. FIELDS

TRIPS 109, 112, 136 - 140 (TO THE EAST)

These trip workings served the many coal sidings on the Manchester Exchange line out to Howe Bridge and via Bickershaw to Kenyon Junction. There was quite a network of collieries radiating out from Bickershaw Junction with associated groups of sidings. Tripper 138 and 139 also ran up from Howe Bridge to Bolton, covering the sidings en route.

Stanier Mogul 2-6-0 No 42968 is signalled to go down onto the GC at Bickershaw. It is presumably en route for Bamfurlong Yard via Amberwood West Junction. **1ST JULY 1964 • ALLAN HEYES**

Passing Bickershaw Junction is an unidentified Super D with a westbound coal train off the Bickershaw branch. **JUNE 1960 • J. PEDEN**

Unusual motive power for a coal train in the shape of Stanier 2-6-4 tank No **42494** approaching Cromptons Siding Signalbox from the Bickershaw coalfield. **19TH JUNE 1964 • JOHN BURGESS**

TRIPS 101 AND 132 (TO THE SOUTH)

Three months away from withdrawal, Super D No 49002 lays a trail of smoke at Golborne with a southbound coal train from the Wigan area. **1ST JUNE 1962** ● **JOHN BURGESS**

Covering the collieries on the main line south of Bamfurlong, namely Cross Tetley, Golborne and Haydock plus Earlestown for the wagon works. By 1959 Trip Working 132 was changed from Golborne to cover the Kirkless branch which had previously been a shunt turn.

The Ivatt 2MT's did see some use on the trip workings and here No **46419** approaches Springs Branch No 1 signalbox with coal from the south. The train is on the down slow line and will probably reverse into North sidings from here. **15TH JUNE 1964** ● **JOHN BURGESS**

TRIP WORKINGS ON THE EX-GC LINES

When Springs Branch took over the ex-GC work there were seven trip workings that all started with light engines off the shed. Two would travel to Lowton St Marys and serve the St Helens Central line collieries and works. Two others went to Glazebrook and one each to Lowton St Marys, West Leigh and Wigan Central Goods plus some turns to and from Dewsnap Sidings. Although there were minor changes, this pattern remained the same over the years until freight working ceased on the line. Much of the trip working on the ex-GC appeared to cease in 1964, although Wigan Central Goods Depot continued to be rail served and saw occasional activity until at least the late 1960's, although this tended to be concentrated on the busy Christmas parcels trade. In 1968, the route from Lowton St Marys to Golborne closed completely and a new curve was created from Cross Tetley, on the West Coast Main Line, to Edge Green. This allowed continued access to Golborne Colliery, Ashton Oil Terminal and Lowton Metals.

The hub of freight activities over the former GC extension to Wigan and St Helens was Lowton St Marys. Passing through the station with a southbound trip working is 0-6-0 No **44076**.

29TH SEPTEMBER 1962 ● **BEV PRICE**

GC Freight - Summer 1964

0T45	06:00 SB - Wigan Cen Gds	06:22
9T46	09:25 Lowton St M - Bamfurlong	
9T46	09:25 Lowton St M - Bamfurlong	
9T46	10:25 Bamf - Lowton St M	11:14
7T46	11:35 Lowton St M - St H Cen	12:05
7T46	16:00 St H Cen - Lowton St M	16:30
7T46	17:30 Lowton St M - Trafford Pk	18:26
7T46	19:20 Trafford Pk - Glazebrook	19:37
0T46	19:52 Glazebrook - Sp Branch	
0T47	06:30 Sp Branch - Lowton St M	07:00
0T47	08:00 Sp Branch - Lowton St M	08:26
9T47	07:30 Lowton St M - St H Cen	08:00 SO
9T47	09:00 Lowton St M - St H Cen	09:15
9T47	09:00 St H Cen - Ashton	09:40 trip
9T47	09:00 St H Cen - Ashton	09:40
9T47	10:45 Ashton in M - Lowton St M	11:20 to Dewsnap
0T47	12:20 Lowton St M - Sp Branch	
0T48	07:05 Sp Branch - Glazebrook	07:53
9T48	08:42 Glazebrook Sdgs - Edge Green	09:11
9T48	09:23 Edge Green - Glazebrook	09:55
8T48	10:20 Glazebrook - Wigan Cen Gds	11:05
0Z00	12:05 Wigan C Gds - Sp Branch. Works Q to Lowton if req	
9T50	08:30 Bamf - Culcheth	09:40
9T50	10:10 Culcheth - Glazebrook	10:30
7T50	11:30 Glazebrook - Ashton in M	12:38
0T50	12:55 ebv Ashton - Lowton St M	13:10
0T50	13:25 Lowton St M - Sp Branch	
7T58	08:47 Lowton St M - Partington	09:44 shunts Culcheth
9T58	10:17 Partington - Edge Green	11:53
0T58	12:05 ebv Edge Gn - Lowton St M	12:15
8T58	12:35 Lowton St M - Glazebrook	13:00
9T58	13:42 Glazebrook - Edge Green	14:06
0T58	14:23 Edge Green - Ashton In M	14:33
9T58	15:05 Ashton - Lowton St M	15:20
0T58	15:40 Lowton St M - Sp Branch	

Standard Class 4 No 75058 shunts wagons into the sidings at Edge Green, on the Lowton to St Helens Central branch, before returning to its train.

15TH MAY 1964 ● **JOHN BURGESS**

Having dropped off wagons at Edge Green, No **75058** recouples to its train before continuing its trip working. **15TH MAY 1964** ● **JOHN BURGESS**

TRIPS AND FREIGHT WORKINGS ON THE EX-L&Y LINES

With the closure of the L&Y shed, Springs Branch engines and men handled the remaining freight and trip workings over the ex-L&Y lines. There had generally been around six freights that worked out of Bamfurlong yard, mostly to the Aintree or Southport areas. In 1965 the shed was working what were now basically 'trippers' to Appley Bridge, Burscough Bridge, Southport, Fazakerley, Horwich Works and Burnden Junction (Bolton). The Gathurst gunpowder traffic was tripped to Wigan Exchange Sidings (by the side of NW station) as part of trip 9T25. The Burscough Bridge trip would collect wagons from the cake factory and also shunt the ROF at Burscough Junction.

Standard Class 4 No 75015 passes the closed Branckers Siding signalbox as it brings the gunpowder vans down from the Roberite factory sidings at Gathurst to Wigan Canal sidings yard. Branckers Sidings were created in the 1960's to serve the nearby Heinz factory but a dispute over costs resulted in the facility never being used.

26TH AUGUST 1964 ● ALLAN HEYES

Stanier 8F 2-8-0 No 48125 heads the Fazakerley to Bamfurlong Trip through Pemberton Station.

1965 ● LES RILEY

OTHER TRIP WORK

The Incline (Springs Branch) had generally been worked by a shunt engine, sometimes two, but occasionally it was also part of a trip working, especially if it involved working out at the Rose Bridge Junction end.

'Super D' 0-8-0 No 48895 leaves the erstwhile Wigan Coal and Iron Company's Kirkless complex with its light load and travels via the re-instated curve up to Rose Bridge Junction on the Whelley line. Dominating the background are the terraced houses of Higher Ince.

c.1962 ● HAROLD HUNT

SHUNT ENGINES

The shed was required to supply shunting engines to the various yards around Wigan, the majority of which were within one mile of the depot. Most of these engines would leave the shed at 6am Monday and some would stay out for a week, only returning for maintenance. Provision had been made for the engines to be coaled and watered on site, so they could remain on duty 24 hours a day. It is interesting to compare the situation in 1920 with that of 1951. In 1920 the shed supplied 14 shunt engines and almost certainly others at Canal goods and NW Station - in 1951 that figure was 11. The LNWR numbers given to the shunt turns remained unchanged except for the addition of 140 (so Shunt 7 became Shunt 147, etc). Note that in 1920 Springs Branch North Sidings was known as Springs Branch Down Sidings and warranted two shunt engines. Springs Branch Up sidings (at the side of the shed) became better known in the BR period as Engine Shed Sidings. Although not given a shed code, there would also be a loco allocated as loco shed shunt/pilot for moving dead engines around and shunting loco coal wagons.

SHUNT ENGINES 1920

	Title	Engine Type	Time of working	Work
1	SB Incline	SCTE	6am - 10pm daily	Trips as required Eng Shed Sdgs/Monks Hall
2	SB Incline	SCTE	6am - 4pm daily	Trips as required Eng Shed Sdgs/Monks Hall
3	Eng Shed Crossing	STE	6am Mon - 2pm Sun	Trips between Eng Shed Crossing/N Sdgs/Incline
4	SB Up Sidings	STE	6am Mon - 6am Sun	Works in SB Up Sidings (side of shed)
5	SB Down Sidings	0-8-2 Tank	6am - 6am daily	Works in SB Down Sdgs (North Sidings)
6	SB Down Sidings	0-8-2 Tank	6am Mon - 2pm Sun	Works in SB Down Sdgs (North Sidings)
7	IM Up & Down Sidings	STE	6am - 2pm Mon/Tue, 6am - 10pm Wed - Sat	Works at Ince Moss, both sides of Liverpool line
8	Bamfurlong N End	0-8-2 Tank	6am Mon - 2pm Sun	Works in North End Yard
9	Bamfurlong N End	STE	6am Mon - 6am Sun	Works in North End Yard, trips S End/Screens
10	Pemberton Corner	STE	6am Mon - 2pm Sun	Trips to South End/Ince Moss
11	Bamfurlong S End (LNW)	0-8-2 Tank	6am Mon - 2pm Sun	Works LNW side of South End Yard
12	Bamfurlong S End (L&Y)	SCTE	9am - 5pm	Works L&Y side of South End Yard
13	Coppull Yard/Hall	SE	7.30am - 8.35pm daily	Coppull Yard N of Wigan on Main Line
14	Roundhouse Sidings		6am - 8pm daily	Roundhouse Sidings on Whelley Line

SHUNT ENGINES 1951

	Title	Time of working	
141	SB Incline	M - F 6am and 12:40pm, Sat 6am	Engine off shed Daily 6am
145	SB North Sdgs	M - S 6am, 2pm, 10pm, Sun 6am, 2pm	Engine off shed Mon 6am. Stays out
147	Ince Moss	7days, 3 turns 6am, 2pm, 10pm	Engine off shed Mon 6am. Stays out
148	Bamfurlong N End	M - F 7 days, 3 turns, 6am, 2pm, 10pm	Engine off shed Mon 6am. Stays out
149	Long Drag	M - F 6am, 11pm, Sat 6am	Engine off shed Mon 6am. Stays out
150	Pemberton Corner	M - S 6am, 2pm, 10pm	Engine off shed Mon 6am. Stays out
151	Bamfurlong S End (LNW)	Mon 6am,10.25am, 4:40pm, Midnight Tue - Sat 6am, 2pm, Midnight, Sun 6am, 2pm	Engine off shed Mon 6am. Stays out
152	Bamfurlong S End (L&Y)	Mon 4pm, 10pm, Tue - Fri 4pm, Midnight, Sat 2pm, 10pm	Engine off shed Daily 4pm (2pm Sat)
154	Ince Moss Tip	Mon - Fri 7.30am, 2.45pm. Sat 6am	Engine off shed Daily on first turn
156	Wigan Canal Gds	Mon - Fri 5am, 4.30pm. Sat 5am & 9am	Engine off shed on each turn
X	Wigan Bank	Mon 5.50am, 11:15am, 4:25pm, 11:30pm Tue - Thur 6:30am, 12:30pm, 11:30pm, Fri 12:30pm, 11:30pm, Sat 6:20 am, 12:30pm, Sun 1:20 am, 6:42 am, 10:45 pm	Engine off shed 11pm (When)

Engine Type	SCTE - Small Coal Tender Engine (DX or SDX)	4F - Fowler 4F	BL5 - Stanier Class 5
	STE - Special Tank Engine	2-6-0* - Stanier Mogul	DS - Diesel Shunter
	SE - Small Engine (Square Tank)	2-6-0** - Ivatt Mogul	

SHUNT ENGINES 1966

	Title	Engine Type	Time of Working
117	North Sidings	2-6-4T	06:00 - 11:00 mo
			16:00 sx - 09:00 mx
119	Bamfurlong N End	350DS	Daily 06:15 - 13:45,
			14:15 - 21:45
			22:15 sx - 05:45 mx
121	Pemberton Corner	204DS	06:15 - 13:45 daily,
			14:15 - 21:45 sx
			22:15 sx - 05:45 mx
122	Bamfurlong S End	2-6-0**	06:00 - 22:00 sx
			06:00 - 21:00 so
123	Ince Moss Tip	2-6-0*	06:00 - 19:00 sx
124	Wigan Canal Goods	204DS	05:00 - 11:20 sx
			13:40 - 20:00 sx
136	Wigan Bank	2-6-0**	04:30 - 18:30 mo
			22:00 sx- 18:30 mx
			22:00 so - 06:00 so

HUMPIES

A *Humpy* was the LNW engineman's pet name for a saddle tank, either of L & Y or LNW parentage. **Driver Tommy Taylor** couldn't resist telling as many outrageous lies as possible so one day, when leaving the shed with a Humpy, he stopped at Cromptons Signalbox to inform the 'Bobby' where he was bound. *To Fleetwood to bring a special of fish for Liverpool* he called. The signalman, noting the type of engine, was incredulous and rang the shed foreman who, on receiving the enquiry, knew what was going on. He asked *And who is the driver concerned?*, Tommy Taylor came the reply. *Well, you silly b-----*, said the foreman, *If you believe him, you will believe anyone.* The Bobby then pulled off to send the engine to its correct destination which was Bamfurlong Sidings on a shunting turn.

◀ **One of the 'Titanic' 0-8-2 Tanks, No 7881** stands in steam in the shed yard. It will shortly move off to commence its next turn of duty which can easily be identified. Affixed to the rear of the bunker is LMS Target Plate No 45 which confirms that it will work at Springs Branch North Sidings as designated shunt engine.

20TH MAY 1938 ● **AUTHOR'S COLLECTION**

INCLINE SHUNT (141)

A good example of a shunt working is the Bridge Hole or Incline shunt which worked from the engine shed sidings (alongside the shed and originally consisting of Springs Branch Up sidings and Brewery Sidings) up the Springs Branch itself and served the various industries along the line. The traffic on the branch was a mixture of coal (from pits) and materials into and out of the various iron and steel industries. The huge Wigan Coal & Iron Company's Kirkless site, one of the largest employers in the North West, would probably be the significant concern requiring large quantities of wagonload traffic, although its coke came in directly off the Whelley line spur. Also creating a considerable amount of traffic would be the numerous wagon works and, combined, this traffic was so intense that, at its peak, four shunt locomotives were needed plus other locomotives working trips to move the wagons to where they were required.

◄ **The shed's last 19" Goods, No 8824** runs back from the Incline towards the shed.

15TH AUGUST 1949 ● LNWR SOCIETY

Looking back to the LNWR period, in 1920 there were 2 locos allocated to these shunt workings and were designated shunts 1 & 2. Both were allocated for 'small coal engines' so Webb 17" coal engines would be undertaking the work. There was also another loco (a Special tank) allocated to the engine shed sidings and another to Springs Branch Up sidings, so this gives an indication of the amount of traffic in this area.

Shunt 1 was rostered to work 6 am to 10pm daily and was expected to run to Monks Hall sidings (Ince Forge) as required. No 2 worked 6am to 4pm daily, mainly shunting the small yards up the incline, many of which were involved with wagon repair and construction. One spin off from this was that enginemen could get blocks of wood (for firewood) from the wagon works off the repaired wagons. The closure of the huge Kirkless Iron Works in the mid 1930's must have been a crippling blow for the Springs Branch and in 1958 the line was cut back to Manchester Road, Higher Ince, but still served the various wagon works that existed on the lower section.

By 1951 there was only one incline shunt, often an ex-L&Y 0-6-0 tender loco, and the working was now SHUNT 141, operating 2 shifts, 6am and (generally) 12:40 pm Monday to Friday with just the early shift on Saturdays. In later BR years a Jinty was booked to the incline shunt but by this time much of the industry up the Springs Branch had ceased. The last section, that from Springs Branch to Central Wagon Works closed in 1973 and a headshunt was all that remained until 1998 when the remaining track was lifted. The headshunt was used chiefly for running round but problems with Warrington Road bridge caused this to be curtailed.

LMS 0-6-0 No 44490 shunts wagons at the shed end of the incline.   **16TH SEPTEMBER 1961 ● D. HAMPSON**

0-8-2T No 47896, still carrying the letters LMS on its tank sides, trundles down the incline and is caught passing under the former L&YR line. Just in view through the bridge is the Central Wagon Works overhead gantry.

5TH FEBRUARY 1949 ● ALLAN BROWN

The diminutive Jinty 0-6-0T's were the regular engines for the Incline Shunt by the mid 1960's and here No **47444** shunts with wagons at either end. In the distance is the magnificent Girder Bridge carrying the L&Y avoiding line.

27TH JUNE 1962 ● JOHN BURGESS

An extract from the RSF log book with regard to Shunt 141 is of interest:

149

SPRINGS BRANCH NORTH SIDINGS SHUNT (145)

An important job in the area was the shunting of the North Sidings, the group of lines curving round from opposite the shed to Ince Moss Junction. At both ends of this yard there are connections into the Ince Moss Colliery which was active until the late 1950's. In 1920 there were two shunt engines at North Sidings, or Springs Branch Down sidings as it was then known (LNWR shunts Nos 5 & 6). Bowen Cooke 0-8-2 tank locos were allocated to the job and both worked 24 hours for 7 days a week apart from the second loco resting from 2pm Sunday until 6am Monday and this gives an indication of the amount of traffic there was to shunt around. By 1951, there was now just one booked shunt engine, usually an ex-L&Y 0-6-0 tender loco, still working 7 days a week until 2pm Sunday.

Veteran 0-6-0 No 52045 goes about its business shunting the North Sidings. Ince Moss Pits and its rail connection are both visible as is Springs Branch North Sidings signalbox. The photograph, taken from the window of a passing train, reveals that the storm sheet has been attached from engines cab roof to tender to protect the crew from inclement weather. **13TH SEPTEMBER 1950 • H.C. CASSERLEY**

Springs Branch North Sidings dispatched trains to the north, generally via the Wigan North Western station route but could, when needed, reverse them to Ince Moss so they could go via the Whelley line. Incoming trains were usually from the Bickershaw Junction line and would reverse at Ince Moss into the North Sidings. A couple of trains from Merseyside also came directly into North Sidings. The odd train would also come from the Manchester Line via Crompton Siding signalbox (the shed side) and across all lines to access the yard although, for obvious reasons, this was avoided whenever possible. North sidings also stabled a little coaching stock and one such example was the ROF train in the 1960's.

In the mid 1960's the North Sidings shunt became '17 Shunt' but was still operating 16:00 to 09:00 in 1966 and was booked for a 2-6-4 tank although it soon became a '350 diesel shunter'. The working finally ceased in 1972.

A fine side view of No 12023 in North Sidings headshunt showing the jackshaft arrangement on these early LMS diesel shunters. This loco arrived in the Summer of 1960 and gave twelve years service here.

17TH SEPTEMBER 1967 • JOHN BURGESS

INCE MOSS SHUNT (154)

Two for the price of one. Heavy shunt engine No **47877** shunts the north side of Ince Moss, whilst a bank engine rests on the south side of the Liverpool line. Although renumbered with the 4 prefix, the engine also retained the LMS lettering on its tanks. Unfortunately this was now the last 'Titanic' in service at Springs Branch and had just six more months left in service. **14TH AUGUST 1952 • STEAM IMAGE**

Originally the tip was at Rainford but later became established at Ince Moss where there was plenty of wasteland to the west of Ince Moss Colliery. Shunt No 154 was the Ince Moss tip shunt engine which operated two shifts, 7.30 am and 2.45 pm Monday to Friday, and one (6am) shift on Saturdays. The tip became an increasingly important site during the late 1950's with 300 wagons of rubbish and spoil arriving daily and being dumped here. This activity continued, at a reducing level, right through until the 2000's. Other building rubble also found its way here, including the remains of at least two local signal boxes and quite a few station buildings. This shunt working was still operating until at least 1992 with an 08 diesel shunter.

Busy scene at Ince Moss. A view of Stanier Mogul No **42954** in charge of a rake of spoil wagons on what looks like a precarious stretch of track. At least three labourers are in evidence assisting with the removal of the wagons' contents.

4TH NOVEMBER 1966 • ALLAN HEYES

INCE MOSS SIDINGS (147)

In the LNWR days this turn was known as Shunt No 7, Ince Moss Up and Down Sidings and was allocated to a special tank loco working 6am - 2pm Monday and Tuesday and 6am to 10pm Wednesday to Saturday. The tip wasn't in existence then so the loco would work both sides of the Liverpool line as required. By 1951 the turn was 'shunt 147' allocated a Super D working 3 shifts, 24 hours/7 days, and only returning to the shed late on Sunday evening. By the mid 1960's this job was a common working for either a BR Standard Class 4, an Ivatt 2MT or a Stanier Mogul. In the later years the Ince Moss tip engine (23 shunt) served both the tip sidings and the yard although the Pemberton Corner shunt loco (21 shunt) could also shunt the yard as required.

BAMFURLONG YARD SHUNT (149 - 152)

Throughout the LNWR and LMS period there were generally five shunt engines here. In LMS days it was reported that there existed a shunt loco at Bamfurlong Screens working two shifts, afternoons and nights, seven days a week. This may have been due to the war situation as no documentation can be found to confirm this. Generally speaking, a loco would be provided for shunting the screens 'as required'. The wood yard behind Pemberton Corner and known locally as the 'Baltic' (the wood came from Russia) or 'Woodside' where pit props were made, has been reported as having, at one time, its own shunt loco, but again this is subject to confirmation. In BR days, the Pemberton Corner loco would generally work the Baltic Sidings, although the Ince Moss pilot was also used on occasion for this purpose The Baltic Yard used casual labour and men would regularly turn up in the hope of work. The Yard Foreman would then select the best from those present.

LNWR 'Small Engine' 0-6-0T No 1096 at work in Bamfurlong Yard.
c.1910 ● STEAM IMAGE

In 1920, Bamfurlong Yard had the following shunt engines:

No 8 - Bamfurlong North End Sidings.
  Working 6.00am Monday - 2pm Sunday. 0-8-2 Tank loco
No 9 - Bamfurlong North End Sidings.
  Working 6.00am Monday - 6am Sunday. Special Tank loco
No 10 - Pemberton Corner Sidings.
  Working 6.00am Monday - 6am Sunday. Special Tank loco
No 11 - Bamfurlong South End Sidings
  (LNWR side). Working 6.00am Monday - 2pm Sunday.
  0-8-2 Tank loco
No 12 - Bamfurlong South End Sidings
  (L&Y side). Working 9.00am - 5.00pm.
  DX or SDX loco

At this time no loco was allocated to what later became 'the long drag' although it was, in essence one of the North End locos.

Shunting at Bamfurlong North End is 'Titanic' 0-8-2T No 47896.
13TH SEPTEMBER 1950 ● H.C. CASSERLEY

By 1951 they had become:

148 Shunt (North End).
  Working 7 days, 3 shifts. Super D loco.
149 Shunt (Long Drag).
  Working 2 shifts, Monday - Friday and one (6am) Saturday. Super D loco.
150 Shunt (Pemberton Corner).
  Working 3 shifts, Monday - Saturday. Ex-L&Y 2F tender loco.
151 Shunt (South End).
  Working throughout from 6am Monday to 10pm Sunday. Super D loco.
152 Shunt (South end L&Y).
  Generally working 4pm and 10pm shifts Monday - Saturday.
  Ex-L&Y 2F tender loco.

The second South End shunt had gone by 1955, leaving four pilots working the yard. The Pemberton Corner Shunt (nicknamed snuffies) was usually a Barton Wright 0-6-0 until the ex-GC locos came to Springs Branch, whereupon a J10 was invariably used. By 1957 the diesel shunters had arrived and they were put on the Bamfurlong jobs - firstly at 'Pemberton Corner' then 'South End' followed by 'North End' which they maintained until the yard ceased operations around 1966. One of the earliest to be observed was D3367 on 10th August 1957.

WIGAN BANK (WIGAN NW STATION PILOT)

The Wigan Bank shunt job had always officially been part of the 'Passenger Links' although it was generally the preserve of the older men or those unfit for main line duty. It was always referred to as 'Wigan Bank' and although it had an official number of 170 Bank, it wasn't used on any documentation. The loco was required to shunt the sidings adjacent to the station (Wallgate side) and also assist any freight train requiring banking up the steep climb to Boar's Head and Coppull. It was rare to bank passenger trains but if the need arose then assistance would be given as far as Standish Junction. It should be remembered that the vast majority of slow freight was routed away from the busy North Western station via the Whelley line, so the demands on the pilot engine for banking became relatively small. In early BR days it was usual to find the older locos on this job and the 'Cauliflowers' were often seen on this turn. Later, when the former GC shed had closed, the J10's would be the favoured locos for the Wigan Bank.

The old order with Cauliflower 0-6-0 No **28580** standing in the platforms. **21ST APRIL 1951** ● H.C. CASSERLEY

After the shed took over the GC workings, a J10 was the usual engine for Wigan Bank. Here No **65192**, one of the very last survivors at the shed, is seen at work.

13TH JUNE 1959 ● RAY FARRELL

The Jinties had occasional spells on the pilot turn in the 1960's and No **47671** is pictured, sat in the centre road of the Liverpool bays. Beyond the loco can be seen the chimneys of Westwood Power Station.

2ND JUNE 1962 ● BEV PRICE

In the 1960's it was the 2-6-4 tanks and the Jinty's and sometimes the Ivatt 2MT's that were employed on Wigan Bank. The diesel shunters finally took over the job in the late 1960's, initially with the ex-LMS variety before the ubiquitous '08's' took control, an era that lasted until the late 1980's before the working finally ceased.

A regular on the station pilot job was Fairburn 2-6-4 tank No **42235**, seen here coupled on to parcels vehicles, the first of which is of Gresley origin.

13TH MAY 1964 • ALLAN HEYES

The Ivatt 2-6-0's were also used regularly and here No **46447** is caught going about her duties at the south end of Platform 5. Judging by the new ballast, access to the old turntable here might now have been disconnected.

11TH AUGUST 1966 • ALLAN HEYES

By 1967 the shed occasionally had Stanier power available to fulfil the Wigan Bank turn. Black Five No **44679** rests between duties in the north end bay platform.

4TH MARCH 1967 • TOM HEAVYSIDE

WIGAN CANAL GOODS

The LNWR goods yard and building was situated just south of the station, close to the canal, and was also known as Chapel Lane Goods. According to official British Railways records, the depot received 56 wagons and forwarded 31 wagons each day in 1963. Although nothing shows in the local shunt loco allocation for 1920, the LNWR would employ one engine here and in later days it became shunt number 156. Canal sidings would also be visited by various trip workings during the day, particularly Trips 133 and 134.

154

BANKING ENGINES

In LNWR days the main requirements for banking were from Ince Moss and of the nine banking turns, five worked from there. In the 1940's, the Garston trains went via St Helens but then they changed, going via Golborne, hence the change in bank engine positions. By 1951 the focus of banking was from Bamfurlong Junction over the Whelley line. At this time there were five banking engine turns from the shed, Nos 160 - 164 of which four were stationed at Bamfurlong Junction for assisting over the Whelley line, usually to Roundhouse Sidings, and often to Coppull, and on at least one East Lancs bound train it would hook up and assist all the way to Brinscall beyond Chorley. Freights over the Whelley line were allowed a maximum of 34 wagons (340 Tons), otherwise a banker was needed.

Until the WD's arrived, Super D's were the usual bank engines and the tender cab version was particularly welcome as these banking jobs always involved a lot of running 'tender first' returning to Bamfurlong Junction. In the 1960's, some 4F's and BR Standard Class 4's also appeared until, in the final years, the Black 8's were in command.

BANK ENGINES 1920

	Title	Engine Type	Time of working	Work
54	Ince Moss Banker	not given	Treble manned, 04:00 - 00:15 MX, 06:00 - 02:15 MO	Ince Moss & Garswood
55	Ince Moss Banker	not given	Double manned, 05:30 - 19:00 MO, Treble 23:00 - 19:15 SX Single manned, 23:00 Sat - 06:00 Sun	Ince Moss & Garswood
56	Ince Moss Banker	not given	Treble manned, 19:15 - 14:30 Daily	Ince Moss & Whelley
57	Ince Moss Banker	not given	Treble manned, 06:00 - 02:15 Daily	Ince Moss & Whelley
58	Ince Moss Banker	not given	Treble manned, 20:00 - 16:15 Daily	Ince Moss & Whelley
59	Bamfurlong Banker	not given	Treble manned, 07:00 - 03:15 Daily	Bamfurlong & Whelley
60	Bamfurlong Jn Banker	not given	Treble manned, 05:00 - 13:15 Daily	as required by control
61	Bamfurlong Sdgs Banker	not given	13:00 - 09:15 Daily	as required
62	Bamfurlong Jn Banker	not given	Double manned, 23:00 Mon - 12:15 Sun	as required

An unidentified 'Super D' assists a freight off the Whelley line through Standish Junction. Having come this far from Bamfurlong, the loco will continue to help to the top of the incline at Coppull before dropping off. From here it will probably be at least 30 minutes before the engine arrived back at Bamfurlong ready for another job. Notice that the loco has 111 chalked on the bufferbeam, presumably from another days trip working.

c.1961 • BOB MAXWELL

All is not as it seems here as Super D 0-8-0 No 49451 is actually the banking engine on a mineral train to Kearsley Power Station on the L&Y. The train would probably have started from Bamfurlong Yard with the train engine on the rear. The bank engine on the front would travel via the Whelley line to De Trafford Junction where the train reversed and the rear engine, in this case Patricroft's Jubilee, No 45600 *Bermuda*, would then become the train engine. After assisting from De Trafford Junction up to Hindley and often to the top of the hill at Chew Moor Sidings, No 49451 would retrace its route back to Bamfurlong for its next task.

(above) approaching De Trafford Junction
(right) Hindley North

16TH SEPTEMBER 1961 ● A.C. GILBERT

Stanier Class Five No 45376 receives banking assistance from WD 2-8-0 No **90148** on the approach to Amberswood East Junction on the Whelley line.

2ND SEPTEMBER 1964 ● BRIAN BARLOW

156

```
.R.(L.M.R.)                              B.R. 358/5    34
              NORTH WESTERN LINES
     FREIGHT ENGINE WORKINGS COMMENCING 14 JUNE, 1965.
        ENGINE & MEN'S WORKINGS           SPRINGS BRANCH : SHEET 62
                                            Book    Book
                                             On     Off      H.M.
        ONE CLASS 8F (WD 2-8-0)             07 35   15 30    7 55
        WEEKLY AVAILABILITY TURN
        ENGINE to Shed for coal at time
        suitable to traffic requirements

Turn 408  No. 126 Bank
          ENGINE PREPARED by Turn 358              MO
          Springs Branch M.P.D.    07 50    LE     MO
          Bamfurlong Sdgs
08 00     BANK                     15 00           MO
          Bamfurlong Sdgs          15 00    LE     MO
15 10     Springs Branch M.P.D.

Turn 409  No. 126 Bank                      22 50   06 50    8 00
          Springs Branch M.P.D.    23 50    LE     SX
          Bamfurlong Sdgs
00 01     BANK                     06 20           MX
          RELIEF 06 20 by Turns 410 (MSX)          MX
                               411 (SO)

Turn 410  No. 126 Bank                      05 50   14 00    8 10
          RELIEVE Turn 409 at 06 20               MSX
06 20     BANK                     13 30          MSX
          Bamfurlong Sdgs          13 30    LE    MSX
13 40     Springs Bch. M.P.D.

Turn 411  No. 126 Bank                      05 50   13 50    8 00
          RELIEVE Turn 409 at 06 20               SO
06 20     BANK                     13 20          SO
          RELIEF 13 20 by Turn 412                SO

Turn 412  No. 126 Bank                      12 40    -        -
13 20     RELIEVE Turn 411 at 13 20               SO
          BANK                     16 00          SO
          Bamfurlong Sdgs          16 35   7F25   SO
17 04     Warrington E.S.                   LE or SO
          Springs Bch. M.P.D.               as reqd
```

The bank engine siding at Bamfurlong Junction holds No **45312**. By this time the Super D's and the WD's had long since gone and although the Black Eights were the normal choice, Black Fives were also used.

3RD JUNE 1967 • TOM HEAVYSIDE

BANK ENGINES 1951

Title	Engine	Time of working	Work
160	Bamfurlong Jn Banker	Super D	3 shifts, Mon - Sat, 2 shifts Sub	Bamfurlong Jn & Whelley
161	Bamfurlong Jn Banker	Super D	4 shifts, Mon - Sat, 2 shifts Sun	Bamfurlong Jn & Whelley
162	Bamfurlong Jn Banker	Super D	4 shifts, Tue - Sat, 3 on Mon	Bamfurlong Jn & Whelley
163	Bank	Super D	4 shifts, Mon, Tue, Fri, others 3	As required
164	Bank	Super D	2 shifts, Mon - Fri	As required

162 bank would normally do the Brinscall banking job, a move that required hooking on. At Brinscall the guard would lift the coupling with a pole. If it was awkward he may need to do this from his steps - such was the demands of the job in those days. Imagine how Health and Safety would view that now.

160-163 banking engines all left the shed on the first turn on Monday morning and would be remanned each shift. 163 bank engine worked from Ince Moss Junction and would bank trains up to Garswood or beyond as required.

164 bank commenced every shift with the engine and men coming off the shed.

An atmospheric view of a couple of Super D's returning from banking jobs. The nearer is No **49451** whilst the other remains unidentified. The pair are held at Platt Bridge Junction (signal box above) and are awaiting a path to Bamfurlong Junction Bank Engine Siding.

JUNE 1962 • TOM SUTCH

An interesting extract from the notebooks of Driver Tommy Taylor:

One night on banking duties at Bamfurlong, the call came through that the Saltley to Carlisle car flat train was in the block. The crew mounted the loco, placed some Garswood Hall coal in the firebox, turned the blower on hard and prayed for a rise in the pressure gauge because the local Garswood Hall coal was the rubbish coal given to Bank and Shunt engines.

The train arrived on the down through line and headed under the main line towards the Whelley line and stopped with the engine under Platt Bridge box. Because the train was very long, the brake van stopped under the long main line bridge. The bank engine crept out of the banking sidings and up to the brake van, however, they were now being choked with fumes from their fire and could not see the train engine, nor would they have been able to hear the answer to their 'two crows' whistle signifying that they were ready to start.

The upshot of this was that it was decided to open the regulator slightly, dismount and walk through the long bridge to watch the train engine start, then at their leisure catch the bank engine as it strolled past. Unfortunately for this crew, the Saltley men felt the slight push of the opened regulator and set off at a rate of knots, leaving the banking crew racing like mad to catch up to their engine. It was fortunate the crew was young and managed to scramble aboard but they spent the trip gasping for breath and vowing never to try that trick again.

In LNWR and LMS days, the bank engines would invariably be one of the variety of Bowen Cooke 0-8-0 tender engines, although the ex-L&Y 0-6-0 saddletanks (Humpies) were occasionally called upon. Once the Super D's had gone, the Ince Moss banker was usually in the hands of a WD 2-8-0 and the other turns usually featured these engines, but occasionally a BR Standard Class 4 was used. In the final period of steam, the Stanier 8F's were in control of all bank duties before they, in turn, handed over to diesel traction, albeit at a reduced level. Classes 25, 40 & 47 were all represented. Local footplatemen reported that Crewe men wouldn't go on the Whelley line without a banker. By 1966 there remained just four banking engine diagrams which appear to have continued until the end of steam. The Wigan NW station bank engine, always known as 'Wigan Bank', was rostered in the passenger link and is described in more detail on pages 153 and 154.

BANK ENGINES October 1966

	Title	Engine	Time of working
126	Bamfurlong Jn Banker	8F	08:00 - 15:00mo, 00:01msx - 13:30msx, 00:01 - 16:00so
127	Bamfurlong Jn Banker	8F	06:00mo - 22:00so
128	Ince Moss Banker	8F (sx)	00:26mo - 14:30so 18:45 - 21:30so (Ivatt Class2 so)
129	Ince Moss Banker	8F	00:26mo - 11:50mo, 15:00mo - 11:50so, 15:00so - 21:50so

Banking duties were also undertaken on the incline from Ince Moss Junction up to Carr Mill. Here 8F 2-8-0 No **48125** has assisted to Garswood and is now running back to Ince Moss. Apparently there was one Bank driver who didn't like the guards and he gave them all a hard time. Because of this he was known as 'Bumper Wright'.

1965 ● LEN BALL

Having dropped down from Coppull after banking, WD 2-8-0 No **90317** drops off extra coal supplies to Standish Junction signalbox.

26TH MARCH 1964 ● ALLAN HEYES

A banker on the front with No 75051 assisting WD No **90204** on a southbound freight. The Standard Class 4 will have been facing north on the bank engine siding when the call for assistance was received, hence the tender first running.

20TH JUNE 1964 ● JOHN BURGESS

ACCIDENTS, INCIDENTS AND FOLKLORE

As with any engine shed, Springs Branch, its men and locomotives, were all liable to occasional mishaps. Those involving the locomotives can be minor, such as derailments on shed, or something of a more serious nature. On 8th April 1941, Black Five No 5425 was badly damaged after a bomb was dropped on the engine whilst it was stopped in a loop at Winsford. The Springs Branch driver was regrettably killed whilst his fireman, Reg Tierney, survived after hastily leaving the footplate. The engine was taken to Crewe Works where it received a new boiler (ex-No 5445) and a Heavy General Overhaul. After 119 weekdays out of traffic, the loco returned to Springs Branch on 23rd August 1941 and subsequently became one of the 'Royal Train' engines *(see page 118)*. Stanier 2-6-4 Tank No 42235 was involved in a serious collision at Ince Moss Junction on 17th February 1958 which is fully described below. Two Black Fives, Nos 45414 (Edge Hill) and Springs Branch's No 45313 were involved in the Bickershaw Junction accident in 1965, and another Black Five No 45094 of Edge Hill shed, ended up on its side after 'running away off shed'. A Super D also ran away and travelled across the turntable and part way up the bank towards the canteen and water tank.

Ince Moss Junction Collision 17th February 1958

A Black Five was travelling light engine from Preston to Edge Hill, following the cancellation of its intended freight. It stopped near the relieving point at Ince Moss Junction as the driver, a passed fireman, hadn't signed the route beyond this point. The signal for his train was in the 'off' position but he was expecting a conductor so, after stopping, went back to the relief cabin to make enquiries. It transpired no request had been received regarding a conductor so 'Control' then had to arrange for Springs Branch shed to provide one (it was a five minute walk away). The driver returned to his engine and waited. Meanwhile, a Springs Branch crew on Fairburn 2-6-4 Tank No 42235 departed from Wigan NW station on the 02:00 express passenger train to Liverpool Lime St. This ran under clear signals to Ince Moss Junction where a collision with the light engine occurred. The fault was put firmly with the signalman at St Helens No 3 who had, in error, mistakenly thought the light engine had passed him and accepted the express. At the time Ince Moss Junction signalbox was unmanned as were other boxes through to St. Helens No 3. The light engine had therefore actually stopped in the block section now controlled by St Helens No 3.

Fairburn 2-6-4T No 42235 heads a Liverpool Lime Street to Wigan NW train under the GC viaduct at St Helens as it approaches Gerards Bridge Junction. Worthy of note is the first coach which is of Gresley origin.

c1957 ● GERRY DROUGHT

Ex-Midland loco runs away on Road 6

Three of the ex-Midland 0-6-0 tender engines came to Springs Branch for a short period, and it was one of these that was reputedly involved in an incident with Driver Bill Hobson, an ex-Furness man. When they first arrived, few drivers had handled them and they had one peculiarity in that the brake handle was not in the usual place, being in the middle of the backhead where you would expect to find the blower handle. On the eventful day, the engine was standing on Road 6, the wheeldrop road, and required moving. A spare driver was asked to undertake this and moved every handle including the regulator but failed to get the engine to budge, so he went to the foreman to seek help. The foreman then asked a driver to move the engine and he, on mounting the footplate, took off the brake. This proved to be a bad mistake as the previous man had put the reversing lever in full gear, shut the taps and opened the regulator thereby filling the steam chest before leaving the footplate. Consequently, the engine moved quickly along the track, over the wheel drop and up the concrete ramp, demolishing some overhead trunking and knocking its chimney off. Fortunately, given the circumstances, little damage was done.

Amberswood Collision

Arthur Edwards describes an accident on the Whelley line.

The Whelley line was like a Big Dipper, with the trickiest bit between Amberswood East and West signalboxes, where there is a dip about mid point which required careful control from both train engine and banker. On one occasion we were banking a freight train through this dip with a Super D running tender first, and I saw the wagons towards the front start to buck and bounce in the air. As my driver was not sighted due to the curvature of the line, I reached for the duplicate brake lever and slammed on the brake. We stopped instantaneously and took action to protect the train by laying detonators on both lines whilst the guard walked forward to check the train. We walked back to Amberswood West signalbox to inform the signalman, who called 'Control'. The emergency crane was called out to clear the wreckage. The cause of the derailment was discovered by the guard, who, on walking the length of his train, found a platelayer's rail jack under the rail.

Runaways from the shed yard

On 18th July 1964, Edge Hill Black Five No 45094 ran away and ended up running through the sand drag at Platt Bridge Junction. The loco ended up on its side and gave the breakdown crew a challenging session.

18TH JULY 1964 ● JOHN BURGESS

Bickershaw Junction Collision February 1965

One accident that is well remembered by Springs Branch men is that at Bickershaw Junction. On this occasion a light engine, No 45313 of Springs Branch, had come up the incline from Hindley South, having worked at Wigan Central Goods yard. On arriving at Bickershaw Junction, the engine would reverse and take the main Manchester Exchange to Springs Branch line back to the shed. It appears that it was held at the box, and the driver, Jimmy Lincoln, went to see the signalman as required by the rules. The delay was to allow a Manchester to Liverpool parcels to clear the line, which it did, whereupon the driver returned to the engine and after a short while the signal was cleared and the light engine moved off. What the crew of Black Five No 45313 didn't know was that the signalman had forgotten their presence and had actually pulled off for another parcels train (believed to be a Manchester to Wigan) with No 45414 at the head. Visibility was poor at the time and although the light engine had a little start, it was only estimated to be running at around 20mph, insufficient to take it clear of the fast moving parcels train, which was running on clear signals and bearing down on it at 60mph.

Edge Hill's Black Five No 45414 suffered serious damage in the accident as a result of which it was withdrawn.

FEBRUARY 1965 ● AUTHOR'S COLLECTION

The first the crew of the parcels train knew of the light engine was a somewhat hazy sighting of the locomotive a short distance in front of them. Impact was inevitable regardless of any action by the footplatemen concerned. Edge Hill Black Five No 45414, not long in service after a major overhaul at Crewe, ploughed into the light engine. As No 45313 was travelling tender first, the two locomotives hit smokebox to smokebox, with the result that both suffered serious front end damage. Certainly No 45414 was totally derailed, as were some of the parcels vehicles. As would be expected in the circumstances, there was considerable damage to the track. After recovery from the site, both engines were taken to Springs Branch shed from where it was decided that neither would be repaired. Both ended their days at the Central Wagon Works scrapyard soon after.

The mangled remains of No 45313 in the shed yard. Parts of the lettering 'Springs Branch, Wigan' remain visible on the bufferbeam - a trademark of Glasgow's Cowlairs Works where this and other English based engines were repaired in the latter years.

FEBRUARY 1965 ● J. DANIELS

161

Other incidents

Engine sheds have always been places with the potential for accidents. In a staff manual from the turn of the century, it is reported that Mr A Southall, a driver who had started in 1893, was killed on shed age 47. In the 1940's a cleaner was killed on No 10 road. There is no doubt other serious incidents occurred but those records are now lost. Some of the less serious episodes, which were probably fairly frequent, are detailed in the Foreman's Log book. An example is shown here.

22nd January 1951. Steamraiser R Lancaster sent to Wigan Infirmary with badly burst left little finger after first aid 5.0. Unable to turn off for 6.0 149 shunt.

7th February 1951. Washout J Brown reported at 3.30 he had fallen into No 10 shed pit and damaged left lower ribs, left arm bruised, also right knee. First aid rendered.

Monday 7th May 1951. Driver T Wood with engine No 7884 on 154 shunt was stood at Fir Tree and was run into by a Garston man with engine No 8327 (6C) causing damage to buffer plate of No 7884.

29th May 1951. Coyle was sent home by ambulance this morning at 3.45. He commenced to vomit blood from his old war wound.

16th June 1951. Stores van M279924 door damaged when being brought into Barracks Sidings, wagons left foul in ARK road.

4th October 1951. Passed Cleaner R Fisher on duty firing for Driver H Morrell on 123 Trip, engine No 52341. Preparing engine on shed 9.5am received injury to face over right eye. Sent to hospital for further attention.

14th October 1951. Steamraiser G Makin, while using the injector on engine 4302 was scalded on both legs through the valve on the slacking pipe being left in the open position. Treated for burns and went home for change of clothing and resumed duty again.

On his last day of employment with BR, Andrew Taylor derailed an 18" Goods

In the 1970/80's, Bert Dixon was playing cards in the mess room and dropped a card. He bent down to retrieve it but didn't resurface and subsequently died of a heart attack. The mess room door wouldn't open wide enough so the window had to be taken out to remove his stoutly body.

Humorous (Tales of events, real or fiction?)

One fireman, known as Shipperbottom, was noted for his humorous ways. Prior to 1948 a railwayman was killed on the main line and it is reported that Mr Shipperbottom took the severed head into Springs Branch No 1 signalbox to enquire if anyone knew him. I doubt he got the reaction he expected.

Railwaymen would constantly play jokes on other men and if they were suitably irked, some devious plan may be put in action. Such was the case when, on a somewhat foggy night, two men decided to repay an awkward signalman. The men proceeded from the shed yard towards Cromptons signalbox, each holding a lamp at a position akin to that of a locomotive. On arriving at the dummy and telephone used to request permission to leave the shed, the men reported that they were 'engine & crew for Bamfurlong' and the signalman subsequently cleared the dummy for them to leave the yard. They continued their pretence, passed the box, switched off their lamps and disappeared into the haze leaving a bewildered signalman wondering what had happened to the engine.

THE FINAL YEARS

From 1965, the sidings alongside No 1 shed were used for stabling both steam and diesel locomotives. In addition to Springs Branch's own allocation, the sidings were constantly receiving locos from further afield destined for the nearby scrapyard of the Central Wagon Works. Some of these stood for months on end before making their final journey down the branch itself.

Very few people pointed their camera over the wall on the shed side of Warrington Road bridge, but this unusual view shows much of interest. The coal wagons, hopper and guards van in the centre are standing on the Up Springs Branch with the Down line to the right clear. Further right are Brewery Sidings, complete with stored locos, at the head of which is Jubilee No 45592 *Indore*, minus its chimney. To the left are engine shed sidings, holding stabled and stored engines, with Springs Branch No 2 signal box beyond. The houses prominent to the right are on Polding Street - ideal locations for budding trainspotters! The engine shed itself is just off the picture to the left.

17TH JANUARY 1965 ● R. FREEMAN

By 1967, British Railways was nearing completion of its quest to replace all steam locomotives by diesel and electric traction. Most of the country had already become completely dieselised and the North West of England was destined to become the final retreat for steam. Springs Branch men watched as local sheds closed, such as Aintree on 12th June 1967 and, even nearer to home, Sutton Oak at St Helens on 19th June 1967. Some of Sutton Oak's engines came to Springs Branch for a short period. When Warrington's Dallam shed closed on 2nd October 1967, Springs Branch knew the end was nigh and, on 4th December 1967, the shed was officially closed to steam. Some of Springs Branch's fleet of steam locomotives moved on to the remaining steam sheds to eke out a few more months service but about 25 engines were withdrawn and stayed on site, some for quite a while. Many of these had their rods removed before a final journey to the scrapyard. Servicing facilities remained available in the short term and interestingly there were seven engines in steam on shed on Saturday 9th December, five days after closure to steam. This continued into the New Year as on Sunday 7th January 1968 eleven locos were recorded as being in steam on the shed.

On Shed Sunday 26th November 1967 (2 weeks before closure to steam)

Withdrawn	44658	44678	44679	44732	44776	45116	45198	45267	45368	48125	48261	48675
	48676	48724	76075	76081								
Stored	45431											
Possibly stored	44682	44873	44920	44962	45331	45449	76077					
Later transferred	44711	44780	44842	45268	45296	48117	48132	48192	48193	48325	48338	48410
	48752	48764										
Visitors		70004 12A	70023 12A	48436 9K	48617 8E							
Diesel shunters	12017	12020	12021	12061	D2088	D2126	D2376	D2860	D2867	D3361		
Diesel Locos	D210	D211	D218	D219	D224	D268	D352	D379	D5199	D5260	D5261	D5286
	D5287	D7553	D7556	D7610	D7674	D1846						
Diesels stored	D2557	D2558	D2561	D2563	D2565	D2568	D2570					**Total 77**

After closure to steam, visiting engines would continue to occasionally appear on shed and this included two Britannia Pacifics, Nos 70023 *Venus* and 70035 *Rudyard Kipling* on 24th December 1967 and No 70004 *William Shakespeare* two days later - all three likely to have arrived off Carnforth or Carlisle to Ince Moss freights. Springs Branch's coaling plant must have stayed in operation until at least January 1968, although it's doubtful that any new supply of coal would have been ordered once supplies were exhausted. When Carlisle Kingmoor MPD closed on 1st January 1968, one of their Britannia Pacifics No 70045 *Lord Rowallan,* found itself on shed. It was withdrawn on the spot and having been noted stored in the sidings at the side of No 1 shed on 3rd January 1968, it was there until at least 18th February.

Ivatt 2-6-0 No 46515 has had its rods removed and these are in the process of being placed in the tender. The loco will then make its last trip to the scrapyard. **22ND MAY 1967 ● ALLAN HEYES**

Ex-Colwick 8F No 48750, now of Northwich, drifts through the sidings alongside the shed. **c1967 ● LES RILEY**

8F 2-8-0 No 48752 is seen at the shed in August 1967. Although it left for further work at Edge Hill, it returned for storage and had the distinction of being the very last withdrawn steam loco at Springs Branch, still being there in November 1968, 11 months after the shed closed to steam. **c1967 ● LES RILEY**

On Shed - Saturday 9th December 1967 (1 week after closure to steam)

Withdrawn	44658	44678	44679	44682	44776	44819	44831	44873	44920	45048	45198	45281
	45267	45331	45368	45431	48125	48676	48724	76075	76077	76079	76080	76084
Later transferred	48206											
Visitors	44878 12A	45187 8A	48012 8A	48340 8E	48507 9F	48765 9F	70021 12A	92212 10A				
Diesel shunters	12004	12013	12017	12020	12021	12031	12038	12063	12076	12097	D2088	D2126
	D2376	D2858	D3184	D3198								
Diesel locos	D217	D219	D255	D269	D290	D310	D388	D5089	D5151	D5202	D5262	D5273
	D5287	D5293	D7550	D7552	D7634	D7635	D7640	D7641	D7677	D1622	D1858	
Diesels stored	D2557	D2558	D2561	D2563	D2565	D2568	D2570					**Total 79**

Visiting 8F No 48340 from Northwich stands under the coaling stage. By this time the shed had been closed to steam for almost four weeks and it's doubtful whether there was still any coal to be had. **28TH DECEMBER 1967 ● ALLAN HEYES**

An Ivatt 2-6-0, believed to be No **46515,** awaits its fate in the sidings alongside the main line. Springs Branch No 2 signalbox lurks in the background. **1967 ● LES RILEY**

The final removal of withdrawn steam locos was quite protracted and there were still twelve on site in April 1968, nine in May and four in June. By July, a single Stanier 8F 2-8-0, No 48752, remained; however, possibly because of some damage, it was still on shed on 3rd November 1968 - an astonishing eleven months after closure to steam.

On Shed Sunday 7th January 1968 (5 weeks after closure to steam)

Withdrawn	44658	44678	44679	44682	44776	44819	44831	44873	44920	45048	45198	45267
	45281	45331	45368	45431	48125	48675	48676	48678	48724	76075	76077	76079
	76080	76084										
Stored	70045 12A											
Visitors	44804 9E	45013 12A	48201 9F	48206 8C	48410 10F	48424 9L	48646 10D	48683 8E	92077 10A	92165 8C	92233 12A	92249 12A
Diesel shunters	12003	12004	12013	12017	12020	12021	12023	12031	12032	12072	D2377	D2378
	D2858	D3198										
Diesel Locos	D200	D211	D214	D233	D248	D337	D5248	D5259	D5264	D5265	D7546	D7551
	D7554	D7557	D7610	D7635	D7639	D7641						
Diesel Stored	D2557	D2558	D2561	D2563	D2565	D2568	D2570			**11 in steam**	**Total 78**	

Steam and diesel rub shoulders in the shed yard during the final year of steam. A visiting Standard Class Five stands alongside diesel shunter No **12070** and Sulzer Type 2 No **D7639**. Stanier Class Five No **45198** is also prominent. **1967 ● LES RILEY**

165

As 1968 dawned, most of the old No 1 shed was filled with stabled diesel locomotives or shunters, although visitors may recall a set of coaches in road six which was a communications train, kept in a state of permanent readiness for unforeseen circumstances! Nothing really changed now until the early 1980's when concrete roof sections of this shed started to deteriorate and the shed was considered unsafe, whereupon locomotives were banned from using it and, soon after, demolition of the building commenced.

English Electric Type 4 2,000 b.h.p. diesel-electric I Co-Co I No **D341** rests between duties in the Engine Shed Sidings at the west side of the shed. **JULY 1968 ● JOHN BURGESS**

Standing in front of No 1 shed are a trio of Derby/Sulzer Type 2's. Nos **D5261, D5204** and **D7637**. Of interest are the early livery variations.

MARCH 1968 ● JOHN BURGESS

BR Class 03 0-6-0 No D2126 stands surrounded by members of the larger variety of diesel shunter at the bottom of the shed. A handful of these diminutive shunters arrived during the summer of 1967, lasting until 1972

1972 ● TOM SUTCH

An impressive aerial view of the shed buildings taken from the top of one of the lighting columns. There is little activity outside the diesel maintenance depot to the right but doubtless men would be hard at work inside. In stark contrast, the yard of No 1 shed is full to capacity with a fine collection of Class 25, 40 and 47 diesels in attendance. The old fuel road is still available at the bottom of the photo.

9TH MAY 1976 • CHRIS COATES

A nightime view inside No 1 shed with Sulzers **D7598** nearer the camera and **D5258** beyond. They are standing on Road 1 which, in steam days, was eventually given over to the servicing of the depot's diesel shunters. Conditions look bleak outside and it was always a policy to stable diesel locos under cover whenever possible.

7TH FEBRUARY 1974 • CHRIS COATES

A daytime view inside No 1 shed looking at the occupants from the slightly elevated corridor which ran the width of the building at the rear of the shed (see page 13). A couple of mineral wagons occupy the shortened Road 1 on the right, beyond which is a Class 25 loco. Those identified are Class 40 No **40133** on Road 3 with Sulzers Nos **25248** and **25207** occupying the end of Road 2 nearest the camera. Note the fitters' workbench in the foreground.

3RD AUGUST 1974 • TOM SUTCH

167

◀ **Class 25 No 25282** stands on road 1 outside No 1 shed. By this time the roof was becoming dangerous and there is a fence across the face of the shed preventing access. The shed was demolished within two years.

31ST JANUARY 1982 ● **DAVE INGHAM**

The view looking north east inside a deserted No 1 shed prior to demolition. **15TH OCTOBER 1983** ● **TOM SUTCH**

Work in progress. The Manchester contractors Connell & Finnigan were charged with demolishing the building. The roads, which were truncated, remained in use throughout, as witnessed in this view looking south, by an assortment of diesels. **OCTOBER 1983** ● **FRED BANKS**

The view looking north-east down the side of the face of the building. **OCTOBER 1983** ● **FRED BANKS**

The Traction Maintenance Depot

The new Traction Maintenance Depot was built as part of the London Midland Region's North West modernisation programme and, upon opening, was the only one of its type on the 141 miles of main line between Crewe and Carlisle. The building measures 282 feet long and 137 feet wide and a staff of around 100 were employed. The depot was now capable of undertaking major repairs, which included body lifts, and although serious repairs to power units were not normally done, the shed did, on one occasion, replace a camshaft on a Class 40 loco, a repair that would only normally happen at Crewe. BR organised a first Open Day on Saturday 22nd August 1970 which attracted 3,000 visitors and the BBC's 'Nationwide' cameras. Rides were available in the cab of Class 25 5207 at 2 shillings each. On Saturday 7th July 1973 the depot held a second such occasion with locomotives on display and demonstrations of railway machinery. Various stands were again in evidence together with a rare appearance of Collectors Corner, the relic sales department of BR. In the meantime Springs Branch became coded SP in May 1973.

In the early days after opening, Sulzer Type 2's (Class 25) and English Electric Type 4's (Class 40) dominated the scene but the large class of Brush Type 4's (Class 47) then became increasingly more in evidence followed by the Class 50's which were regular visitors for servicing and repair. During the 1970's there was still a considerable amount of coal traffic and the Bickershaw complex was the major hub of this. In 1978 approximately 50 additional staff and 6 supervisors came to the depot, mainly from Allerton, to undertake work on overhead line maintenance. Initially they were housed in various places within the depot building before moving into the upper floor of a new office block that was built 50ft from the north end of the depot. The lower floor of this block became the new offices for the 400 traincrew working from the shed and this situation continued until they moved to Warrington on closure of the depot.

The three road Maintenance Depot was capable of undertaking servicing and repair on any class of loco and Class 50's became common visitors. Here No **D406** receives attention within the building. 12 main line locomotives could be accommodated under cover.

MARCH 1968 ● JOHN BURGESS

Brush Type 4 No 47119 dominates this general view within the depot. Other classes are in evidence, as is a small overhead crane for lifting cylinder heads to the left.

c1973 ● FRED BANKS COLLECTION

A pair of unidentified Class 40's, both on 4 x 20 ton Matterson jacks, have been lifted clear of their bogies. This third road is fitted with specially reinforced concrete jacking strips running the full length of the depot. It was also equipped with a specially designed mobile straddler crane, capable of lifting half a ton, but for heavier duties, a Coles mobile diesel crane stands in the distance, and this could handle up to six and a half tons. In addition, each of the three pits are fitted with fluorescent lighting and power points.

c1973 ● FRED BANKS COLLECTION

By the 1970's, the Class 47 diesels were now hauling MGR wagons out from Abram North sidings, (the exchange sidings for Bickershaw Colliery), the wagons having been brought up from the colliery by the NCB steam or diesel locos. A major change now occurred when a new bunker, loading facility and rail layout was created at Bickershaw and in May 1984, the first of the Type 1's (Class 20's) arrived for crew training, and soon commenced their legendary top and tail formation, utilising two pairs of locos. By this time the Class 25's and 40's were being withdrawn and the Class 47's found other work. The depot also had Class 31's allocated in the 1990's and they performed duties other than the MGR trains.

Brush Type 4 No 47366 awaits its next duty in the shed yard. The loco, which is carrying the pleasing two tone green livery, was previously numbered D1885.

24TH FEBRUARY 1975 ● CHRIS COATES

Standing at the side of the new depot on land which had previously been occupied by the turntable is Class 40 **40010**. The two storey building contains workshops, stores, offices and staff amenities. Two well equipped classrooms enable the training of the maintenance staff to be undertaken and adjacent is a large mess room, locker room, drying room and showers.

JULY 1981 ● MALCOLM CAPSTICK

From the mid 1970's the depot undertook repair and servicing work on track tamper machines and, a little later, on the long welded trains. By 1984 there was a reduction in the workload on loco repair but, fortunately, more work was obtained on the long welded trains and small cranes, resulting in many men transferring across, and this work continued until 1994. A concrete test bed for 75 ton cranes was also created at the side of the shed with the intention of undertaking repairs, servicing and testing on these large cranes but sadly this work never materialised.

A Track Tamper Machine in what can only be described as brand new condition stands on what are now the stabling roads, but were once inside No 1 shed

c1985 ● FRED BANKS

There was now a brief spell with Class 56's on the MGR trains (generally on the Gladstone Dock traffic) which lasted until 1991, when the arrival of new motive power occurred in the shape of the Class 60. During the first few months of 1992 the shed received an allocation of 'Coal sector' Class 60's and thereafter the standard formation for the Fiddlers Ferry MGR trains seemed to be a Class 60 with two Class 20's on the drawbar. Unfortunately Bickershaw Colliery closed in March 1992 and all operations had ceased by May 1992, ending a long association with this pit. This now left Springs Branch with little alternative work and although the shed actually acquired a new overhead crane gantry, enabling lifts up to 15 tons, incoming work was diminishing.

Class 20 No 20073 is standing on tracks that were once inside No 1 shed. A Class 47 No **47191** brings up the rear.

c1985 ● FRED BANKS

The shed had a brief spell servicing Class 56's. Here Nos **56080** and **56085** stand in front of the Diesel Depot. Note once more the livery variation.

c1985 ● FRED BANKS

The Class 60's have arrived and Nos **60066 *John Logie Baird*** and **60073** stand on the old No 5 road.

1991 ● FRED BANKS

Trainload Freight had been formed in 1987 as a sector of BR and existed until privatisation of the railways in 1994. In 1994 Train-Load coal became Trans-Rail, a new trainload railfreight operator which was subsequently purchased by EWS (English, Welsh & Scottish Railways) in 1996. By this time EWS was owned by a consortium led by the American Company Wisconsin Central. Unfortunately, by 1997 the writing was well and truly on the wall for the depot, and it closed on 4th May of that year, with loco servicing being transferred to the new depot at Warrington Arpley.

This may well have been the end of the story but, at that time, EWS was beginning to realise the value of recycling locomotive components and so Springs Branch entered its next phase of life as Wigan CRD (Component Recovery Depot). During this time diesel locomotives would be brought to Springs Branch and left in the yard. Gradually each locomotive would enter the depot and be stripped of any useful components before being dumped in the sidings. The retrieved components would be wrapped, stacked and stored for dispatch as required. The carcass of the locomotive would then be cut into pieces, put in a skip and removed by road transport and it was not uncommon to see a locomotive body mounted on a flat rail wagon or similar support awaiting stripping. Class 37's, 47's and 56's seemed to be the main provider of spares although Class 31's were also noted around the shed yard, as was the occasional Class 08 shunter. Around this time the depot had also been repairing and scrapping wagons

The next change was in 2001 when Canadian National bought Wisconsin Central and so EWS had yet another owner. Unfortunately the CRD operation on locomotives ceased in 2005 and the few remaining carcasses were removed by low loaders. Wagon repairs, modifications and servicing continued and, shortly after, work commenced on refurbishing and servicing MPV vehicles. These were Multi Purpose Vehicles that could undertake various functions whilst travelling a given route, such as Sandite track cleaning and deicing fluid or weedkiller application. During this EWS period the depot also undertook the odd repair to Class 08's and to the Class 37 locomotives used for the MPV trains, although this petered out in 2008. Also locomotives would be sent from Warrington for moderate repairs that could be undertaken with the facilities at the shed, such as cylinder head removal to facilitate gasket replacement. EWS was finally acquired by Deutsche Bahn AG in June 2007, and two years later rebranded as DB Schenker Rail (UK). At the time of writing (2010) the depot was still performing work on the MPV vehicles and undertaking occasional loco repairs to ex-EWS engines.

Class 31 No 31304 stands behind the imposing Transrail Traction Maintenance Depot, Wigan Springs Branch, signboard.
FEBRUARY 1997 ● MALCOLM CAPSTICK

The body of Class 47 No 47555 sits on a flat wagon, its bogies possibly removed for immediate reuse. **18TH APRIL 1999 ● BRIAN ROBERTS**

The general view of the stabling sidings looking south. The depot is busy once again during these component recovery days.
18TH APRIL 1999 ● BRIAN ROBERTS

Final ride for No 56121 after it had caused chaos by being taken over Cemetery Road bridge in error. It was despatched to Springs Branch for component recovery; however, despite police escort, the loco was mistakenly taken to an industrial complex. Here it was turned, but was unable to climb up the incline back over the bridge. At this point Railtrack grounded the loco as it had passed over a weight restricted bridge in Cemetery Road. Over the next couple of days the bridge was inspected and, with assistance from an additional tractor unit, the loco again crossed the bridge, whereupon it was grounded once again as its route to the shed, a mere 100 yards, entailed crossing yet another even weaker bridge in Warrington Road. After another day or two the loco and low loader returned to its source, probably Carlisle Kingmoor.
FEBRUARY 1999 ● MALCOLM CAPSTICK

LOCOMOTIVE ALLOCATIONS

LOCO	FROM	DATE	TO	IW: IN WEEK
40003	Preston	IW 14/02/53	Stockport	IW 15/08/53
40103	Carnforth	IW 26/02/49	Wrexham GC	IW 25/02/50
40144	Rugby	IW 26/02/49	Edge Hill	IW 29/04/50
40397	Upperby	IW 18/01/47	Preston	IW 10/12/49
40561	Trafford Park	IW 20/08/49	Patricroft	IW 01/10/49
42102	Willesden	On 20/06/65	Withdrawn	On 14/12/66
42119	Stoke	IW 16/03/57	Barrow	IW 20/06/59
42120	Stockport	IW 16/03/57	Barrow	IW 20/06/59
42121	Watford	IW 12/09/53	Brunswick	IW 24/10/53
42174	Stockport	IW 25/01/64	Withdrawn	IW 07/08/65
42233	Southport	On 12/06/66	Wakefield	On 06/11/66
42235	Stoke	IW 16/03/57	Bangor	On 21/07/59
	Bangor	IW 05/09/59	Wakefield	On 06/11/66
42266	Crewe North	IW 29/04/50	Greenock	On 27/02/54
42295	Blackpl C	IW 19/09/64	Lostock Hall	IW 14/08/65
42303	Stafford	IW 22/03/47	Bletchley	IW 13/11/48
	Chester Ngt	On 03/01/60	Northwich	IW 13/08/60
	Northwich	IW 15/10/60	Withdrawn	On 21/10/62
42317	Chester Ngt	On 03/01/60	Carlisle Canal	IW 06/05/61
42327	Stafford	IW 23/06/62	Stockport	IW 07/12/63
42343	Stockport	IW 22/05/65	Trafford Park	IW 04/09/65
42348	Alsager	IW 17/01/48	Bletchley	IW 13/11/48
42369	Gorton	IW 08/05/65	Withdrawn	IW 15/05/65
42374	Stockport	IW 01/05/65	Trafford Park	IW 11/09/65
42379	Stoke	IW 11/10/47	Stockport	IW 20/03/48
42423	Greenock	On 05/03/54	Trafford Park	IW 12/03/55
42426	Upperby	IW 10/02/62	Bolton	On 20/11/64
42427	Longsight	IW 29/08/53	Longsight	IW 05/09/63
42428	Carnforth	IW 23/10/48	Carnforth	IW 06/11/48
42442	Bletchley	IW 13/11/48	Patricroft	IW 30/10/54
42453	Edge Hill	IW 05/11/49	Patricroft	IW 25/09/54
42454	Patricroft	IW 01/10/49	Stoke	IW 16/03/57
42455	Patricroft	IW 16/03/40	Chester	IW 08/01/49
42456	Dallam	IW 13/12/47	Withdrawn	IW 24/04/65
42460	Bolton	On 21/09/64	Fleetwood	IW 30/01/65
42462	Longsight	IW 05/09/53	Parkhead	On 29/01/61
	Parkhead	On 06/11/61	Withdrawn	IW 14/05/66
42463	Stockport	IW 16/03/57	Preston	IW 08/11/58
42465	Bletchley	IW 14/01/39	Chester	IW 13/11/48
	Chester	IW 20/11/48	Chester	IW 16/06/56
	Chester	IW 07/07/56	Withdrawn	IW 13/02/65
42471	Alsager	IW 22/06/57	Withdrawn	IW 07/10/61
42494	Wigan L&Y	On 12/04/64	Fleetwood	IW 09/01/65
42539	Patricroft	IW 06/02/43	Stockport	IW 16/03/57
42554	Wigan L&Y	On 12/04/64	Bolton	IW 21/11/64
42555	Wigan L&Y	On 12/04/64	Bolton	On 27/11/64
42558	Blackpool C	IW 19/09/64	Withdrawn	IW 17/04/65
42560	Trafford Park	IW 08/02/64	Withdrawn	IW 18/04/64
42563	Polmadie	IW 03/06/44	Patricroft	IW 20/09/52
42564	Edge Hill	IW 23/10/48	Edge Hill	IW 20/11/48
	Rugby	IW 25/06/60	Stoke	IW 09/12/61
42565	Bolton	On 21/09/64	Withdrawn	IW 28/11/64
42571	Bushbury	IW 16/02/57	Willesden	IW 21/12/57
	Willesden	IW 04/01/58	Lancaster	IW 11/06/60
42572	Patricroft	IW 28/02/42	Withdrawn	IW 11/01/64
42577	Willesden	On 18/07/65	Withdrawn	IW 14/01/67
42587	Kirkby	IW 14/11/64	Birkenhead	IW 12/11/66
42588	Edge Hill	IW 07/03/42	Chester	IW 17/09/49
42589	Wigan L&Y	On 12/04/64	Withdrawn	IW 12/09/64
42601	Bangor	IW 09/11/63	Withdrawn	IW 03/04/65
42607	Dallam	IW 15/04/61	Withdrawn	IW 01/02/64
42610	Bletchley	IW 13/11/48	Chester	IW 21/07/56
42611	Willesden	On 18/07/65	Tebay	IW 23/07/66
42631	Wigan L&Y	On 12/04/64	Withdrawn	IW 12/09/64
42634	Wigan L&Y	On 12/04/64	Withdrawn	IW 09/01/65
42647	Wigan L&Y	On 12/04/64	Birkenhead	IW 23/07/66
42663	Bangor	On 27/11/52	Stockport	IW 12/12/53
	Stockport	IW 19/12/53	Stoke	IW 16/03/57
42664	Upperby	IW 10/02/62	Low Moor	On 29/11/64
42665	Stoke	IW 21/06/58	Southport	IW 02/10/65
42666	Crewe North	IW 17/01/53	Barrow	IW 20/06/59
42670	Longsight	IW 03/10/64	Withdrawn	IW 05/12/64
42680	Wigan L&Y	On 12/04/64	Carnforth	IW 09/05/64
42730	Wigan L&Y	On 12/04/64	Birkenhead	IW 23/05/64
42734	Wigan L&Y	On 12/04/64	Stockport	IW 27/06/64
42751	Kingmoor	IW 21/07/62	Gorton	IW 03/10/64
42777	Stoke	IW 21/07/62	Birkenhead	IW 14/12/63
42878	Wigan L&Y	On 12/04/64	Gorton	IW 24/10/64
42894	Stoke	IW 21/07/62	Birkenhead	IW 15/08/64
42948	Stoke	IW 14/12/63	Gorton	IW 29/05/65
42952	Aintree	IW 25/07/64	Withdrawn	IW 12/09/64
42953	Aintree	IW 25/07/64	Withdrawn	IW 15/01/66
42954	Nuneaton	On 09/08/64	Withdrawn	IW 11/02/67
42956	Aintree	IW 25/07/64	Withdrawn	IW 19/09/64
42959	Stoke	IW 21/12/63	Withdrawn	IW 25/12/65
42960	Aintree	IW 25/07/64	Gorton	IW 15/05/65
42961	Aintree	IW 25/07/64	Gorton	IW 15/05/65
42963	Stoke	IW 22/05/64	Withdrawn	IW 16/07/66
42968	Mold Junction	On 17/05/64	Gorton	IW 15/05/65
	Heaton Mersey	IW 08/01/66	Withdrawn	IW 31/12/66
42977	Stoke	IW 14/12/63	Gorton	IW 15/05/65
43973	Alsager	IW 09/01/60	Withdrawn	IW 09/07/60
44041	Skipton	IW 06/04/63	Skipton	IW 30/11/63
	Skipton	IW 11/01/64	Kingmoor	IW 04/04/64
44069	Longsight	IW 22/03/58	Withdrawn	IW 12/10/63
44076	Northampton	IW 22/04/61	Dallam	IW 13/07/63
44110	Aston	IW 14/07/62	Buxton	IW 15/09/62
44121	Upperby	IW 29/04/61	Withdrawn	IW 16/01/65
44125	Upperby	IW 29/04/61	Skipton	IW 12/01/63
44246	Stoke	IW 10/11/62	Withdrawn	IW 12/12/64
44280	Sutton Oak	IW 15/03/58	Withdrawn	IW 14/12/63
44301	Aston	IW 14/07/62	Withdrawn	IW 28/03/64
44302	Bescot	IW 17/08/63	Withdrawn	IW 21/03/64
44303	Sutton Oak	IW 15/03/58	Withdrawn	IW 31/08/63
44348	Bescot	IW 17/08/63	Workington	IW 21/03/64
44355	BR Barrow Rd	IW 24/10/59	Bangor	On 01/11/59
44395	Stoke	IW 09/11/63	Withdrawn	IW 23/11/63
44438	Sutton Oak	IW 14/06/58	Withdrawn	IW 12/03/60
44444	Aston	IW 14/07/62	Withdrawn	IW 31/08/63
44445	Speke Junction	IW 17/09/60	Carnforth	IW 28/10/61
44486	Wigan L&Y	IW 02/11/63	Skipton	IW 30/11/63
	Skipton	IW 25/01/64	Gorton	IW 04/04/64
44490	Buxton	IW 28/01/61	Withdrawn	IW 28/08/65
44492	Aston	IW 14/07/62	Heaton Mersey	IW 22/06/63
44500	Crewe South	IW 26/12/64	Barrow	IW 04/12/65
44514	Aston	IW 14/07/62	Heaton Mersey	IW 06/07/63
44517	Aston	IW 14/07/62	Stoke	IW 10/11/62

LOCO	FROM	DATE	TO	IW: IN WEEK
44536	Stoke	IW 09/11/63	Sutton Oak	IW 29/02/64
44537	BR Barrow Rd	IW 24/10/59	Barrow	On 01/11/59
44548	Stoke	IW 09/11/63	Lower Darwen	IW 14/12/63
44658	Nottingham	On 28/02/65	Dallam	IW 10/04/65
	Dallam	IW 20/05/67	Withdrawn	IW 18/11/67
44678	Speke Junction	IW 22/01/66	Withdrawn	IW 25/11/67
44679	Speke Junction	IW 22/10/66	Withdrawn	IW 23/09/67
44682	Stoke	On 06/08/67	Withdrawn	IW 02/12/67
44683	Crewe South	IW 24/06/67	Lostock Hall	On 03/12/67
44708	Preston	IW 30/09/50	Crewe South	On 25/10/60
44710	Banbury	On 14/08/66	Withdrawn	On 19/12/66
44711	Shrewsbury	On 05/03/67	Edge Hill	On 03/12/67
44732	Speke Junction	IW 28/05/66	Withdrawn	On 13/07/67
44737	Bank Hall	On 16/10/66	Withdrawn	IW 14/01/67
44758	Crewe North	On 15/06/59	Longsight	IW 18/06/60
44761	Crewe South	IW 24/06/67	Lostock Hall	On 03/12/67
44776	Croes Newydd	On 23/05/67	Withdrawn	IW 21/10/67
44779	Bury	IW 20/03/65	Dallam	IW 26/06/65
44780	Lancaster	On 02/11/59	Longsight	IW 18/06/60
	Birkenhead	On 13/08/67	Newton Heath	On 03/12/67
44819	Dallam	IW 20/05/67	Withdrawn	IW 02/12/67
44823	Agecroft	IW 14/09/63	Withdrawn	IW 20/11/65
44827	Crewe North	IW 28/01/56	Crewe South	IW 18/02/56
44831	Chester	IW 20/05/67	Withdrawn	IW 02/12/67
44842	Mold Junction	On 30/01/66	Stockport	On 03/12/67
44864	Speke Junction	IW 22/06/63	Edge Hill	IW 13/07/63
44873	Crewe South	On 18/07/65	Withdrawn	IW 02/12/67
44892	Newton Heath	IW 01/12/45	Preston	IW 10/06/50
44918	Nottingham	On 28/02/65	Lostock Hall	IW 03/07/65
44920	Dallam	IW 20/05/67	Withdrawn	IW 02/12/67
44930	Dallam	IW 30/01/65	Dallam	IW 10/04/65
44935	Dallam	IW 30/01/65	Dallam	IW 10/04/65
44962	Burton	On 27/03/66	Newton Heath	On 03/12/67
44971	Edge Hill	IW 20/06/53	Crewe South	IW 04/07/53
44985	Stoke	IW 20/05/67	Withdrawn	IW 04/11/67
45004	Crewe South	IW 21/11/53	Bletchley	IW 26/02/55
45017	Carnforth	IW 02/05/59	Southport	IW 20/07/63
45019	Preston	IW 24/03/45	Edge Hill	IW 10/02/51
	Carnforth	IW 02/05/59	Withdrawn	IW 13/05/67
45024	Crewe South	IW 09/12/61	Longsight	IW 16/12/61
	Longsight	IW 30/12/61	Withdrawn	IW 13/05/67
45026	Patricroft	IW 30/09/50	Blackpool C	IW 27/07/63
45030	Preston	IW 18/11/44	Crewe South	IW 23/10/48
45045	Crewe North	IW 08/01/49	Chester	IW 28/05/49
45048	Holyhead	On 04/12/66	Withdrawn	IW 02/12/67
45055	Patricroft	IW 20/09/52	Mold Junction	IW 07/05/55
	Mold Junction	IW 15/09/62	Southport	IW 20/07/63
45057	Chester	IW 25/08/56	Newton Heath	IW 27/07/63
45069	Trafford Park	IW 22/06/63	Edge Hill	IW 06/07/63
45070	Willesden	IW 24/04/48	Chester	IW 08/05/48
	Mold Junction	IW 15/09/62	Dallam	IW 26/06/65
45073	Speke Junction	IW 21/07/62	Newton Heath	IW 27/07/63
45091	Crewe South	On 18/07/65	Withdrawn	IW 10/09/66
45092	Holyhead	IW 27/09/58	Crewe South	IW 02/04/60
	Crewe South	IW 25/06/60	Upperby	IW 16/06/62
45108	Longsight	IW 12/09/59	Withdrawn	IW 11/12/65
45109	Longsight	On 06/09/59	Newton Heath	IW 27/07/63
45116	Chester	IW 20/05/67	Withdrawn	IW 29/07/67
45128	Crewe South	On 18/07/65	Withdrawn	IW 10/09/66
45129	Upperby	IW 07/02/48	Upperby	IW 23/10/48
45135	Crewe South	IW 21/11/53	Holyhead	IW 13/11/54
	Holyhead	IW 27/11/54	Southport	IW 17/08/63
45140	Speke Junction	IW 21/07/62	Withdrawn	IW 01/10/66
45141	Upperby	IW 21/06/47	Carlisle Canal	IW 02/06/51
45181	Speke Junction	IW 22/06/63	Carnforth	IW 13/07/63
45188	Holyhead	IW 15/09/62	Edge Hill	IW 17/08/63
45198	Croes Newydd	IW 11/03/67	Withdrawn	IW 30/09/67
45218	Wigan L&Y	On 12/04/64	Rose Grove	IW 27/06/64
45221	Nottingham	On 28/02/65	Dallam	IW 26/06/65
45235	Crewe South	IW 10/04/48	Carnforth	IW 13/05/50
	Carnforth	IW 24/06/50	Preston	IW 05/07/52
	Preston	IW 20/09/52	Crewe North	IW 07/02/53
45244	Upperby	IW 22/06/63	Edge Hill	IW 13/07/63
45249	Patricroft	IW 26/01/52	Edge Hill	IW 20/06/53
45267	Colwick	On 06/11/67	Withdrawn	IW 14/10/67
45268	Stoke	IW 20/05/67	Newton Heath	On 03/12/67
45278	Holyhead	IW 15/09/62	Withdrawn	IW 10/06/67
45281	Crewe South	IW 09/12/61	Withdrawn	IW 02/12/67
45282	Chester	IW 11/03/67	Edge Hill	On 03/12/67
45289	Longsight	IW 30/09/50	Edge Hill	IW 20/06/53
	Edge Hill	IW 12/09/53	Patricroft	IW 09/06/56
45296	Patricroft	IW 26/10/63	Edge Hill	On 03/12/67
45305	Chester	On 15/08/65	Speke Junction	On 03/12/67
45310	Crewe South	IW 24/06/67	Newton Heath	On 03/12/67
45312	Speke Junction	IW 22/06/63	Edge Hill	IW 06/07/63
45313	Holyhead	01/10/1949	Edge Hill	IW 11/11/50
	Edge Hill	IW 25/11/50	Withdrawn	IW 06/02/65
45314	Crewe South	IW 21/11/53	Withdrawn	IW 06/11/65
45321	Crewe South	On 18/07/65	Withdrawn	IW 07/10/67
45329	Speke Junction	IW 22/06/63	Carnforth	IW 13/07/63
45331	Banbury	On 14/08/66	Withdrawn	IW 02/12/67
45340	Preston	On 02/11/59	Preston	IW 15/04/61
45347	Trafford Park	IW 18/06/55	Blackpool C	IW 20/07/63
45350	Speke Junction	IW 11/03/67	Rose Grove	On 03/12/67
45368	Agecroft	IW 08/01/66	Withdrawn	On 06/11/67
45372	Longsight	On 06/09/59	Withdrawn	On 23/11/66
45373	Crewe North	On 15/06/59	Blackpool C	IW 20/07/63
45375	Speke Junction	IW 22/06/63	Southport	IW 06/07/63
	Southport	IW 13/02/65	Dallam	IW 26/06/65
45380	Dallam	IW 30/03/63	Newton Heath	IW 27/07/63
45385	Patricroft	IW 26/10/63	Withdrawn	IW 05/11/66
45388	Bletchley	IW 05/11/60	Newton Heath	IW 27/07/63
45394	Lancaster	IW 24/09/60	Carnforth	IW 31/12/60
45395	Mold Junction	On 30/01/66	Edge Hill	On 03/12/67
45408	Patricroft	IW 22/12/51	Stoke	IW 05/08/61
	Stoke	IW 19/08/61	Withdrawn	IW 26/11/66
45413	Preston	IW 01/11/47	Patricroft	IW 13/06/53
	Speke Junction	IW 22/06/63	Patricroft	IW 06/07/63
45425	Preston	IW 30/11/40	Patricroft	IW 07/07/51
	Patricroft	IW 26/01/52	Withdrawn	IW 21/10/67
45431	Carnforth	IW 07/11/59	Withdrawn	IW 02/12/67
45449	Preston	IW 11/04/42	Withdrawn	IW 02/12/67
45454	Carlisle Canal	IW 02/06/51	Preston	IW 22/06/57
45495	Holyhead	IW 01/10/49	Patricroft	IW 21/01/50
45521	Edge Hill	IW 16/09/61	Withdrawn	IW 28/09/63
45531	Edge Hill	IW 19/10/63	Upperby	IW 25/07/64
46110	Edge Hill	IW 29/06/63	Kingmoor	IW 06/07/63

LOCO	FROM	DATE	TO	IW: IN WEEK
46115	Longsight	IW 06/06/64	Upperby	IW 25/07/64
46128	Crewe North	IW 15/09/62	Kingmoor	IW 03/11/62
46161	Preston	IW 09/09/61	Crewe North	IW 14/07/62
46165	Preston	IW 09/09/61	Crewe North	IW 14/07/62
46167	Preston	IW 09/09/61	Crewe North	IW 30/06/62
46168	Preston	IW 09/09/61	Withdrawn	IW 02/05/64
46402	Derby	On 17/05/64	Bank Hall	IW 03/07/65
46419	Lees (Oldham)	On 12/04/64	Aintree	IW 22/01/66
46422	Widnes	IW 28/04/56	Kirkby Stephen	IW 09/04/60
	Kirkby Stephen	IW 17/06/61	Lancaster	IW 10/02/62
46423	Rhyl	IW 22/03/58	Nuneaton	IW 06/12/58
46428	Preston	IW 24/03/51	Lower Ince	IW 09/06/51
	Lower Ince	On 24/03/52	Rhyl	IW 05/06/54
	Rhyl	IW 02/10/54	Bescot	IW 10/02/62
46430	Preston	IW 24/03/51	Rhyl	IW 07/07/51
	Rhyl	IW 27/10/51	Preston	IW 15/12/61
46432	Willesden	IW 12/07/52	Rhyl	IW 05/05/56
	Workington	IW 30/04/66	Withdrawn	IW 06/05/67
46434	Rhyl	IW 24/10/53	Upperby	IW 07/05/60
46440	Derby	On 17/05/64	Speke Junction	IW 07/11/64
46447	Workington	IW 12/12/59	Llandudno Jn	IW 18/06/60
	Derby	On 17/05/64	Withdrawn	IW 31/12/66
46448	Workington	IW 13/02/54	Rhyl	IW 29/05/54
	Rhyl	IW 05/06/54	Uttoxeter	IW 16/01/60
	Uttoxeter	IW 12/03/60	Bescot	IW 10/02/62
46457	Workington	IW 10/12/55	Workington	IW 24/12/55
46459	Chester	IW 02/06/56	Chester	IW 07/07/56
46470	Kirkby Stephen	IW 17/09/60	Aston	IW 10/02/62
46484	Lees (Oldham)	On 12/04/64	Bank Hall	IW 03/07/65
46486	Lees (Oldham)	On 12/04/64	Lancaster	IW 14/08/65
46487	Lees (Oldham)	On 12/04/64	Northwich	IW 19/02/66
46489	Preston	IW 29/11/52	Workington	IW 30/01/54
46499	Nottingham	IW 23/05/64	Barrow	IW 27/06/64
46503	Northwich	IW 08/08/64	Speke Junction	On 05/11/64
46506	Nottingham	On 17/05/64	Barrow	IW 27/06/64
46515	Speke Junction	IW 28/05/66	Withdrawn	IW 06/05/67
46517	Northwich	IW 08/08/64	Withdrawn	IW 26/11/66
47270	Stoke	IW 27/02/60	Withdrawn	IW 08/09/62
47281	Stoke	IW 27/02/60	Kingmoor	IW 05/11/60
47314	Speke Junction	IW 21/07/62	Lostock Hall	IW 23/07/66
47392	Dallam	IW 09/01/60	Sutton Oak	IW 05/05/62
47395	Crewe South	IW 28/01/61	Withdrawn	IW 17/04/65
47398	Crewe South	IW 28/01/61	Lancaster	IW 25/02/61
47444	Sutton Oak	IW 21/01/61	Aintree	IW 07/05/66
47493	Speke Junction	IW 21/07/62	Edge Hill	IW 04/09/65
47517	Barrow	IW 25/11/61	Withdrawn	IW 27/06/64
47520	Barrow	IW 21/01/61	Barrow	IW 04/02/61
47603	Dallam	IW 06/10/62	Sutton Oak	IW 22/10/66
47659	Dallam	IW 09/01/60	Widnes	IW 11/02/61
	Widnes	IW 18/03/61	Birkenhead	IW 08/04/61
47669	Camden	IW 09/01/60	Dallam	IW 17/09/60
47671	Camden	IW 09/01/60	Sutton Oak	IW 22/10/66
47877	Speke Junction	IW 12/08/50	Withdrawn	IW 21/02/53
47881	Speke Junction	IW 12/02/49	Speke Junction	IW 19/02/49
	Speke Junction	IW 23/04/49	Withdrawn	IW 21/07/51
47884	Speke Junction	IW 25/03/50	Withdrawn	IW 09/06/51
(4)7885	Speke Junction	IW 02/05/42	Withdrawn	IW 18/03/50
(4)7888	Birkenhead	IW 04/11/44	Withdrawn	IW 04/12/48
47896	Edge Hill	IW 05/09/42	Withdrawn	IW 04/11/50
48033	Sutton Oak	On 17/06/67	Patricroft	On 03/12/67
48082	Unallocated	On 20/06/66	Withdrawn	IW 15/04/67
48114	Kirkby	On 29/11/64	Withdrawn	IW 01/04/67
48117	Colwick	On 04/12/66	Heaton Mersey	IW 03/12/67
48125	Toton	IW 05/12/64	Withdrawn	IW 28/10/67
48132	Colwick	IW 04/02/67	Newton Heath	On 03/12/67
48153	Sutton Oak	On 17/06/67	Speke Junction	On 03/12/67
48165	Unallocated	On 20/06/66	Withdrawn	IW 18/03/67
48167	Sutton Oak	On 17/06/67	Rose Grove	On 03/12/67
48187	Nottingham	On 29/11/64	Withdrawn	IW 07/01/67
48192	Sutton Oak	On 17/06/67	Stockport	On 03/12/67
48193	Sutton Oak	On 17/06/67	Heaton Mersey	On 03/12/67
48206	Sutton Oak	On 17/06/67	Speke Junction	On 03/12/67
48221	Northwich	IW 19/06/65	Withdrawn	IW 04/02/67
48261	Buxton	IW 09/01/65	Withdrawn	IW 19/08/67
48275	Buxton	IW 09/01/65	Withdrawn	IW 24/06/67
48278	Buxton	IW 02/01/65	Patricroft	On 03/12/67
48279	Sutton Oak	On 17/06/67	Withdrawn	IW 14/10/67
48319	Fleetwood	On 13/02/66	Patricroft	On 03/12/67
48325	Croes Newydd	IW 11/03/67	Patricroft	On 03/12/67
48338	Fleetwood	On 13/02/66	Patricroft	On 03/12/67
48362	Sutton Oak	On 17/06/67	Edge Hill	On 03/12/67
48379	Kirkby	On 29/11/64	Withdrawn	IW 18/03/67
48410	Unallocated	On 17/07/66	Rose Grove	On 03/12/67
48494	Nottingham	On 29/11/64	Withdrawn	On 29/03/67
48614	Sutton Oak	On 17/06/67	Edge Hill	On 03/12/67
48675	Kirkby	On 29/11/64	Withdrawn	IW 16/09/67
48676	Sutton Oak	On 17/06/67	Withdrawn	On 17/10/67
48678	Colwick	On 08/11/66	Newton Heath	On 03/12/67
48705	Oxley	IW 04/02/67	Withdrawn	IW 04/03/67
48715	Aintree	IW 26/06/65	Edge Hill	On 03/12/67
48724	Oxley	On 05/03/67	Withdrawn	On 25/10/67
48752	Oxley	IW 04/02/67	Edge Hill	On 03/12/67
48764	Northwich	IW 19/06/65	Bolton	On 02/12/67
(4)8824	Sutton Oak	IW 06/12/41	Withdrawn	IW 04/02/50
(4)8834	Sutton Oak	IW 07/03/36	Withdrawn	IW 31/12/48
48895	Bescot	IW 27/05/50	Bushbury	IW 18/08/62
48905	Walsall	On 08/06/58	Withdrawn	IW 06/06/59
48915	Watford	IW 07/07/56	Withdrawn	IW 07/10/61
48929	Stockport	IW 20/11/48	Withdrawn	IW 29/07/50
48930	Crewe South	IW 03/10/42	Bescot	IW 30/09/50
48942	Speke Junction	IW 15/08/59	Withdrawn	IW 07/10/61
(4)8962	Crewe South	IW 28/02/48	Withdrawn	IW 18/12/48
48964	Bletchley	IW 23/09/50	Bletchley	IW 30/09/50
49002	Edge Hill	IW 09/09/61	Withdrawn	On 14/09/62
49007	Bletchley	IW 10/03/51	Stockport	IW 04/02/56
	Stockport	IW 21/04/56	Withdrawn	IW 07/10/61
49008	Speke Junction	IW 15/08/59	Withdrawn	On 04/12/62
49009	Bescot	IW 21/02/59	Withdrawn	On 27/11/59
49018	Crewe South	IW 29/05/48	Shrewbury	IW 12/08/50
	Shrewsbury	IW 26/08/50	Withdrawn	On 04/09/59
49020	Walsall	On 08/06/58	Withdrawn	IW 07/10/61
49023	Willesden	IW 08/01/44	Carnforth	IW 24/04/48
	Carnforth	IW 31/07/48	Withdrawn	IW 07/10/61
49024	Crewe South	IW 18/11/44	Stockport	IW 30/09/50
49025	Bescot	IW 15/09/51	Crewe South	IW 03/11/56
	Crewe South	IW 05/01/57	Withdrawn	On 14/09/62
(4)9026	Shrewsbury	IW 26/02/44	Withdrawn	IW 17/09/49
49029	Shrewsbury	IW 26/02/44	Withdrawn	IW 13/05/50
49030	Plodder Lane	IW 07/12/40	Withdrawn	IW 23/06/51
49032	Speke Junction	IW 12/11/49	Withdrawn	IW 03/06/50
49034	Stafford	IW 19/08/50	Plodder Lane	IW 28/10/50

LOCO	FROM	DATE	TO	IW: IN WEEK
(4)9043	Stockport	IW 11/10/47	Withdrawn	IW 24/09/49
49049	Rugby	IW 18/01/58	Withdrawn	On 27/11/62
(4)9050	Bescot	IW 17/06/50	Withdrawn	IW 07/10/50
(4)9053	Bletchley	IW 04/08/45	Sutton Oak	IW 27/11/48
49073	Widnes	IW 26/05/56	Withdrawn	On 07/01/58
49079	Widnes	IW 08/11/58	Nuneaton	IW 07/11/59
49082	Birkenhead	IW 08/04/50	Edge Hill	IW 23/09/50
49090	Springs Branch	At 05/01/35	Withdrawn	IW 16/12/50
49092	Buxton	IW 19/02/49	Bescot	IW 03/03/51
49093	Dallam	IW 09/07/55	Bletchley	IW 21/09/57
49104	Preston	IW 09/09/61	Withdrawn	On 27/11/62
49109	Carnforth	IW 24/01/48	Carnforth	IW 13/03/48
49122	Willesden	IW 28/01/61	Withdrawn	On 30/11/62
(4)9124	Sutton Oak	IW 03/02/45	Withdrawn	IW 21/01/50
49125	Willesden	IW 08/01/44	Birkenhead	IW 25/06/49
49129	Crewe South	IW 18/01/41	Withdrawn	On 30/11/62
49134	Springs Branch	At 05/01/35	Preston	IW 24/04/48
	Speke Junction	IW 15/08/59	Nuneaton	IW 07/11/59
49139	Willesden	IW 19/04/58	Withdrawn	On 14/09/62
49140	Speke Junction	IW 27/12/47	Speke Junction	IW 10/01/48
49141	Shrewsbury	IW 25/09/37	Preston	IW 24/04/48
	Preston	IW 12/12/59	Withdrawn	On 20/07/62
49142	Edge Hill	IW 11/03/61	Edge Hill	IW 17/06/61
49143	Speke Junction	IW 15/08/59	Withdrawn	On 21/10/59
49144	Carnforth	IW 18/09/54	Nuneaton	IW 21/09/57
49145	Watford	IW 07/07/56	Withdrawn	On 01/01/58
49149	Shrewsbury	IW 12/06/43	Dallam	IW 24/04/48
49150	Widnes	IW 08/11/58	Withdrawn	On 09/11/59
49154	Bletchley	IW 15/09/51	Withdrawn	On 27/11/62
49155	Speke Junction	IW 06/02/54	Edge Hill	IW 27/08/60
(4)9159	Bletchley	IW 05/05/45	Withdrawn	IW 14/05/49
49160	Bescot	IW 17/06/50	Preston	IW 28/10/50
	Preston	IW 31/10/53	Withdrawn	IW 14/11/59
49163	Willesden	IW 28/10/50	Withdrawn	IW 08/12/51
49164	Willesden	IW 28/01/61	Withdrawn	IW 14/10/61
(4)9176	Sutton Oak	IW 12/06/43	Withdrawn	IW 14/01/50
(4)9190	Nuneaton	IW 28/02/48	Patricroft	IW 28/08/48
49191	Stockport	IW 02/01/60	Withdrawn	IW 14/10/61
(4)9192	Farnley Junction	IW 12/05/45	Preston	IW 24/04/48
(4)9197	Northampton	IW 23/11/46	Withdrawn	IW 29/05/48
49203	Plodder Lane	IW 09/10/54	Withdrawn	On 09/11/59
(4)9207	Patricroft	IW 29/03/41	Withdrawn	IW 02/07/49
(4)9208	Bletchley	IW 05/06/48	Walsall	IW 11/03/50
(4)9221	Buxton	IW 13/12/47	Speke Junction	IW 10/01/48
49228	Mold Junction	IW 21/01/50	Withdrawn	IW 04/04/59
49253	Speke Junction	IW 10/03/51	Withdrawn	IW 15/03/52
49257	Stockport	IW 12/02/44	Plodder Lane	IW 05/06/48
(4)9259	Bescot	IW 21/08/48	Sutton Oak	IW 02/10/48
(4)9263	Crewe South	IW 05/06/48	Withdrawn	IW 26/03/49
49264	Nuneaton	IW 23/10/48	Withdrawn	IW 13/01/51
49267	Preston	IW 30/03/57	Withdrawn	On 27/11/62
49268	Nuneaton	IW 22/04/50	Withdrawn	On 09/11/59
49277	Willesden	IW 29/03/58	Willesden	IW 19/04/58
49288	Bletchley	IW 10/03/51	Sutton Oak	IW 05/05/51
49306	Abergavenny	IW 18/01/47	Crewe South	IW 09/10/48
	Crewe South	IW 27/11/48	Speke Junction	IW 21/09/57
49310	Patricroft	IW 07/12/40	Bletchley	IW 15/09/51
49311	Preston	IW 02/05/42	Withdrawn	On 06/10/59
49314	Nuneaton	IW 05/05/62	Withdrawn	On 30/11/62
49315	Plodder Lane	IW 09/10/54	Buxton	IW 21/09/57
49321	Northampton	IW 18/01/58	Withdrawn	On 23/06/60
49322	Longsight	IW 10/03/51	Withdrawn	IW 10/03/56
49323	Watford	IW 07/07/56	Dallam	IW 25/08/56
49331	Buxton	IW 24/01/48	Withdrawn	IW 28/10/50
(4)9338	Dallam	IW 24/01/48	Dallam	IW 13/03/48
49341	Speke Junction	IW 13/03/48	Withdrawn	IW 23/03/57
49344	Willesden	IW 28/01/61	Withdrawn	On 27/11/62
49346	Edge Hill	IW 08/10/49	Bushbury	IW 26/08/50
49352	Nuneaton	IW 15/01/49	Sutton Oak	IW 11/04/59
	Edge Hill	IW 04/03/61	Edge Hill	IW 11/03/61
(4)9369	Crewe South	IW 24/01/48	Crewe South	IW 03/04/48
49378	Mold Junction	IW 21/01/50	Withdrawn	On 09/11/59
49381	Nuneaton	IW 11/03/50	Withdrawn	On 30/11/62
49385	Bletchley	IW 15/09/51	Withdrawn	On 20/12/57
49393	Watford	IW 28/10/50	Withdrawn	IW 22/06/57
49394	Farnley Junction	IW 12/03/49	Edge Hill	IW 23/09/50
49401	Rugby	IW 20/01/51	Stockport	IW 02/01/60
49402	Bescot	IW 21/05/49	Withdrawn	On 30/11/62
49408	Rugby	IW 16/12/50	Withdrawn	On 30/11/62
49422	Preston	IW 14/07/45	Bletchley	IW 12/03/49
	Pontypool Road	On 23/02/58	Withdrawn	IW 02/09/61
49424	Birkenhead	IW 12/02/44	Nuneaton	IW 16/10/48
49431	Nuneaton	IW 05/05/62	Withdrawn	On 27/11/62
49436	Nuneaton	IW 06/01/51	Withdrawn	On 21/05/59
49438	Carnforth	IW 14/02/59	Withdrawn	On 30/11/62
49444	Mkt Harboro	IW 06/08/60	Edge Hill	IW 27/08/60
49447	Mkt Harboro	IW 09/07/60	Withdrawn	On 27/11/62
49450	Crewe South	IW 24/01/48	Crewe South	IW 03/04/48
49451	Speke Junction	IW 15/08/59	Withdrawn	On 31/11/62
52021	Barrow	IW 20/07/35	Withdrawn	On 24/08/55
52022	Barrow	IW 20/07/35	Patricroft	IW 24/09/49
52023	Barrow	IW 20/07/35	Patricroft	IW 27/03/48
	Patricroft	IW 02/10/48	Withdrawn	IW 08/04/50
52024	Preston	IW 17/04/37	Patricroft	IW 28/02/48
12032	Wigan L&Y	IW 15/02/36	Withdrawn	IW 10/01/48
52045	Springs Branch	05/01/1935	Patricroft	IW 08/11/52
52051	Preston	IW 26/02/49	Withdrawn	IW 04/02/56
52053	Preston	IW 13/07/46	Wakefield	IW 20/09/52
52063	Preston	IW 17/04/37	Withdrawn	IW 04/09/48
52064	Springs Branch	05/01/1935	Preston	IW 27/03/48
52098	Moor Row	IW 04/06/49	Withdrawn	On 28/10/53
52107	Nuneaton	IW 12/11/49	Rhyl	IW 26/01/52
	Rhyl	IW 26/04/52	Withdrawn	IW 07/03/53
52118	Edge Hill	IW 27/09/52	Withdrawn	IW 04/09/54
52126	Sutton Oak	IW 18/02/50	Withdrawn	IW 26/05/51
52140	Dallam	IW 27/03/48	Sutton Oak	IW 15/09/51
52143	Sutton Oak	IW 21/03/53	Withdrawn	IW 26/10/57
52172	Preston	IW 04/02/39	Rhyl	IW 17/01/48
12208	Birkenhead	IW 03/10/42	Chester	IW 28/02/48
52230	Bangor	On 07/11/57	Newton Heath	IW 14/06/58
52233	Shrewsbury	IW 27/03/48	Dallam	IW 01/10/49
52250	Dallam	IW 27/03/48	Withdrawn	IW 27/10/51
52269	Preston	IW 19/04/47	Shrewsbury	IW 28/02/48
	Shrewsbury	IW 27/03/48	Bangor	On 23/06/49
	Bangor	On 08/11/57	Lees (Oldham)	IW 14/06/58
52322	Nuneaton	IW 23/08/52	Sutton Oak	IW 07/07/56
52341	Preston	IW 22/01/49	Newton Heath	IW 22/12/56
52366	Sutton Oak	IW 18/09/54	Sutton Oak	IW 07/07/56
52393	Sutton Oak	IW 18/02/56	Sutton Oak	IW 09/02/57
52449	Nuneaton	IW 08/11/52	Withdrawn	IW 02/11/57
52551	Hereford	IW 31/05/52	Bangor	IW 04/08/56
	Bangor	IW 06/10/56	Withdrawn	IW 23/03/57

LOCO	FROM	DATE	TO	IW: IN WEEK
52598	Preston	IW 15/12/51	Withdrawn	IW 09/08/52
58120	Northwich	IW 21/11/59	Northwich	IW 13/08/60
	Northwich	IW 10/09/60	Rugby	IW 01/04/61
58123	Northwich	IW 21/11/59	Monument Lane	IW 29/10/60
58203	Patricroft	IW 11/02/56	Walsall	IW 17/03/56
28345	Bushbury	IW 14/10/50	Withdrawn	IW 30/06/51
28403	Bushbury	IW 21/12/46	Widnes	IW 27/11/48
58376	Barrow	IW 30/11/46	Upperby	IW 28/05/49
58377	Stockport	IW 15/03/52	Withdrawn	IW 21/06/52
58381	Rugby	IW 20/09/47	Bangor	IW 11/03/50
58396	Workington	IW 15/12/51	Widnes	IW 12/07/52
58398	Workington	IW 27/05/50	Llandudno Jn	IW 20/01/51
	Llandudno Jn	IW 20/01/51	Withdrawn	IW 16/02/52
58400	Stoke	IW 28/05/49	Widnes	IW 21/04/51
58415	Aston	IW 14/02/48	Workington	IW 17/04/48
28580	Sutton Oak	IW 27/01/51	Rhyl	IW 03/11/51
28592	Shrewsbury	IW 13/12/47	Bangor	On 08/02/50
28594	Walsall	IW 15/05/48	Withdrawn	IW 12/06/48
58427	Monument Lane	IW 08/04/50	Stoke	IW 29/04/50
7703	Edge Hill	IW 11/10/47	Withdrawn	IW 31/07/48
65131	Northwich	IW 25/02/56	Withdrawn	On 25/03/59
65138	Widnes	On 08/12/56	Withdrawn	On 05/08/59
65140	Chester Ngt	On 08/12/56	Withdrawn	On 02/12/59
65144	Lower Ince	On 24/03/52	Trafford Park	On 13/12/52
65146	Chester Ngt	On 08/12/56	Withdrawn	On 08/12/58
65148	Lower Ince	On 24/03/52	Darlington	On 02/12/56
65156	Chester Ngt	On 08/12/56	Withdrawn	On 10/02/58
65157	Widnes	IW 07/11/59	Withdrawn	On 23/08/61
65159	Lower Ince	On 24/03/52	Withdrawn	On 20/12/57
65162	Lower Ince	On 24/03/52	Darlington	On 02/12/56
65164	Lower Ince	On 24/03/52	Trafford Park	On 20/12/52
65170	Lower Ince	On 24/03/52	Trafford Park	On 06/12/52
	Chester Ngt	IW 08/12/56	Withdrawn	On 25/06/58
65173	Lower Ince	On 24/03/52	Darlington	On 02/12/56
65175	Lower Ince	On 24/03/52	Withdrawn	On 31/03/58
65176	Lower Ince	On 24/03/52	Darlington	On 02/12/56
65177	Walton	On 20/12/58	Withdrawn	On 22/09/59
65189	Lower Ince	On 24/03/52	Withdrawn	On 22/09/52
65192	Walton	On 20/12/58	Withdrawn	On 11/05/60
65196	Lower Ince	On 24/03/52	Brunswick	On 07/03/53
65198	Widnes	IW 15/08/59	Withdrawn	On 23/08/61
65199	Lower Ince	On 24/03/52	Withdrawn	On 08/12/58
65203	Lower Ince	On 24/03/52	Darlington	On 02/12/56
75011	Derby	IW 07/11/63	Skipton	IW 20/03/65
75015	Aintree	IW 25/04/64	Skipton	IW 20/03/65
75017	Southport	IW 14/12/63	Skipton	IW 20/03/65
75019	Southport	IW 14/12/63	Skipton	IW 20/03/65
75039	Derby	On 21/11/63	Skipton	IW 20/03/65
75041	Derby	On 18/11/63	Skipton	IW 20/03/65
75042	Derby	On 22/11/63	Skipton	IW 20/03/65
75044	Derby	IW 23/11/63	Skipton	IW 20/03/65
75051	Derby	On 21/11/63	Skipton	IW 06/03/65
75057	Derby	IW 23/11/63	Skipton	IW 06/03/65
75058	Derby	On 19/01/64	Skipton	IW 06/03/65
75059	Derby	On 22/11/63	Skipton	IW 06/03/65
76022	Lancaster	IW 10/02/62	Aston	IW 14/07/62
76051	Lancaster	IW 10/02/62	Aston	IW 14/07/62
76075	Sutton Oak	On 17/06/67	Withdrawn	On 05/10/67
76077	Sutton Oak	On 17/06/67	Withdrawn	IW 02/12/67
76079	Sutton Oak	On 17/06/67	Withdrawn	IW 02/12/67
76080	Sutton Oak	On 17/06/67	Withdrawn	IW 02/12/67
76081	Sutton Oak	On 17/06/67	Withdrawn	On 20/07/67
76084	Sutton Oak	On 17/06/67	Withdrawn	IW 02/12/67
78017	Kirkby Stephen	IW 30/04/60	Rhyl	IW 10/06/61
78019	Kirkby Stephen	IW 30/04/60	Northwich	IW 10/06/61
78020	Wigan L&Y	On 12/04/64	Derby	On 17/05/64
78027	Wigan L&Y	On 12/04/64	Derby	On 17/05/64
78037	Skipton	IW 21/03/64	Derby	On 17/05/64
78057	Wigan L&Y	On 12/04/64	Derby	On 17/05/64
78061	Wigan L&Y	On 12/04/64	Derby	On 17/05/64
78062	Wigan L&Y	On 12/04/64	Nottingham	On 17/05/64
90125	Aintree	IW 13/07/63	Lostock Hall	IW 14/09/63
90140	Widnes	IW 16/03/63	Agecroft	IW 08/06/63
90147	Sutton Oak	IW 06/07/63	Withdrawn	IW 02/05/64
90148	Stourbridge	IW 14/07/62	Sutton Oak	IW 13/03/65
90157	Widnes	IW 23/03/63	Withdrawn	IW 04/07/64
90173	Birkenhead	IW 09/04/60	Lancaster	IW 03/11/62
	Lancaster	IW 13/07/63	Withdrawn	IW 11/07/64
90183	Newton Heath	IW 07/12/63	Frodingham	On 23/05/65
90192	Widnes	IW 23/03/63	Withdrawn	On 03/05/63
90214	Chester (West)	On 09/04/60	Westhouses	IW 02/07/60
90242	Gorton	IW 01/06/63	Fleetwood	IW 16/11/63
90257	Birkenhead	IW 09/04/60	Withdrawn	IW 01/08/64
90261	Stourbridge	IW 07/07/62	Agecroft	IW 01/06/63
90268	Stourbridge	IW 07/07/62	Agecroft	IW 01/06/63
90283	Aintree	IW 25/07/64	Frodingham	On 06/09/64
90316	Bolton	IW 29/02/64	Colwick	On 06/09/64
90317	Birkenhead	IW 09/04/60	Withdrawn	IW 13/03/65
90369	Carnforth	IW 25/04/64	Doncaster	On 06/09/64
90399	Aintree	IW 25/04/64	Withdrawn	IW 27/03/65
90423	Widnes	IW 16/03/63	Colwick	On 06/09/64
90440	Dawsholm	On 15/07/62	Withdrawn	On 17/08/63
90493	Dawsholm	On 15/07/62	Frodingham	On 11/04/65
90507	Woodford Halse	IW 07/03/59	Withdrawn	On 29/06/63
90509	Woodford Halse	IW 14/03/59	Staveley BH	On 06/09/64
90533	Agecroft	IW 17/10/64	Aintree	IW 13/02/65
90535	Aintree	IW 13/07/63	Lostock Hall	IW 14/09/63
90561	Aintree	IW 25/07/64	Withdrawn	IW 27/03/65
90574	Woodford Halse	IW 07/03/59	Withdrawn	IW 15/02/64
90585	Banbury	IW 14/07/62	Gorton	IW 06/04/63
	Gorton	IW 01/06/63	Withdrawn	IW 03/04/65
90632	Agecroft	IW 17/10/64	Aintree	IW 30/01/65
90667	Woodford Halse	IW 14/03/59	Withdrawn	IW 02/05/64
90669	Woodford Halse	IW 25/04/64	Retford GN	On 11/04/65
90686	Chester (West)	On 09/04/60	Gorton	IW 30/03/63
	Gorton	IW 01/06/63	Withdrawn	IW 03/04/65
90687	Aintree	IW 08/08/64	Aintree	IW 22/08/64
90697	Newton Heath	IW 08/08/64	Canklow	On 06/09/64
90702	Mold Junction	IW 02/04/60	Preston	IW 27/08/60
90724	Bolton	IW 18/07/64	Aintree	IW 30/01/65
90725	Agecroft	IW 17/10/64	Rose Grove	IW 07/11/64

A fine panoramic view of Pocket Nook with the Shaw Street avoiding lines on the far left, together with the sidings of Rockware Glass and its sheeted wagons. Stanier 2-6-4T No **42571** and Jubilee 4-6-0 No **45652** *Hawke* head the 18:00 Liverpool Lime Street to Wigan NW service whilst a Jinty shunts the St Helens Shaw Street Goods Yard. In the late 1950's, prior to the introduction of the DMUs, this train was booked for two locos. The first was a Springs Branch engine and the second came from Crewe North which was their Turn 56. This often produced an engine fresh off the works as is the case here. It returned on the 21:05 to Lime Street. c1958 ● GERRY DROUGHT

Two final views from Taylor's Lane bridge illustrating the changes of motive power in the area within a decade. Super D 0-8-0 No **49381** ambles by, light engine, at Manchester Junction. A somewhat desolate shed yard is prominent in the background.   **5TH MAY 1962** ● **BRIAN BARLOW**

A pair of Class 47 diesels, D1741 and D1744 move off shed. D1741 became 47148 in February 1974 and was cut up at MC Metals, Glasgow in September 1989. D1744 became 47151 in March 1974, then 47648 in February 1986 and finally Inter City 47850 in January 1990. It was cut up at Crewe Works in July 1997.   **9TH MARCH 1968** ● **JOHN BURGESS**

The full front vista is caught at a quiet moment.   **MAY 1964** ● **TOM SUTCH**

FRONT COVER

Springs Branch shed viewed from the top of the ash disposal hoist. A good representation of LNWR and LMS classes are seen in the yard in front of Nos 1 and 2 shed. The old coach body *(bottom left)* which is in use as an oil store, is a remnant of the tragic 1873 accident at Wigan North Western station. In the distance stand the chimneys of Westwood Power Station, opened in 1953 and closed in 1986.

24TH JUNE 1961 ● **RAY FARRELL**

BACK COVER

No 42102. Standish Junction.	**1ST JUNE 1966** ● ALLAN HEYES	**No 7894.** Springs Branch MPD.	**30TH JULY 1933** ● H. F. WHEELER
No 47395. Incline Shunt.	**10TH APRIL 1964** ● JOHN BURGESS	**No 2246.** Springs Branch MPD.	**c1918** ● AUTHOR'S COLLECTION
No 48125. Hoghton.	**27TH SEPTEMBER 1967** ● PETER FITTON	**Gordon Wilkinson and No 45431.**	**FEBRUARY 1965** ● TOM SUTCH
No 8824. Springs Branch MPD.	**c1946** ● STEAM IMAGE		

Steam
IMAGE